P9-AGV-684

EDITING FOR PRINT

EDITING FOR PRINT

Geoffrey Rogers

A QUARTO BOOK

Published in North America by
North Light, an imprint of Writer's Digest Books
9933 Alliance Road
Cincinnati, Ohio 45242

ISBN 0-89879-184-7

This book was designed and produced by
Quarto Publishing Ltd
The Old Brewery, 6 Blundell Street, London N7 9BH

Editor Michelle Newton
Art Editor Marnie Searchwell
Designer Andy Luckhurst
Art Director Alastair Campbell
Editorial Director Jim Miles

Copy-editing principles text Celia Hall
Magazine text Yvonne Rees, Mary Forsell
Computer text Hildi Hawkins
Origination, imposition, finishing and binding text David Bann

Phototypeset by AB Consultants, London
Color separation by Universal Color Scanning Limited, Hong Kong
Printed by Leefung-Asco Printers Limited, Hong Kong

The publishers would like to thank the following companies, people and organizations for their help in preparing this book: Linotype-Paul Ltd, Scitex Europe SA, Crosfield Electronics Ltd, Dimension Ltd, Visutek Graphic Products Ltd, (representing Scangraphic, Dr. Boger GmbH), Book House Training Center, David Evans, Paul Barnett, Robert Payne and Microware, London

Contents

INTRODUCTION

The editorial process — in common with many working activities today — has been touched by the magic of the microchip. Computers influence all aspects of publishing, from the capture of the author's original thoughts on relatively cheap microcomputers running word processing programs, and the use of computers in stock control and financial organization, to the world of digital typesetting and the transmission of color images via satellite links. In such an expanding, high-tech environment change is inevitable: change in working methods; change in speed of operation; change in attitude.

And yet in the eye of this whirlwind of change the essential nature of the editorial role remains constant: to convey the message with clarity and style. Since the written word is still read at the same speed as it has been for centuries, the care and consideration the editor gives it will continue to be appreciated, however rapid and sophisticated is the technology used to make it accessible.

Editing however is not simply concerned with words. Particularly in the field of color, illustrated reference books, magazines and partworks, which are the central concern of this book, you will be surrounded as much by images of various kinds — photographs, diagrams, artwork illustrations — as by rows of typeset characters. Understanding the interrelation of text and pictures, captions and annotation is not only the designer's domain; you will need to learn 'layout speak' and be able to cope with the various elements of design.

This book, therefore, extends the boundaries of the editor's traditional province — an abiding concern for the content and expression of the text — to encompass a host of tasks and responsibilities that may never appear in your job description, but which editors tackle each day in publishing companies all over the world. Thus, the opening chapter deals not only with the fundamentals of schedules and budgets, contracts and editorial research, but also discusses the generation of new ideas, finding and briefing prospective authors and the value of consultants. The majority of the strictly 'editorial' processes receive due attention in the second chapter, from the principles of editing to the practices of typesetting — all the while trying to offer fresh insights, for example, how does the editorial 'desk' and the activities that take place at it differ between book publishers and magazine and partwork publishers; what impact are computers actually having; what exactly is digital typesetting?

Design considerations are aired in chapter three: the basic processes involved in design; organizing picture research; acquiring artwork references; arranging location photography; working on layouts. Here the working relationship between editor and designer receives attention, as do the intricacies of choosing pictures and writing captions. The mechanical processes involved in printing — often a mysterious 'blur' to editors — are clearly explained in chapter four. This is followed by a chapter that explores the amorphous territory of promotions, publicity and presentation — looking at blurb writing, book fairs and sales conferences.

The closing chapter sheds light on that almost unmentionable area of publishing — rehashing existing material for new projects. How and why is it done and what role are computers playing in this field? The chapter answers these and other questions.

Thus *Editing for Print* is more than a reference point for standard publishing procedures, it is a guide to the increasingly varied business of international publishing, a business that, above all, relies upon the strength, character and insight of the human mind.

Consider the following. I am preparing my first draft of this introduction in longhand. It will then be typed into the memory of a modest microcomputer, edited on screen and printed out at lightning speed. The publishing editor will read and style it and then send it for typesetting by a computerized system that appears to owe little to the techniques that emerged during the Middle Ages. When the text proofs are checked and positioned on the design layout, when the printing plates are made and the presses have stopped turning, then you can begin to read these words on the printed page. Paradoxically, this introduction is my final contribution to the book. Thus, as my job as one of the authors draws to a close, your journey, as one of the readers, is only just beginning.

Geoffrey Rogers

1
THE FUNDAMENTALS

The editorial role / The print production process / How books and magazines are produced / Budgeting / Scheduling / Generating ideas / Authors / Contracts / Consultants / Research / Flat plans

The word 'edit' literally means 'give out' or 'set in order for publication'; the derived word 'editorial' describes the cutting, revising and reshaping that takes place before publication. 'Editing', therefore, refers to the processing of the written word during its transformation from author's manuscript to printer's plate. The 'editor' is thus the guardian of a book's style, content and logic, fulfilling this role on behalf of the eventual reader, who may not even notice that such care and attention has been lavished upon it.

The editorial role

A concern for the quality and 'fitness' of the text is at the heart of all editorial responsibilities, but being an 'editor' of books or magazines usually involves taking a wider view. This wider view

EDITORIAL JOB TITLES

The definitions given below are a rough guide to editorial job titles, as titles and allocation of work responsibilities will vary from house to house and from one type of publishing house to another.

An editor The basic job title for anyone working on editorial matters in all kinds of publishing. It usually implies an overall responsibility for the 'nuts and bolts' of the editorial process — from finding and briefing authors to overseeing the final result on the printing machine. More precise job titles, such as Military Editor, Cooking Editor, Natural History Editor and so on, refer to the subject area each editor oversees.

The editor A title generally applied to the person who is ultimately responsible for the editorial output and 'angle' of a newspaper or magazine (see below) and who also acts as a 'figurehead' for the publication.

Managing editor In many companies this is synonymous with editor, for most fully-fledged publishing editors manage a wide range of processes and people at the same time. It can also involve the supervision of other less senior editors.

Production editor This individual trafficks material between the editor, copy-editor, proof-reader, and production department, and therefore is involved in several projects at once.

Editorial director Here the responsibility shifts from control of individual projects toward the overall publishing stratagem — the type and number of books or magazines to be published in a given season for example.

Acquisitions editor An editor principally concerned with finding and signing up authors.

Coordinating editor Since coordinating is part of every editor's work, this usually specifically refers to an editor who has brought together the skills of several contributors to prepare a particularly complex publication. It often refers to someone outside the publishing company.

Series editor Quite simply, an editor in charge of a series of publications.

Editor-in-chief An editor who is responsible for an editorial team.

Desk editor Literally an editor who

includes the discussion of ideas and concepts before the author starts to write, the mechanical processes of modern four-color printing, the stratagems of sales and marketing, budgeting and scheduling. Fulfilling these responsibilities involves a complex and rapidly changing series of tasks that make up the 'editorial role'.

The print production process

Having detailed a few of the many editorial duties, we now look at the entire chain of events by which books and magazines are produced.

The production of printed matter can be seen as a kind of 'creative conveyor belt'. Ideas plus materials plus labor are loaded on at one end and completed publications are off loaded at the other. The speed of the conveyor belt varies considerably from books to magazines and also within these categories according to subject, content, budget and a number of other factors.

Some insight into the processes of print production can be gained by examining a finished book or magazine. Open a book to its fullest extent, look down on it from above and it is clear that the pages are bound together by thread or glue into batches (sections, or signatures) of equal size. The outer hard cover (case) of a hardback book is attached to the pages by an extra folded sheet at the front and back (the endpapers). Looking through the pages of any book or magazine it is evident that the text has been produced in a particular style by a mechanical process (typesetting). And, if looked at closely, the photographs appear to be made up of tiny dots that range in size and color — these are halftones which are usually printed using offset lithography but can also be printed using other processes.

Some details of the manufacturing processes involved are

works mainly at a desk. A desk editor is responsible for close control of the text from the author's manuscript through to the finished book.

Content editor A content editor brings about the greatest changes in an author's manuscript, influencing the content and the flow of ideas. The most extreme result of this editor's work is a total rewrite.

Copy-editor When the content editing has been completed the copy-editor checks the text for style, spelling, punctuation, consistency and accuracy — a wide spectrum of important details that need a keen eye and an impartial approach. The copy-editor often marks up the manuscript for typesetting.

Assistant editor or editorial assistant This is usually regarded as the first rung on the editorial ladder. In companies with a well-structured hierarchy, an assistant editor works in close collaboration with an editor, often carrying out the more routine aspects of the editorial workload.

THE MAGAZINE EDITOR

Depending on the size of the magazine and the number of staff members, an editor's role can cover anything from producing it virtually single-handed to a purely supervisory position, but the responsibilities remain the same. It is the editor's job to run the magazine efficiently, consulting the production department or checking the schedule, perhaps daily, to make sure every page and piece of copy (text, caption, chart material) is where it should be and is being produced according to plan. A lost or forgotten section would be disastrous so it is important to maintain a detailed record of every item as it passes between departments or to and from the typesetters.

Checking and approving every stage of the magazine from raw copy and layouts to final proofs is equally essential if good standards of production and continuity of style are to be maintained, and it helps to keep an eye on how the issue is shaping up. In the initial planning stages, a brainstorming of creative ideas from contributors, staff, the advertising department and management have to be collated into a workable, interesting publication. A practical budget must then be worked out and adhered to, and a flat plan has to be drawn up to provide the skeleton of the magazine for everyone to work from.

therefore clearly discernible in the finished product. Evidence of the activities of editors and designers, however, is a little harder to find.

If the text reads fluently and appears to be accurate and relevant then it would seem that the author has responded well to a clear briefing from the editor. It could be the case, however, that the content editor has worked long and hard on a totally unsuitable author's manuscript and succeeded in producing a text that is logical and accessible to the intended readership. The influence of copy-editor and proof-reader may only be discernible in a negative sense, for example, if an error has been missed. If there are no inconsistencies of language, punctuation and style and if the pages are free from typographical errors, then their work has been successful.

The designer tries to be anonymous, for good design, like good film music, should not be apparent on its own, only as a vital and integral contribution to the overall effectiveness of the product. The element of design most discernible to the untutored eye is the organization of the text and illustrations into an overall pattern. The invisible guidelines of this pattern stem from the designer's 'grid'. A grid is a plan of the empty page that sets out the design parameters for a particular project: the style, width and position of the text; the width and position of captions; the maximum extent of photographs; the position of chapter headings and so on.

It is possible to consider the price of a book or magazine in terms of 'value for money', but this provides no real clue as to how the price was arrived at in relation to the costs involved in its production. In common with other manufacturing processes, time and money are inextricably linked in the publishing world and the twin considerations of scheduling and budgeting are therefore important aspects for the editor to heed.

Having examined the final product to discover something of what was involved in its production, we now need to go right back to the beginning and put these events in their logical order. Since books are the most complex products within our view we shall explain the production sequence with books in mind and then show where magazines differ in any significant way. The broad sequence of events described below will form the plan for the rest of this handbook.

How books are produced

Book publishing activities divide into four major areas and include:

1 Editorial
2 Design
3 Production
4 Sales/marketing

And, conveniently, this sequence of headings reflects the overall direction in which the creative conveyor belt moves, although all departments are involved to a greater or lesser extent at every stage of a book's development. Two other areas — management and accounts — are also part of the formula but they are controlling influences rather than directly involved in the production process.

Editorial It is an editorial responsibility to generate ideas for new projects or to respond to those submitted by outside contributors. In the world of full-color, illustrated reference books most ideas are initiated within a publishing company, and an author or authors are contracted to prepare them.

The first fruit of the editor/author collaboration is a synopsis, or outline, detailing what is to be included in the proposed book. The synopsis becomes the universal 'currency' of information for all other departments during the early stages: the designer scans it to formulate a design approach; the production manager considers it in the light of the processing and printing requirements; and the sales and marketing people discuss the sales potential of it with their sales representatives. They also glean advance information from the synopsis for promotional purposes.

If the synopsis is accepted, and here all departments, including management and accounts, have their say, the editor draws up a contract with the author (or the author's agent).

At this stage three basic plans are set into operation: a production schedule, a budget and a flat plan (a page-by-page 'story-board' of the whole book). These plans are discussed and influenced by all departments.

The editor usually maintains regular contact with the author throughout the manuscript development period, discussing and monitoring each stage.

Once the author's manuscript starts to arrive, and it often comes in batches, the whole process moves ahead with some urgency in order to meet the publication date set by the production schedule. As batches of text arrive, the editor will edit it for content and logic or arrange for this to be done, elicit the expert reactions of any suitable consultants, and then organize detailed copy-editing for style and consistency. The editor, designers and sometimes the author, will generate a list of the photographs and illustrations that will be required.

Having originated or fine-tuned an idea, engaged an author, planned the general approach of the book and edited the text, the editor's initial push is now over and the impetus passes to the design department.

Design The designer's first task is to decide on the typestyle for the text and send sections of text for sample typesetting. When the designer has decided on the fonts to be used he or she will style the whole manuscript and send it to be set. In some companies the editor will do this. In the meantime, attention turns toward designing the layout grids that will serve as the working 'blueprint' for all departments during the rest of the production period. Picture research, photography and illustration are usually commissioned by the designer, but always in close association with the editor. Using the typeset text (in galley form — long strips of photographically produced paper that has the typeset characters exposed on it), photographs chosen from those provided by the author or picture researcher and ideas for illustrations, the designer produces the layouts — a full-size visual record of the whole book in the form of flat 'double page spreads' (sheets showing the left- and right-hand pages in a book). Sometimes the designer will work out just a few spreads which will be used to style the rest of the book. Now the editor becomes actively involved again, writing captions, cutting or extending the text to make it fit the grid exactly, inserting headings and other elements.

At this point in the sequence the boundary between design and production becomes a little blurred. In companies without a production department, the designer will send the photographs

Producing books is a fine blend of creative and mechanical processes (**below**). Activity centers around the work of the design, editorial and production teams, molding the raw material supplied by authors into books that are the shape, size and price demanded by the retailers and readers. Along the way, the efforts of many specialists — typesetters, picture researchers, photographers, artists, separators and printers — provide crucial support.

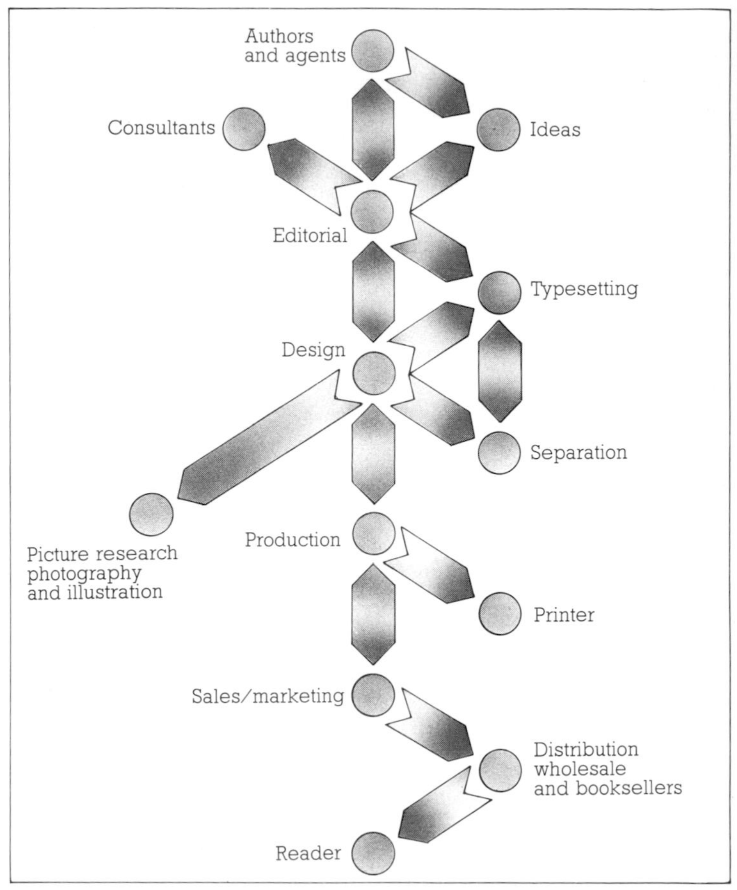

and illustration artwork off for separation into the color films needed for printing and will also check the color proofs.

Production Traditionally, the production department is concerned with all the mechanical aspects of the production process rather than with the artistic ones. This may include sending the styled text for typesetting and certainly involves dispatching photographs and artwork for preparation and separation. It is the production manager's job to secure the highest quality work for the time and money available.

When all the text and illustration films are assembled the production manager 'chaperones' it through printing, binding, delivery and warehousing. Where a distinct production department does not exist, the designer (or even the printer) will perform these roles. It is rare for an editor to become involved with the printing stage itself, although checking the final imposed proof (blueprints are the most common) before the book is passed for press and printing starts is an important editorial task.

Sales/marketing Having publicized the book in advance, based on the synopsis and other information from the editor, the promotion side of the sales/marketing department sends finished copies for review, buys advertising space and arranges any publicity campaigns, competitions and signing sessions that are considered suitable. In general, the sales/marketing department oversees the distribution of the book to bookstores and also sells the rights to book clubs, foreign publishers and others. A company engaged in international publishing may have foreign rights staff who will be responsible for selling language rights to different areas of the world. The various book fairs held throughout the year are focal points for this selling activity.

At this stage the author or editor may be asked to champion the book at sales conferences and book fairs, and will certainly be required to write enticing blurbs for catalogs and other publicity material.

Management/accounts Throughout this period of activity, the management and accounts departments have been badgering the editor, designer, production and sales managers about schedules and budgets, vital areas that form the subject of later sections.

How magazines are produced

What is a magazine? A magazine is what is also called, more accurately, a 'periodical' — a publication that comes out 'periodically' whether that be weekly, bi-weekly, bi-monthly or quarterly.

The main attraction of a magazine to the reader is a relatively low selling price and a combination of regular or serialized features which encourage him or her to buy the next issue (columns by personalities and fiction are good examples), supported by up-to-date news and information. A specialty magazine will aim to keep its readers informed on current trends and products, covering the subject in some detail and providing professional advice; a more general publication will concentrate on good entertainment value — a blend of informative articles, personal advice, fiction, news and picture features depending on its readership.

Magazines can be divided into two types: trade and consumer. The trade magazines are often directly distributed and provide a vital link between manufacturers/craftsmen, retailers and wholesalers, keeping well ahead of trends with news and features; consumer publications have a far broader appeal, without such a captive audience, and rely on attracting spontaneous purchases at the news-stand as well as a core of regular readers who buy their copy by subscription or by placing a regular order with their newsagent. Both trade and consumer magazines have a certain percentage of 'hidden readers' in that an issue is passed on from one person to another.

Unlike books, a magazine usually relies completely on advertising that is directly aimed at the estimated interests and inclinations of the readers and linked closely to the editorial content.

Another important aspect of magazines that differs from most other types of publication is reader involvement. This can take the form of competitions, magazine sweepstakes or even simply a problem column.

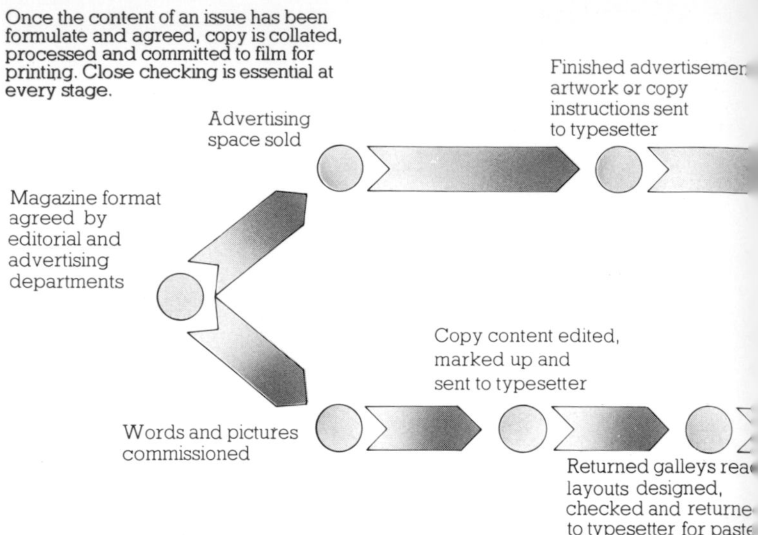
Advertising
space sold
Finished advertisemen
artwork or copy
instructions sent
to typesetter
Magazine format
agreed by
editorial and
advertising
departments
Copy content edited,
marked up and
sent to typesetter
Words and pictures
commissioned
Returned galleys rea
layouts designed,
checked and returne
to typesetter for paste
Once the content of an issue has been formulate and agreed, copy is collated, processed and committed to film for printing. Close checking is essential at every stage.

As publishers continue to pinpoint reader interest in their advertising and editorial content, additional specialty magazines are constantly being introduced. The subjects they cover are wide ranging and even focus on the concerns of specific age groups. These specialty magazines offer helpful how-to and anecdotal information on a subject and present it in depth.

Perhaps even more significant is the noticeable rise of the regionalized magazine. Regionalization is an attempt to improve the editorial service to the readers, providing them with specific information that applies to where they live. Such magazines are developed as a result of demographic and geographic research. A questionnaire is generally mailed to subscribers of the magazine, which is intended to bring to light subjects of importance and relevance to the reader.

This regionalization of magazines is the result of the inflow of magazine circulation into smaller geographic areas. Magazines will split their circulation into regional editions and certain pages will appear in only one region. This may be accomplished by incorporating one regionally slanted article of four to eight pages as a self-contained insert to the edition. The geographic divisions generally include four major areas: the Midwest, the West, the Northeast and the South.

More sophisticated production and distribution techniques are predicted for the near future. With the advent of word-processing equipment that interfaces with typesetting equipment and outside computers, it is quite likely that the process of going from manuscript to camera-ready copy will greatly accelerated, and less costly. These trends indicate that magazine publishers will have more money for individual growth and more time and flexibility to experiment with new formats in the future. The results will most likely cater to almost every special interest imaginable.

The principles of budgeting

It is not intended that this section be an in-depth analysis of financial strategy, more a simple introduction to the concepts of budgeting in books and magazines as they apply to the working editor.

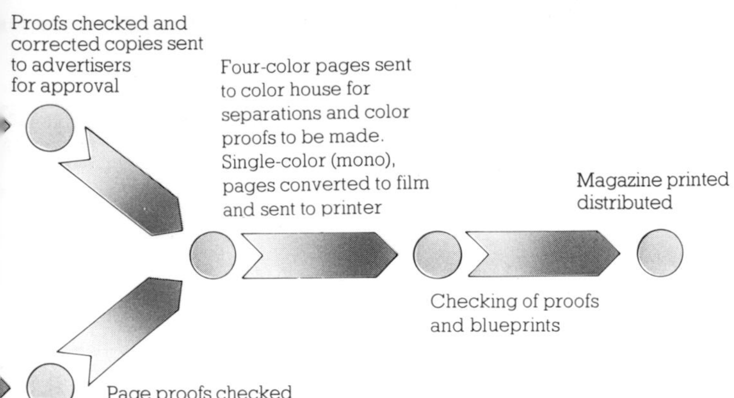
Proofs checked and corrected copies sent to advertisers for approval
Four-color pages sent to color house for separations and color proofs to be made. Single-color (mono), pages converted to film and sent to printer
Magazine printed distributed
Checking of proofs and blueprints
Page proofs checked and corrected

Basic elements in a book budget
The stages in the production schedule form a useful framework for itemizing the cost of a book up to the printing stage. The individuals and companies whose services may be employed during the production of a book are paid in various ways:
Author/text Depending on the type of contract arranged (see page 29-30) an author is either paid a flat fee according to the total number of words in the book, which is by far the most common method for general illustrated books, or receives an advance payment (an advance on royalty) and then a percentage (a royalty) of the book's retail price or net receipts from sales, usually on some form of sliding scale according to the number of books sold.
Consultant reader A flat fee is usual here, although a fee to a 'name' consultant might seem high in relation to the work done.
Freelance editing/proof-reading Usually paid on a time basis, per hour or at a daily rate.
Typing Charged at a rate per hour or per thousand words.

On magazines the activities of the design and editorial teams are paralleled by the advertising department's endeavours to sell money-earning space.

Typesetting Typesetters usually base their first galley charges on the number of characters in the text, (usually per thousand ens or by the number of keystrokes needed to complete the job. They will correct their own typographical errors free of charge, but charge for author's alterations and the publisher's changes. Making the text up into pages may be charged per page or per double page spread. Complicated or display setting is charged separately. Different typesetters offer different services, so check with them what they do and whether they do it manually or electronically as this will affect factors of time and cost.

Picture research Picture researchers usually either negotiate a flat fee with the publisher involved or work on an hourly basis and invoice the publisher for the work done.

Photograph copyright fees Publishing a photograph invariably involves paying a copyright fee. It may be a relatively small sum or even merely a hire fee paid to a museum, or a seemingly exorbitant amount paid to a top picture agency or photographic library. The exact amount paid depends on a number of factors: whether the photograph is used in color or black-and-white (the latter is cheaper); where and how it is used in the book: quarter-page, half-page, full-page, chapter opener, or cover shot (the larger and more prominent it is the higher the cost will be); what rights are required (one language rights worldwide, for example, are cheaper than world rights in all languages); and usually on the total number of photographs used from one source (using more than a certain number constitutes a 'bulk deal' and lowers the price for all the pictures). Picture researchers generally endeavor to secure the best deal for the publisher. If photographs are not returned in a specified time period, picture agencies charge holding fees on a daily or weekly basis. Since the aim is to avoid attracting holding fees, these are not usually included in budgets.

Commissioned photography Most photographers charge a daily rate, which may or may not include film stock, processing costs and expenses, depending on individual arrangements.

Illustrations An artist or artist's agent will quote a price for each individual piece of artwork based on the time involved in producing it, although an overall fee may be agreed for a large job entailing many illustrations. The fee usually includes the preparation of a pencil rough for the publisher's editor and designer to approve. Artwork illustrations range from simple line diagrams to elaborate 'paintings', the latter being more expensive and time-consuming than using photographs.

Preparation (color separations and halftones) A separation house will quote a price for processing each piece of artwork or photograph into films depending on the number and size of the images. Special work, such as silhouette halftones or vignetting, will increase the price. Where a large number of images is involved a uniform price is usually agreed for each piece.

These are the broad categories of expense that go into a typical preprinting budget. The costs involved in printing, binding, shipping and distribution are usually the province of the production department.

Fixed costs and variable costs These terms will come up in any conversation about budgets. Quite simply, fixed costs remain unchanged however many copies of a book are printed and variable costs are directly linked to the number of books printed. Typical fixed and variable costs are shown right.

How to set out a book budget

Most publishing companies provide standard forms for recording budgetary information, often incorporating the book specifications as well. These forms may also be used to calculate and record print runs, sales revenue, break-even point, royalties earned at home and abroad, and other ramifications of publishing at a profit. For an editor working in an illustrated book house, however, the initial aim is to prepare a simple statement of cost up to the printing stage arranged in logical categories. Starting with a blank piece of paper, the following example shows a possible layout.

SAMPLE BUDGET: BOOKS

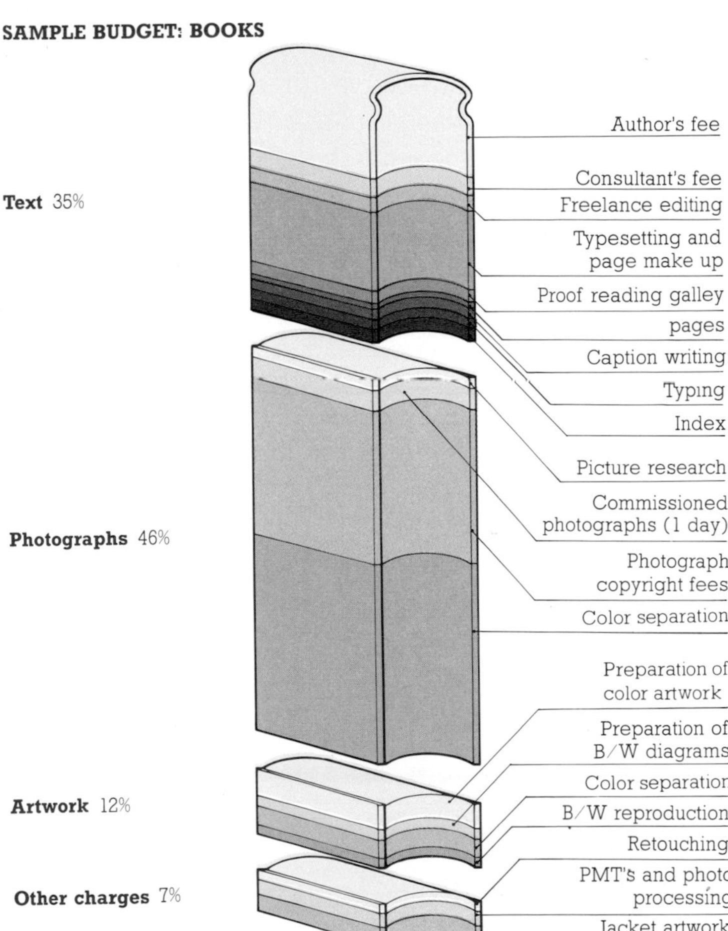

Fixed costs
- Author's fee (if flat fee)
- Picture research
- Typesetting and page make up
- Freelance editing, proof-reading
- Indexing
- Photograph copyright fees (if world rights for all editions bought)
- Commissioned photography
- Artwork illustrations
- Reproduction, separation
- Making printing plates (unless reprint needs new plates)

Variable costs
- Author's fee (if on royalty basis)
- Paper
- Printing
- Binding
- Shipping
- Distribution

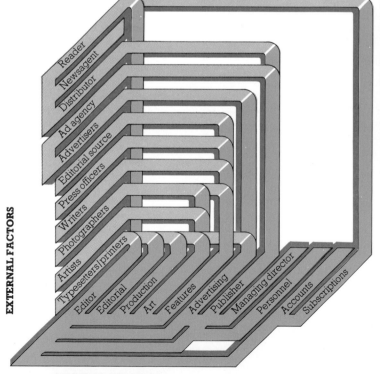

Internal and external factors in magazine publishing

Internal factors fall easily into two groups: management and staff directly concerned with producing the magazine. Management, headed by the publisher, who is responsible for any major magazine decisions and its overall profitability, includes personnel staff who handle stationery, employment details and so on; accounts staff who deal with salaries and expenses, contributor's fees and sponsorship; and a subscription department, which is often separate from the main publishing company. Those more directly concerned with the magazine are the staff in the advertising and the editorial departments. They operate alongside each other and are directly answerable to the publisher via their department managers. The number of staff members in the editorial team will be geared to the size of the magazine: content editors, layout artists, designers, assistants and secretaries as they are required.

Externally, the readers and advertisers are the magazine's *raison d'être*; freelance writers, artists and photographers provide a large portion of the creative material in the issue; press officers and other research sources offer raw material and the typesetters and printers physically produce it.

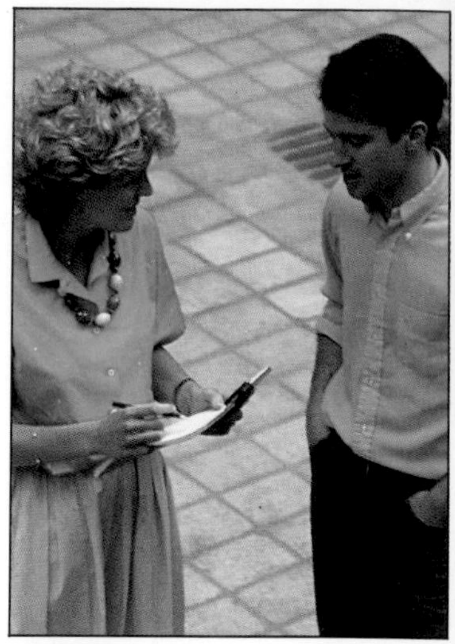

Editorial research is a vital element in the planning of any new publication. How the consumer reacts to the idea is all important, and one of the best ways of finding out is by conducting surveys (**above**).

The purely mechanical element of the fixed costs, that is typesetting, paging, color separation, platemaking, and so on are known as 'plant' costs. The mechanical costs involved in a reprint are called 'running costs'.

Mark-ups and discounts How are the costs involved in producing a book reflected in the retail price? In general terms, the production cost of each book is multiplied ('marked-up') to arrive at the retail price. The crucial point here is what the production cost includes. If a publishing company wishes to make a profit on the first edition of a book then it will add the fixed costs to the variable costs and divide by the number of copies printed. This usually results in an unreasonably high retail price, unless the first print run (number of copies printed) is unusually large. The usual strategy is to use just the variable costs in this formula. This may mean that the first edition does not recover the fixed costs, but printing further editions (perhaps foreign ones) may recover the fixed costs and move the book into profit. The in-house editorial work is usually not included as a cost against each project. It is considered as part of the overheads and the general running costs of the company, with other in-house activities such as promotion, sales, distribution, and accounting.

How much does a bookseller pay for each book? Normally, publishers give booksellers a discount of 40 percent to 45 percent on the retail price, depending on the type of book and the number being ordered. Discounts on exported books may range up to 70 percent of the retail price.

Budgeting in magazines

A magazine is a very visual, commercial and flexible medium. Its budget can be apportioned in many different ways or even augmented by sponsorship to provide the best result. The total sum will often be divided, not necessarily equally, between art and editorial: the editorial budget will be mainly concentrated on writing and research — freelance writers for anything that cannot be handled in-house, expert advisers and interviewers. Specialty writers or researchers and personalities such as actors, authors and top humorists naturally charge higher rates and are less readily available; they are consequently used sparingly and where they will create the most effective impact. In the case of a specialist publication you may well have to cut back on illustration to be able to afford the expert text.

Illustration, be it photographic or commissioned artwork, is expensive and usually forms a large part of the magazine's budget. There are many ways this can be adjusted to create a good-looking issue — for instance, using the money to devise a couple of very good features and spending more time and thought on the design of the other cheaper, often monochrome, pages. Imaginative typography, tints and design can make the most of these pages.

Both color transparencies and monochrome halftones are readily available free of charge from companies and can be used to illustrate more product-oriented features in return for a credit in the caption. These are not always ideal as they often lack quality or good composition but, used with imagination, they can provide a valuable free source of illustration. Original commissioned photography is expensive and should be used wisely to achieve value for money: plan it well in advance with the art

The illustration (**right**) provides a general guide as to how the retail cost of a book is broken down. The author's royalty may account for approximately 10% of the retail price. If the author is paid a flat fee then this will be reflected in the unit production cost — broadly the publisher's expenses divided by the number of copies produced. The discount given to retailers varies, but hovers around 40%. The overhead/profit segment refers to the publisher's in-house costs — salaries, taxes and energy bills — and a contribution to profit for new publishing investment.

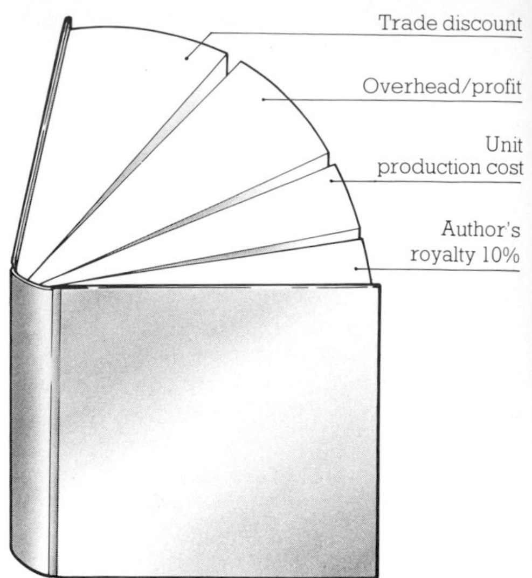

department or designer and make sure you choose the right photographer for the job. If you will be featuring a wide range of products it is always worth approaching some of the manufacturers for possible sponsorship to offset all or some of your costs.

Existing photographs available from photographers' libraries and picture agencies are obviously less expensive if the picture researcher can find a suitable shot. The researcher can often agree a reduced fee if a whole series of photographs is used in one issue.

In order to stay within the budget, the magazine must have defined limits and be strictly enforced. For this reason, the overall budget must be strictly apportioned to each department. Within each department, a certain amount of money will need to be allocated to individual tasks. For example, the editorial budget may consist of freelance writing, proof-reading, consultational reading, copy-editing and research fees. When assigning material to a freelance, it is best to provide clear budget limitations, particularly when hourly rates and additional expenses are involved. The freelance should be instructed that if he or she is about to exceed a certain amount of money, then the editor for the project should be contacted before further work proceeds. This is important so that there is money left over if needed for extra freelance writers, temporary help, and worker overtime.

Likewise, the art director must recognize that he or she may need to bring in freelance paste-up and design people at the end of a production cycle. The production budget will also have to allow for overtime bills: it is less expensive, for example, to hold the presses and pay overtime charges in order to get an issue out on time with all the necessary copy and advertising than to lose several pages of advertising — and the revenue that a magazine needs to survive.

Just as it is the most deadline-conscious of departments, the production department is also the most cost-conscious group in the magazine. The production manager should keep reevaluating the kind of preparation suppliers the company is using. With the new systems of electronic page make up the functions of the preparation process and the printer are no longer completely separate. Extremely advanced production techniques are constantly being developed: for example, it is becoming increasingly cheaper to produce a standard-sized issue rather than an odd-sized one; satellites can now deliver digitized information to the printers so that plates can be made faster; and new developments in web printing result in huge savings in labor and manufacturing costs for the customer, since the presses run faster and more efficiently. Although the transition to such seemingly futuristic equipment may at first be intimidating, it will very soon produce returns on investment.

Working out a basic schedule

A schedule is simply a timetable for the various activities that go into making a book or magazine. Since these activities represent a blend of creative skills and highly sophisticated technical processes it is not surprising that accurate schedules are difficult to prepare and even more difficult to keep.

A book schedule

In principle, preparing a production schedule for a book involves working backward from the publication date, allowing a prescribed period of time for each stage along the way. For even a modest full-color illustrated book these stages may add up to a

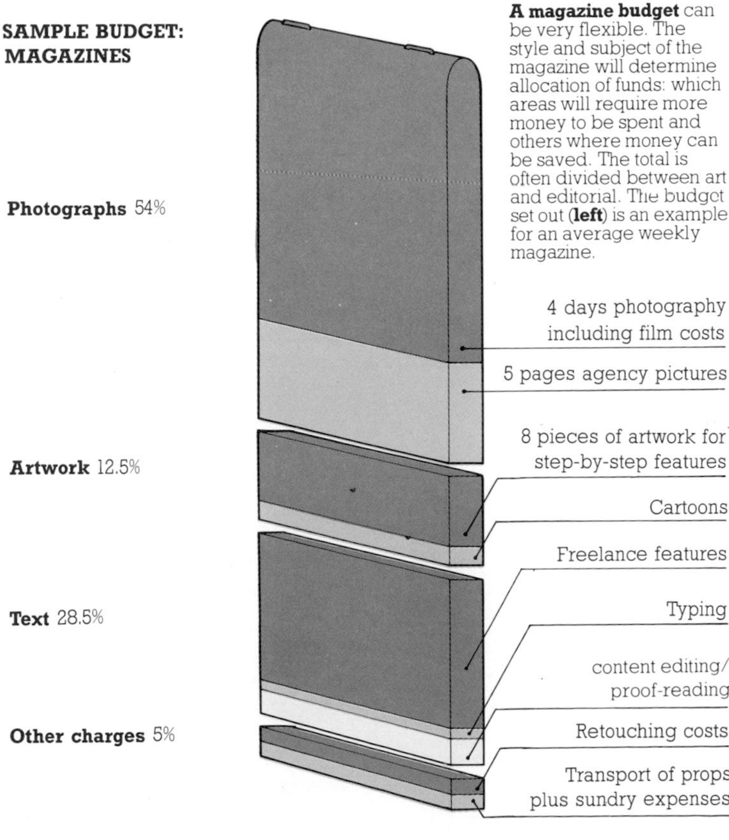

A magazine budget can be very flexible. The style and subject of the magazine will determine allocation of funds: which areas will require more money to be spent and others where money can be saved. The total is often divided between art and editorial. The budget set out (**left**) is an example for an average weekly magazine.

period of between nine months and a year. In simple terms, the stages for a typical illustrated book are:

1 Writing
2 Editing
3 Typesetting
4 Design
5 Color separation
6 Printing
7 Shipping to warehouse
8 Distribution

As we have seen, many of these stages in themselves involve several sequences of activity that must be allowed for in the schedule. Some of the activities in the list above can proceed in parallel, while others cannot begin until the previous stage is complete. And since the schedule represents a real situation, rather than a theoretical exercise in logistics, it must also take into account holidays, allowances for possible problems with an author, expected plant shutdowns, conflicting schedules and other factors, for it to be a true picture of expected progress.

Drawing up a reasonable schedule is therefore a complex task. The publication dates for all the year's forthcoming books are usually worked out during a meeting involving all departments. The last three stages in the production sequence (printing, delivery and distribution) cannot overlap, and it is possible to estimate reasonably accurate dates for these processes from previous experience with similar books printed at the same printing company. This information will usually be supplied by management or from the production department. What really concerns the editor is the schedule up to the printing stage. The deadlines listed below are crucial for the editor:

- Text complete date
- Typesetting complete date
- Artwork to separation house date (for separation into films)
- Final films to printer date.

The text completion date is reflected in the deadline given to the author. It sometimes happens that working backward from a publication date produces a text completion date that allows the author barely enough time to write the book. Here, some forward

Setting out a basic schedule
Schedules are of great importance in publishing, as they are for most commercial production processes. If correctly worked out and properly presented, a book schedule gives the editorial teams a plan of action to follow. Visual representation of each important phase as a horizontal bar, set against the calendar (**right**), clearly shows any overlap between projects moving on parallel courses and is far more effective than a sterile list of dates.

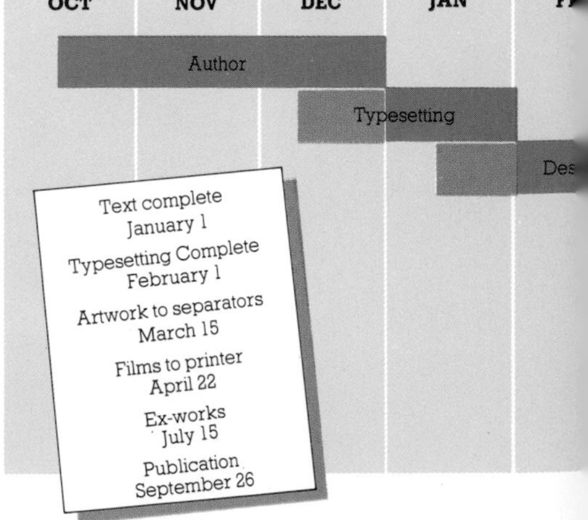

planning is needed to arrive at a realistic schedule. It is always advisable to allow more time for each stage in a schedule than the absolute minimum, and nowhere is this more vital than at the writing phase. Problems with authors do arise, particularly with inexperienced authors new to the commercial pressures of publishing, and the text completion deadline must allow for some 'false-starts' or other problems.

Between the text completion and the typesetting completion dates lies the broad sweep of the actual editing work. Here the editor must consider the logistic of sending out the text for content editing, consultational reading and copy-editing. An editor working in an illustrated book house supplying the 'impatient' international market does not usually have the time to attend to these tasks personally so it is a question of seeing who is free and building their time into the schedule. The problem with this is that when the schedule is drawn up it is difficult to anticipate how much editing a text will need.

The time taken for typesetting is usually fairly easy to calculate, although often several books will be on parallel schedules and arrive at the same typesetting house at the same time. This is one of the practical difficulties that is not visible when 'theoretical' schedules are drawn up.

If the manuscript was cleanly edited before typesetting then proof-reading (again likely to be a freelance task) should not take too long. Usually, the author checks the first galleys and returns them promptly. The concern at this stage is that the author might want to rewrite the book having seen his or her words set into type. This should be discouraged politely in a cover letter to the author; heavy rewriting on the proofs not only delays the schedule but pushes up typesetting costs alarmingly.

When the first text proofs arrive they are given to the designer, who begins working toward the next key deadline: artwork to separation house. Time must now be allowed for picture research, picture selection, illustration briefs to be sketched and final artwork to be prepared. All these elements, together with the text, must then be incorporated in the final design. In some publishing companies, photographs and artwork are sent for separation in batches; in this case the artwork to separation house

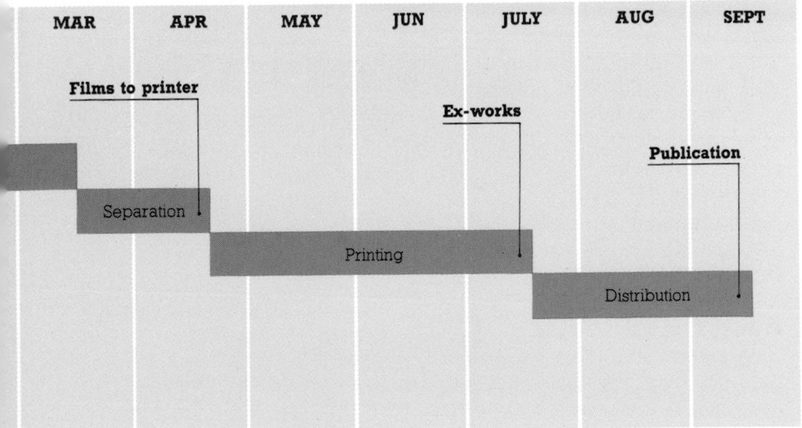

The schedule (**right**) for an average, color weekly magazine reflects the steps from raw copy to printing and publication. It is quite usual to be working to three deadlines for the production of one issue: the cover and the color pages in section 1 need to be prepared first as these take longer to reproduce. Often the first section is printed in four-color on one side of the web and in mono on the other. Section 2 follows as it contains areas of color. Section 3 has a later deadline as monochrome pages are simpler to reproduce.

		Cover meeting	Manuscripts delivered	Photography or artwork commissioned	Manuscripts to types
Section 1	colour pages		**7/6** 10am	**10/6** 6pm	**11/6** 6pm
	mono pages		**10/6** 10am	**12/6** 6pm	**12/6** 6pm
Section 2	spot colour		**13/6** 10am	**14/6** 6pm	**14/6** 6pm
Section 3	mono pages		**20/6** Noon	**20/6** Noon	**20/6** 6pm
	late mono pages		**24/6** 11am		
Front cover		**7/6** 10am		**7/6** 6pm	**12/6** 6pm

deadline refers to the last batch to be sent.

The sending of final films to the printer is the major deadline for all concerned. It means that the text should be in final page form (as film or correct proofs stuck down in the right positions on boards, depending on the method used) and all the illustrations and photographs should be in the form of separated films ready for the printer. Accompanying these is the 'master paste-up'. This is a series of design layouts that show the whole project in spread by spread form and it is used as a final positional guide by the printer. Some printers will not start their work until they have all the materials for the book and one or two vital pieces always seem to be late!

How to set out a schedule Perhaps the least effective way of recording important deadlines is simply to put dates next to each category. There are few people who can recall a list of random dates. Also important are the dates chosen: it can lead to a false sense of security if dates such as May 1 are used instead of the seemingly much more 'pressing' date of April 30.

The most effective presentation, at least for the editor, is to record the deadlines and activities as separate lines on a horizontal bar chart. Showing them to scale, and in relation to the calendar gives a realistic picture of the time periods involved and highlights any overlapping activities. Comparing one book schedule with another one that is represented in the same way will reveal any obvious clashes.

Many publishing companies have standard forms to carry schedule information from the beginning of the editorial process right through to printing and delivery. These are effective *aide memoires* for all departments, but the conscientious editor will be concentrating primarily on the preprinting deadlines and will appreciate an interpretation that focuses on the important dates from the editorial and design points of view.

A magazine schedule

The basic schedule is generally worked backward from the proposed on sale date and the printers' available machine time. It must be realistically calculated to fit in with the magazine and typesetter's capacities, remembering to allow for public holidays, weekends and any likely staffing problems during the summer and Christmas periods. If the publishing house uses a

Galleys back to editorial	Galleys and briefing to studio	Make up to typesetter	Color artwork to separation house	First page proofs to editorial	First page proofs to typesetter	Second page proofs to editorial	Cromalin proofs to studio	Pages passed/ cover approved
13/6 10am	**13/6** Noon	**14/6** 6pm	**14/6** 6pm	**18⅙06** 10am	**18/6** 6pm	**19/6** 2pm	**19/6** Noon	**19/6** 6pm
14/6 10am	**14/6** Noon	**17/6** 6pm		**19/6** 10am	**19/6** 6pm	**20/6** 2pm		**20/6** 6pm
18/6 10am	**18/6** Noon	**19/6** Noon		**20/6** 10am	**20/6** 6pm	**21/6** 2pm		**21/6** 6pm
21/6 Noon	**21/6** 3pm	**21/6** 6pm		**24/6** Noon	**24/6** 3pm	**24/6** 5pm		**24/6** 6pm
	24/6 Noon	**24/6** 3pm		**24/6** 7pm	**24/6** 8pm	**24/6** 9pm		**24/6** 10pm
14/6 Noon			**14/6** 6pm				**19/6** Noon	**19/6** 6pm

foreign color separation house or printer, their holiday patterns are often different and this must be borne in mind when the schedule is being made.

The basic schedule within this framework will be determined by allowing sufficient time for: the material to be written and illustrated; typesetters to turn around copy and layouts; proofs to be read; color separations to be made; distribution of the magazine.

The scheduling process is instituted at a general staff meeting that includes key members of the art and editorial departments. At this meeting, a general brainstorming occurs and many ideas are discussed for a particular issue that is three months away. If a theme or series of article themes is not arrived at in this meeting, a second meeting is held the following week in which the ideas are further shaped and given a concrete form. The managing editor will start to draw up a schedule of who he or she should be expecting copy from, since the editor-in-chief will be assigning articles to editors who will either be writing them themselves, assigning them to staff writers, or using freelances, depending on the organization of the magazine. At this time, the photography and artwork are conceptualized so that they can quickly be commissioned or assigned to staff artists and designers.

By the third week, the issue for the following month has been mechanicalized and color separations have been made. The managing editor and the editor-in-chief generally give final approval to these boards so that they can be dispatched to the printer. By the beginning of the fourth week, the printer should have delivered blueprints or page proofs for one last check. Then, the issue can be printed, bound and delivered. Since the on-sale date of a magazine is usually the third week of the month before the cover month, this four week process is adjusted to this schedule. Work will continue on forthcoming issues.

When the copy for the next issue begins to arrive, the managing editor will often give a copy of the article to the fact-checking/ research department first for verification of all factual information. Then it will go to the copy department where it will be copy-edited and worked on by the content editor. The article is then transmitted to the art department where a designer writes up specifications for the typesetter. After it has been typeset, it will be transmitted back to the managing editor who will have it proof-read, and the layout process can start. After final galley corrections are made, the content editor, the editor-in-chief, or possibly the managing editor will make final cuts and fills on the boards and write any final heads and crossheads. After the mechanicalized boards and all visual materials have been sent out and returned for approval, the process starts again with a new issue.

This hypothetical framework seems to run smoothly enough, but scheduling snags do seem to crop up often. Most production managers cite late editorial copy and late advertising as the main culprits for an issue being late. Identifying problems that cause schedule setbacks can be confusing because the stages of the production schedule are so intertwined. Therefore, it is important that a production manager stay on top of the printing schedule, because a late print date can cause heavy overtime charges, and a late issue means a potential loss of news-stand sales. Many advertisers wait until the last minute to send in their copy, which can be a production manager's nightmare. However, it is a necessary evil since ad copy generates significant revenue. Another major problem caused by late advertising is that there is often no room for it in the layout, or the advertiser may not be able to receive his desired space. Oftentimes, mechanicals need to be reassembled to accommodate late advertising.

Generating ideas

New ideas for illustrated books offered on the international market are usually generated from within a publishing company and first see the light of day as proposals (with impressive mock-ups) at the various book fairs throughout the year, and in particular at the Frankfurt Book Fair in October. From this platform many a flier (a proposal based more on hope than on certainty) takes wing to become a firm project for the following year. The approach of the Frankfurt Book Fair and other book fairs — notably in London, America (ABA) and the children's book fair at Bologna — tends to concentrate the editorial mind on the search for innovative ideas.

Generating ideas is a constant concern for editors. Often the most successful ideas are to be found very close to existing ones; a variation on a theme may be more rewarding than searching for a new theme. A period of completely free-ranging thinking can sometimes lead to a severe bout of desperation, a feeling that nothing new exists and that everything has been done before. The quest is not so much for new subjects, however, as for new ways of presenting existing subjects. Add to this the commercial constraints of cost, schedule and intended market and an idea can begin to take shape and form.

Keeping in touch with new trends and developments in the world is high on the list of an editor's general responsibilities. Editors who specialize in certain subjects, such as natural history, cooking, crafts, health and so on will find countless sources for new books in their reading, in their contact with existing authors and experts, from radio and TV programs, and through proposals sent in from contributors. In many cases, new books are additions to a series and here the established format will help to shape the editor's thinking constructively.

When an idea for a new book begins to crystallize in an editor's mind, the first move should be to visit libraries and bookstores in search of existing books on the subject. These not only show how competing publishers have tackled the same or related subjects, but also provide those first exploratory forays into that most difficult country of all for editors — finding someone good and reliable to write the book.

Generating ideas for magazines While the editor has overall say on the content of the magazine and the basic framework, ideas are best generated and discussed by as many people as possible. Week-by-week contact with material, companies and people in the same field will help stimulate the imagination; press releases, clippings, suggestions from freelance writers and even letters from readers are all good material for feature ideas. Most picture agencies will be able to provide a selection of foreign magazines on a regular basis, useful not only for ideas, but most features are available for syndication complete with pictures and translation.

A full editorial meeting held at the early planning stages of an issue is the best way to assimilate and develop such ideas: throw them open to general discussion and see what transpires. Remember that art and editorial staffs should be working closely together even at this stage and some cross fertilization of ideas should be encouraged.

Not unimportantly, the research department might have some excellent suggestions for article ideas. Based on the kind of information they collect in readership polls, it will be easier for the editorial staff to come up with good and relevant ideas. Keeping up-to-date on social and economic trends by subscribing to market research publications will give you an even sharper idea of how you can help fill peoples' needs. Perhaps most important of all, the editor must get to know his or her readership intimately.

There are dozens of other ways to generate exciting articles. Try culling ideas from past articles that sparked reader interest. It has been argued that there is really no such thing as a new idea, just new ways of presenting them. So do more with your articles than simply present them as text and brainstorm with editorial and art departments. Another fertile ground for providing new ideas is the Sunday paper: it is always an accurate reflection of trends and is often the first to preview and review fashion and cultural events.

Another tested and true technique of drawing reader attention is to preview an important social or sporting event, and feature it boldly on the cover. There will already be an excitation in the air surrounding this event, so most of the publicity is already done for the magazine by the media. Since the movie, television, and music culture always draws eager spectators, you can expect a ready-made audience for the celebrity interview, or have the celebrity model for the magazine. Since the magazine must relate to people's everyday needs, it should draw its material from vital, everyday issues and be accommodating enough to respond to changing styles and tastes.

Finding an author

The boundary between crystallizing an idea and finding an author is a movable one. Talking with a possible writer often leads to substantial changes in the idea itself. Simply telephoning authors of existing books often brings results, if only to provide an opportunity to talk over the subject area in a general way.

If the new book is to be part of a series or closely related to other books on the publisher's list, then contacting a previous author is an obvious first step, either as a possible writer or for advice on likely candidates. Most authors are quite happy to suggest someone more suitable than they for a particular task. This is based on the simple assumption that sooner or later one of their colleagues will be asked the same question and will, in turn, recommend them.

If the subject represents new territory to the editor then contacting the relevant association or society can prove rewarding. Every aspect of human inquiry, however obscure, will usually have an official body to represent and further its activities. Appropriate magazines and journals are also a valuable source of names.

Finding several authors for an extensive project may be a task for an outside consultant. If time is short, this is often the best way of short-cutting the learning curve involved in starting from scratch. Literary agents can also help. They attempt to match authors and projects to everybody's satisfaction. Some agents specialize in one type of work — fiction, non-fiction or children's books, for example — and/or are particularly well represented in specific subject areas.

Finding a magazine writer Finding a writer for a particular article is not as easy as it may seem: if it cannot be handled in-house (and it is important not to overload in-house writers in the interests of cutting costs as this is a false economy), you will have to find a freelance writer who is not only experienced in the subject you want to cover, but will write the piece for the right price. Good, specialist writers are not cheap but it is always worth paying for quality and reliability. After a while you will build up your own file of contacts but, initially, they can be found through recommendation from other magazine editors, introductions at press functions or by likely candidates approaching your magazine or company directly for work. For specialized subjects it is sometimes worth approaching staff members of the specialized magazines, the press officers of specialized companies or associations (not guaranteed to have a good writing style, but whose facts are reliable) or consult a freelance journalist directory.

Briefing an author

When the search for an author starts to bring promising results, it is best for the editor and the author to meet. In a discussion, the editor can see how much original material and freshness of approach the possible author brings to the germ of the idea.

If the meeting is fruitful the next stage is to ask the author to prepare a synopsis of the proposed book. This should show how the idea translates to the printed page, detailing the length and subject of the chapters, the angle of approach and listing the main areas for illustration — in short, a fairly detailed outline of the book as the author would write it.

The synopsis is the first real building block in the editorial process. Passed for comment to the design, management, production and sales departments, it provides the necessary sounding board for initial reactions. If the synopsis completely misses the point, it is possible to pay the author a rejection fee for the time spent on it. If the synopsis shows promise but the author is inexperienced, it is usual to request a text sample of at least 2-3,000 words as the next step. This sample should come from the heart of a book rather than, say, the introduction or first chapter, which may be untypical. At this delicate stage in the proceedings, the editor may wish to send the text sample and synopsis to a consultant for a considered opinion. It is essential to feel confident in an author before preparing a contract for the book; once the contract is signed, time and money are at a premium and the chances of finding an alternative author are much more limited.

Briefing a magazine writer Good communication is vital when briefing a freelance writer; receiving an article that is not quite what you wanted makes extra work for the content editor and wastes both time and money. Worse, it may have to be returned or rewritten. Make sure you are clear in your own mind how the feature or article is to be structured, what sort of detail it will go into and any points you feel should be covered. Alternatively you may prefer to start with a loose idea and work it out in more detail with your writer — it all depends on the person you have in mind and the kind of relationship you have with him or her.

Make contact, either by telephone or in person, to confirm that the writer is willing and available to write the piece; then discuss the feature thoroughly making sure you both agree on what is required. If any new suggestions or slants come up which you feel are worth considering make a note of them so that you have some record of how the original plan was amended. Agree on a fee for the feature; usually the magazine will have a set rate per thousand words but a writer may feel in some cases that a commission warrants further negotiation for research, telephone calls and other expenses. Also, decide on a mutually realistic deadline.

It is very important to follow up these verbal discussions with a proper commissioning form or letter (see Arranging an author contract below and example on page 31).

Arranging an author contract

An author contract can range from a simple one-page letter of agreement, to a lengthy and almost incomprehensible piece of legal phrasing. Publishing companies usually have a standard author contract with spaces left for details of the fee, number of words, delivery date and so on. The order and content of clauses in such contracts vary from company to company and may be modified for particular projects.

Arranging a writer contract After briefing a writer, confirm what you have agreed immediately by letter. This constitutes a formal contract and saves possible disputes and misunderstanding on either side. The letter should summarize the work to be done as discussed, including any necessary special points; fee per thousand words with any expenses if negotiated; deadline for copy and rights bought: either full copyright or first serial rights. Some publishing companies have a standard duplicated form for commissioning writers and photographers, which not only saves time and helps the accounting system but allows the freelancer to sign and return one copy as acceptance.

Engaging a consultant

Once the author is signed up and writing the text, the editor may engage a consultant. There are three reasons for enlisting a second opinion:

- The subject of the book may be so complex and/or controversial that a detailed reaction and some constructive advice are essential in order to ensure the credibility of the finished book.

TYPICAL CLAUSES IN A BOOK CONTRACT

Definition and extent of project A simple statement of the task involved, usually with a provisional title for the book or project (called 'The Work' from then on) plus the number of words and whether or not the author should prepare the captions and provide illustrations.

Synopsis/sample chapter Some contracts have the synopsis and sample chapter stages built into them. A delivery date is given for each and a statement included that the publisher can ask for suitable revisions or, if necessary, end the agreement at this point if either is unsuitable.

Main deadline The final delivery date for the complete text, usually with a request for two copies of the typescript, double-spaced, plus a reminder that the main body of the text should match the standard of the sample chapter.

Revisions and editing An obligation for the author to revise the text and, in turn, to allow the publisher to edit the text as necessary.

Other requirements At this point most contracts hold the author to a number of promises, such as helping to find illustrations, supplying a list of books used in the preparation of the work, helping with the index and captions (if this is not stated clearly at the beginning of the contract), and checking the typeset proofs.

Cost of proof corrections A simple but important statement that the author agrees to pay the cost of his or her proof corrections if they exceed a certain percentage (usually 10%) of,the total typesetting cost. This is to deter authors from rewriting the book at the proof stage.

Publisher's obligation A statement that the publisher has the right to decide on all matters of price, content, production, promotion and distribution. Also that the publisher is not obliged to actually publish the book.

Author's warranty The author warrants (guarantees) that the text is original (not copied from another author's work), is not libelous or obscene, that statements of fact are true to the best of the author's knowledge and that any recipes or instructions are not harmful to the reader. This exacting clause may be further backed up by a statement that the author indemnifies (will compensate) the publisher against any legal cost arising out of these matters.

Rights granted to the publisher This clause deals with copyright. In its most all-embracing form, the author assigns to the publisher the copyright for the text throughout the world for the full term of the copyright (the author's life plus 50 years). In some contracts the ramifications of this broad statement are spelled out in more detail — in addition to publishing the work in its original volume form, a publisher buying the whole copyright can sell the rights to other companies for:

- Foreign editions
- Publication in newspapers and magazines (serial rights)
- Publication of extracts
- Book club, paperback and condensed editions
- Film or theatrical use or for TV or radio program
- Merchandising

Arrangements, including royalties, for any of these subsidiary rights can be the basis for further clauses in a contract.

Competing publications This clause requires the author not to produce a book that will compete with the present one, usually within three years from the manuscript being finished or two years from publication. This clause is usually interpreted in a fairly relaxed way by most publishers; professional writers or popular experts produce similar books for competing publishers all the time. The clause really protects a publisher from seeing exactly the same material appearing in a competitor's list.

Payment Authors writing for a flat fee — normally based on a rate per thousand words — are usually paid in installments spread out over the production period as follows:

1 On signature of contract
2 On delivery of text
3 On return of final proofs, checked and corrected as necessary
4 On publication.

Authors paid on a royalty basis receive an advance payment and then a percentage of the published price for sales in home markets and a percentage of the money received by the publishers for foreign editions. The percentage paid to the author usually increases in stages according to the number of copies sold. Royalty payments are normally made every six months. This fairly straightforward process becomes more complicated when subsidiary rights are involved.

Revision of text The author is required to edit or revise the text of any new edition and will receive further payment for any new material.

Credit The publisher has the right to credit the author or not.

Termination In some contracts the rights revert to the author if the publisher allows the work to go out of print for a certain period of time.

Option on new books The author offers the publisher the option to publish his or her next book or books.

Free books Most contracts include the promise of a number of free books (usually six) for the author and the opportunity to buy further copies (but not for resale) at a specified discount (usually 50%).

Signature The author signs the contract on the understanding that it correctly records his or her agreement with the publisher. Normally there are two copies; the publisher countersigns them and returns one to the author.

A CONTRACT LETTER

Dear John,

Further to our discussions yesterday, I am writing to confirm that we would like you to prepare 2,000 words on basic decorating techniques for our next March issue, on sale February 26.

Ideally the feature should cover correct preparation and application techniques for bothe papering and painting with professional tips and hints. It would be useful if you could also provide about six artwork references for specific tasks such as painting doors, papering around a light switch, preparing a wood surface etc.

As agreed the fee will be $150 based on our standard rate of $75 per thousand words and the deadline for copy is December 16. Fee is in respect of First Serial Rights.

Please let me know if there are any problems.

Yours sincerely,

M Alexander

M Alexander (Editor)

Requesting copy for a magazine article is best confirmed in the form of a simple contract letter (**above**). This should set out the subject of the article, the extent, price and deadline clearly and succinctly. Such a letter usually follows an exploratory discussion over the telephone.

- The support of a known name in the subject area can lend integrity to the final result, even though the consultant might not be involved to a very great extent.
- A series of books may have a Series Consultant or Series Editor to oversee and maintain a consistent approach.

Enlisting advice in the first instance usually involves sending the author's first draft to the consultant. A conscientious adviser will then make notes on the manuscript and return it to the editor with a separate list of comments. Consultation in the second instance may happen later in the production sequence, often when the text has been edited and typeset and therefore looks more presentable. A relatively cursory glance through the proofs and a foreword extolling the value of the book may complete the work.

Both approaches have their merits. If an editor is unfamiliar with a subject, then constructive advice is vital. If the book is one of many being published on the same subject, then an internationally known name can often help sales and is particularly impressive to foreign publishers who are considering buying the rights to translate and publish the book in their own language. Naturally, a combination of both types of consultation is ideal.

Finding a suitable consultant is in fact very similar to finding an author — a process that entails researching books and journals and talking to people involved in the subject area. Some authors are quite happy to suggest a candidate, especially a first-time author who may be anxious about how good the finished book will be. It is advisable where possible to preserve the anonymity of both author and consultant in the early stages. It may be, for example, that the work is not published on the consultant's advice, in which case it is better that the author never knows who the consultant was.

Editorial research
The onus of checking the author's text does not, however, fall solely on outside consultants. In many cases, the editor acts as the most important 'consultant' in the whole process. An editor working on various subjects in a general non-fiction publishing company should become a mini-expert on each one, at least for the duration of the projects.

Editorial research begins at the ideas and synopsis stage but quickens in pace once the author begins writing. The editor enters a kind of intellectual race with the author, striving to be at the finish primed with sufficient basic knowledge to appreciate the manuscript on its own terms. Simply becoming acquainted with the jargon of a new subject is reason enough for the editor to indulge in some extra reading. Each subject has its own terms, for example, breed names of cats, dogs and horses; Latin names of trees and garden plants; code names for stars and galaxies — all should become like a second language to the editor. This not only enables the editor to discuss the text with the author on at least a basic level of understanding and to make appropriate suggestions but is also useful later on in the production schedule when the editor may need to write captions and fill out lines on the page proofs.

Magazine research With magazine features prepared anywhere from one to six months in advance, all information should be as accurate as possible, however tedious the research may seem. Facts must be checked thoroughly even if a previous feature is being rehashed; the magazine will lose credibility if an article is dated, inaccurate or sketchy. News stories need to be verified by the most senior personnel you can persuade to talk to you; features should be researched through reference books, publicity information or specialist organizations. Even personal interviews require a certain amount of background preparation — biographical research and some knowledge of the interviewee's particular field of interest, for instance.

Some editors prefer to use a small tape recorder, others a notebook for recording interviews. Use whichever you can work from most easily but never rely on memory. This can lead to inaccuracies unless you write up the interview immediately. Written or taped notes are also useful for proving your case if the interviewee disagrees with your interpretation.

Merchandise features need particularly intensive research: comb the shops and catalogs to find your initial material and follow this up by persistently calling the manufacturers to obtain the necessary details, prices and stockists likely to be current a few months on from the issue in which this information will appear With informative features it is a good idea to send it to the relevant specialist body for approval if you have time to do so or want to be sure it is accurate.

Drawing up a flat plan
As the author writes, the editor prepares a plan of the book. Soaking up some knowledge of the subject must go hand-in-hand with making a flat plan of the book. A flat plan is literally a flat sheet of paper with the double page spreads of the book drawn out as boxes, with the page numbers marked. Since the flat plan is a visual representation of how the book is organized in page-by-page terms it forms a working interface between the editor and designer. Both understand it and use it as a valuable reference from this point on until the book is finished.

In its most valuable form a flat plan should take account of two specifications of the finished book: the sections and where the color falls.

Sections The pages of a book are bound together in batches called sections or signatures. A single sheet folded once in the middle, for example, forms a four-page section. The number of pages in each section depends on the method of printing and binding to be used (see pages 109-112). Books are commonly printed in 16, 20, 24, 32, 48 or 64 page sections. Thus, a book printed in 16 page sections may have a total length of, say, 128, 144, 160, 176, 192, 208 pages or more, following the same pattern. It is easy to check the length of the sections by looking down at the top edge of a book and carefully separating and counting the pages in each section. This book, for example, is printed in 16 page sections.

The flat plan should display the pages in horizontal rows, each equivalent to one complete section of the finished book. The middle two pages of each section form a 'true double', that is, the paper is continuous across the double page spread of the finished book. It is useful to be able to pick these out easily on a flat plan because both editor and designer know they can run an illustration across the spread without the risk of one side not matching the other in position or color balance, as would be likely anywhere else in the book.

Color fall For books containing color printing, the flat plan is vital not only to show the number of pages in each section, but also to record the 'color fall' — this simply means on what sections or pages color printing can be used. Many combinations are possible, depending on the printing and binding strategy. Many books, for example, have a section of four-color printing alternating with a section of one-color printing (black only). This strategy can be shown on the flat plan by shading in alternate rows of boxes. Alternate spreads of four-color and one-color printing, another common strategy, can be shown by shading in alternate spread boxes. Introducing two-color printing on some spreads or sections adds another layer of complication. (More on printing and binding techniques can be found on pages 114-123).

Once the flat plan has been marked up in accordance with the printing and binding decisions, the editor can begin to transfer on to it the contents of the book. Since the four-color pages, one-color pages and true doubles are clearly shown, it is possible to juggle with the position and length of various chapters or sections to maximize the use of color — to put the bulk of the text on one-color pages and ensure that chapter opening illustrations are in color, for example. The editor or designer writes in the subject of each spread in the appropriate box or indicates the extent of each chapter by sketching in chapter openings. The result tends to look a little untidy and the first draft is usually one of many. Once

A book flat plan provides the 'map' for the editorial, design and production teams. When the decisions have been made about where the color sections will fall and how many there will be, they can be marked onto the flat plan. At this stage the way in which the book is going to be bound must also be taken into account. Once these things have been indicated the editor or designer can take over. It is their task to transfer the contents of the book page by page onto the flat plan, fitting the chapters and juggling with their length to ensure full use of the color sections.

agreed and spruced up for all to understand, the flat plan is an indispensable aid to the whole team.

A magazine flat plan

Editors either like juggling with a flat plan or they do not. The restrictions can be particularly limiting if you have an inflexible pagination and strict advertisement requirements.

Every magazine is limited to some extent by a pre-set pattern of pages: mono and color sites that are determined by cost and the way they are printed — most commonly falling into sections of 32, 16 or even 8 pages.

Superimposed on this framework are the advertisements estimated for the issue: some already booked, others calculated on previous records and targets set. Special request advertisements have to be accommodated wherever possible: in the pages within a particular feature, in the front half of the magazine or maybe on a right-hand page. It is important to maintain a

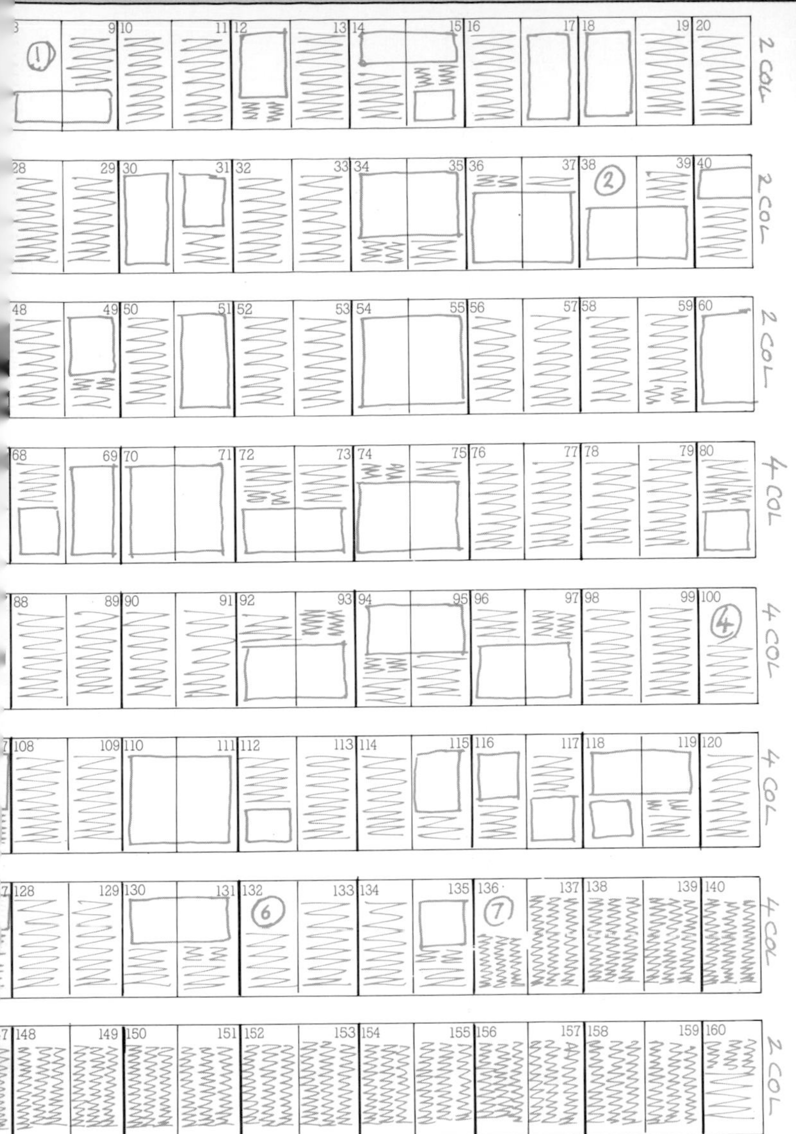

variety of sizes and shapes in advertisement space within the set grid of the page layout to allow greater flexibility for selling and greater interest.

The proposed features will have to be integrated into the remaining spaces: never an easy task. They should ideally run in a logical, easy-to-read way with a good balance of mono and color pages (if used). A 'graveyard' effect at the back of the magazine should be avoided, that is, too many advertisements and the duller editorial items relegated to the later pages. The features themselves should read well too, maintaining interest from one to the other and taking care that they 'open' and 'close' in an obvious way. Change of pace is important too: highly colored, expensive photographic items are best interspersed with more sober pages or line artwork illustrations to create a change of interest and tempo. All these restrictions may make it seem impossible to start at first, but if you block in the items that appear in each issue — the introduction page, stockists, editor's letter or whatever — the more arbitrary features can be pencilled in roughly and juggled around until they all fall into place.

If an editor has trouble determining the flat plan, it might be helpful to approach it in a step-by-step format. Make a list of all the regular columns used. Aside from the ones already mentioned there may be a column written by a specific author, letters to the editor, a question-and-answer page, monthly reports, news summaries, horoscope predictions, fashion spreads, and photo layouts. With these constraints in mind, the editor should then start thinking about how to add interest to the look of the magazine.

There are a number of things to keep in mind when plotting the flat plan. In addition to the editorial copy, the advertising must occupy premium space to keep the clients happy. The ratio of editorial copy to advertising varies but the first few pages of the magazine are often excellent places to showcase advertising. The editor and designer must remember to reserve logical space for

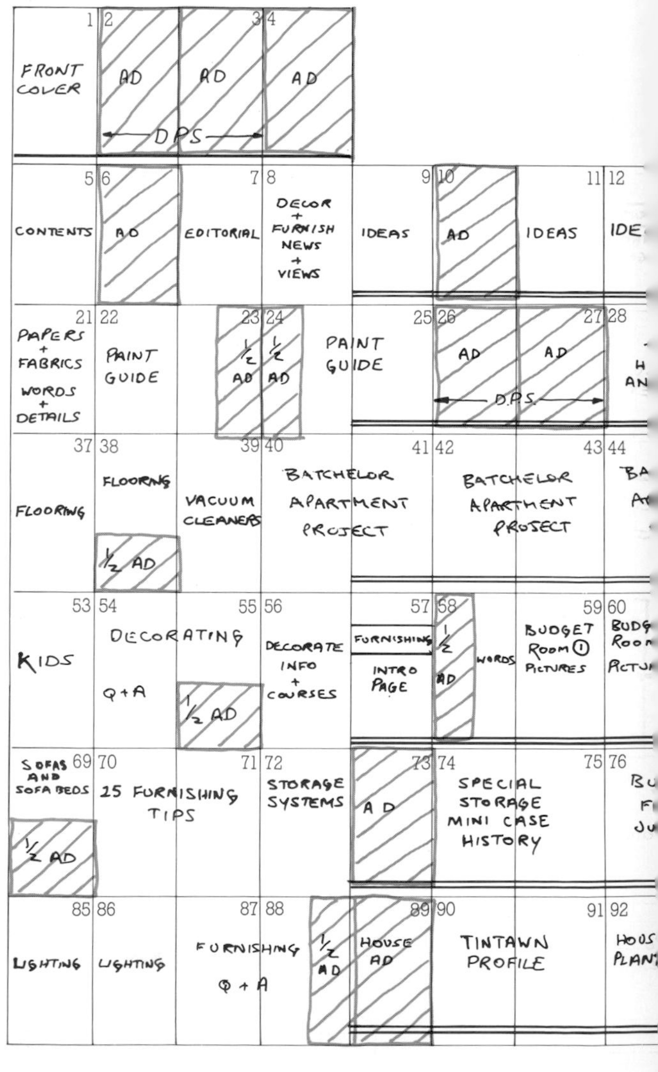

the editorial copy as well as to minimize the number of jumps in a story. People tend to thumb through a magazine from back to front, so the back of the magazine should contain several lively columns instead of blocks of advertising.

Sometimes even the best thought out flat plans will not prevent a set of mechanicals from being restructured. Many of the late ads usurp carefully planned copy progression and cause major positioning problems. At the stage of drawing up the flat plan, major chunks of advertising will usually not have been sold. In this case, the publisher's advertising director will supply a list of sold and unsold ad pages to the production department so that the size of the magazine can be determined and the design department can proceed with laying out the editorial and the sold ad copy. It is at this time that the advertising sales staff will call up potential clients and offer them the advertising space that is still available. When space is left over, an in-house advertisement or public service advertisement is used.

A magazine flat plan is essential for monitoring the balance and progress of an issue. Advertising and editorial areas must be entered on the flat plan, a page-by-page chart, taking care to maintain a logical and interesting sequence for the reader and conforming to the mono/color breakdown of the issue. Care must be taken to avoid relegating uninterrupted advertisements or duller editorial copy towards the back of the issue, and with the placing of specially requested advertisments pages. Everyone involved in the production of the magazine from the editor to the printer should have an updated copy for reference.

13 …RATING …TRO …GE	14 DIY INTERIOR DESIGN	15 AD	16 DIY INTERIOR DESIGN	17 PAPERS + FABRICS	18 PAPERS + FABRICS	19 PAPERS + FABRICS	20 BORDERS
29 …S …ES	30 HOW TO	31 MAKE ½ AD	32 BLINDS	33 BLINDS	34 FLOORING	35 FLOORING	36 AD
45 …R …ENT	46 ENERGY SAVING	47 GADGETS AND MATERIALS	48	49 AD	50 KIDS	51 KIDS	52 AD
61 ½ AD	62 THE FURNISHING	63 ½ AD	64 STORES	65 FURNISHING STORES ½ AD	66 SOFAS AND	67 SOFA BEDS	68 SOFAS AND SOFA BEDS ½ AD
77 …OPS	78 HOUSE CONTENT INSURANCE	79 ½ AD	80 DINING ROOMS WORDS	81 DINING ROOMS	82 PICTURES AND PRODUCTS	83 ½ AD	84 LIGHTING
93 HOUSE PLANTS	94 HOUSE PLANTS	95 BOOK SHELF	96 STOCKISTS	97 NEXT ISSUE	98 PARENTS AD	99 AD	100 AD

2
EDITING AND TYPESETTING

Working out a management plan/ Copy-tasting/Style sheets/ Content editing/Copy-editing principles and practice/Typography/Marking up/ Typesetting processes/Proof-reading/ Computers and the editor

A not inappropriate analogy can be made between producing a book or magazine and producing a play. The author provides the basic script; the editor reshapes it as necessary to heighten its impact and relevance; designers provide a setting of appropriate style and color; production and sales people attend to every detail of its promotion and final presentation. And publication day can evoke a thrill similar to that of an opening night.

In this chapter we look at editing and typesetting — the first and most important parts of the editorial process.

THE DESK AS A WORKBENCH

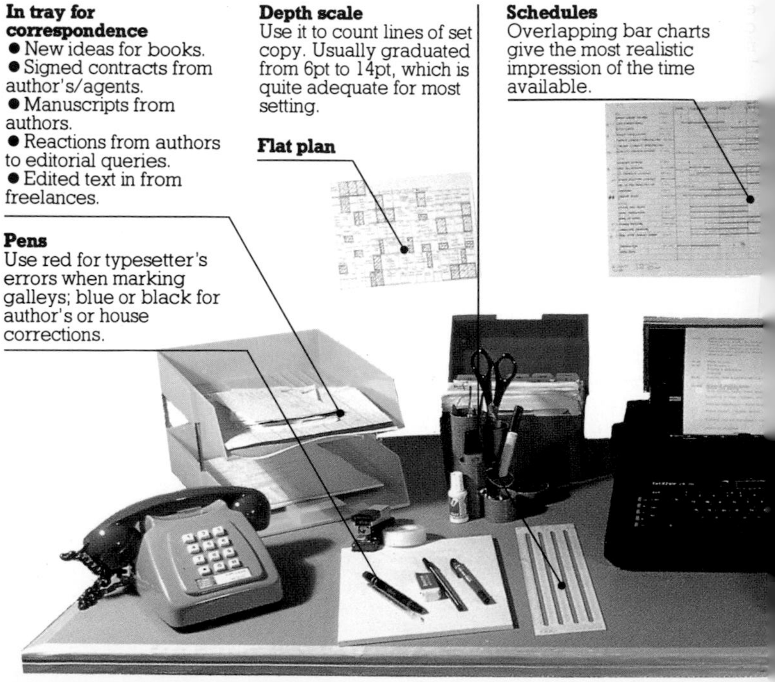

In tray for correspondence
- New ideas for books.
- Signed contracts from author's/agents.
- Manuscripts from authors.
- Reactions from authors to editorial queries.
- Edited text in from freelances.

Pens
Use red for typesetter's errors when marking galleys; blue or black for author's or house corrections.

Depth scale
Use it to count lines of set copy. Usually graduated from 6pt to 14pt, which is quite adequate for most setting.

Flat plan

Schedules
Overlapping bar charts give the most realistic impression of the time available.

Working out a management plan

Before the first batch of raw text arrives at a book publishing house the editor should be thinking about a management plan for the project — who is available in and out of house to work on various aspects of the job. This involves discussing the project with the design and production departments to interpret the sequence of events in the schedule in terms of who will do what and when.

First thoughts must go to the editing process itself. It can be difficult to estimate the time that will be needed to edit a text. However carefully schedules are worked out in the first place, there always seems to be too little time between the author's final deadline for delivery of the text and the date for typesetting to begin. Editing therefore usually starts before the author has finished the text.

Many busy book editors seek the help of a freelance or in-house content editor to style the text in broad terms and rely on the close attention of a copy-editor to refine it ready for typesetting. The availability and speed of such editorial help must be incorporated into the management plan, plus the time needed to send batches of text to and from freelancers in other parts of the country or the world.

In formulating a plan of action, it is never too early to nominate people to prepare indexes, glossaries, appendices and other seemingly distant requirements. Many of these activities can proceed in parallel with the main editorial process; if they are neglected at the outset they may lead to delays in the later stages of the schedule when time is measured in terms of hours and days rather than in weeks and months. Allow time also for caption writing as authors rarely have the time and/or motivation to write their own captions.

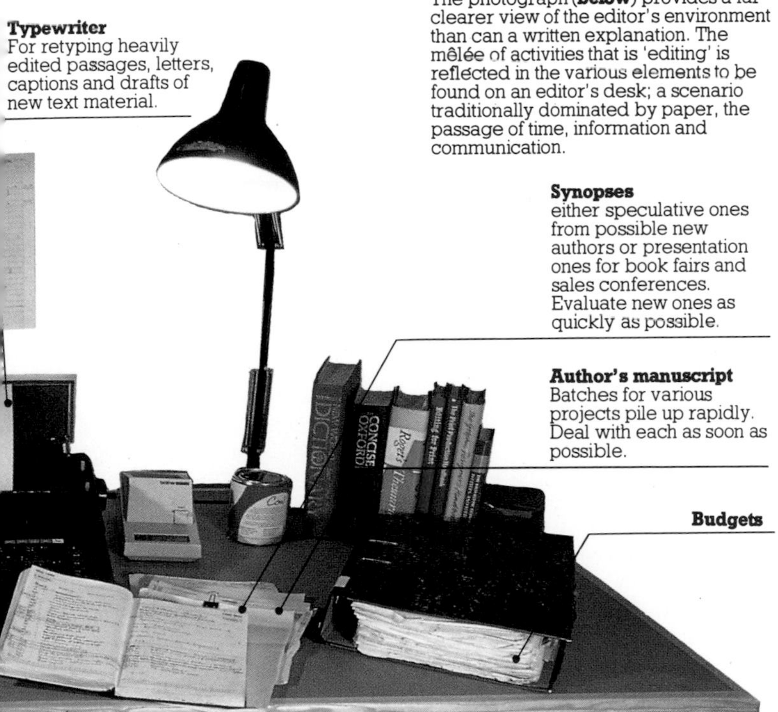

Typewriter
For retyping heavily edited passages, letters, captions and drafts of new text material.
Synopses
either speculative ones from possible new authors or presentation ones for book fairs and sales conferences. Evaluate new ones as quickly as possible.
Author's manuscript
Batches for various projects pile up rapidly. Deal with each as soon as possible.
Budgets
CONCISE OXFORD

The photograph (**below**) provides a far clearer view of the editor's environment than can a written explanation. The mêlée of activities that is 'editing' is reflected in the various elements to be found on an editor's desk; a scenario traditionally dominated by paper, the passage of time, information and communication.

A management plan (**right**) overlays the production schedule with the human and mechanical resources available to realize it. It shows the various disciplines involved as parallel tracks and plots the projects progress as critical path against time. Its great value is in demonstrating which activities can proceed at the same time and which ones must await the completion of an earlier process. Such a plan reflects the roles of everyone involved over the entire production period, starting from the author's initial synopsis and following through to the final date of publication.

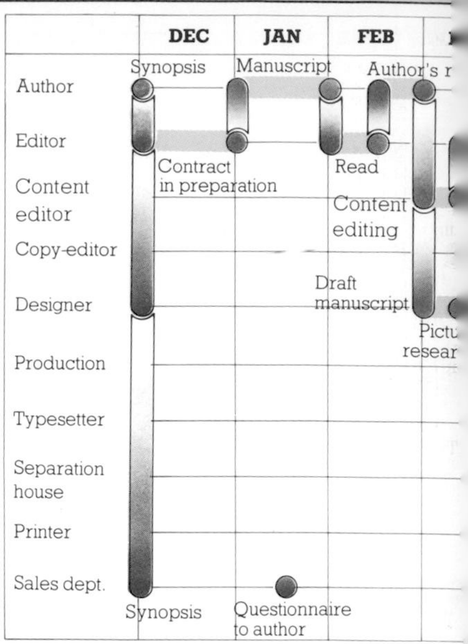

In collaboration with the designer and production team, the editor is involved in planning the typesetting schedule and making sure that the copy-editor and/or proof-reader are available to check the galleys. Artwork preparation, commissioned photography and jacket design must be planned well in advance, given that gremlins seem to disrupt the scheme of things particularly when time is short. Picture research, design time, working on layouts, checking color proofs, pasting up — time and reliable hands must be allotted to all these activities.

Committed to paper, a management plan or progress chart looks like a schedule with the human element sketched in — the broad sweep of the publishing process overlaid with tangential notes referring to specific tasks, individuals and time intervals. This mêlée of activity can be represented in the form of a horizontal bar chart with parallel tracks for author, editor, designer, typesetter, sales, production and all the other departments involved. The book's progress can be plotted as a critical path across the page, split into several channels or different colors to represent simultaneous activity in the various departments.

All this planning may appear to be stealing valuable time from actually producing the book. Experience proves, however, that lack of planning and cracking on with all speed and no direction causes more hold-ups than does spending some time organizing the tasks in the initial stages. So many of the activities rely on the completion of previous stages — typesetting on editing, layout on galleys, for instance — that a clearly laid out form of logical sequence and responsibility is essential to the smooth running of such a complex procedure.

Working out a management plan: magazines Once an issue has been planned and agreed on, it only remains to act as speedily and efficiently as possible. The editor must first assess how much can be handled in-house; this will depend on the number of staff members and their particular skills. Experience shows how much they cope with in the time allotted so the tasks have to be apportioned accordingly, making sure each individual knows

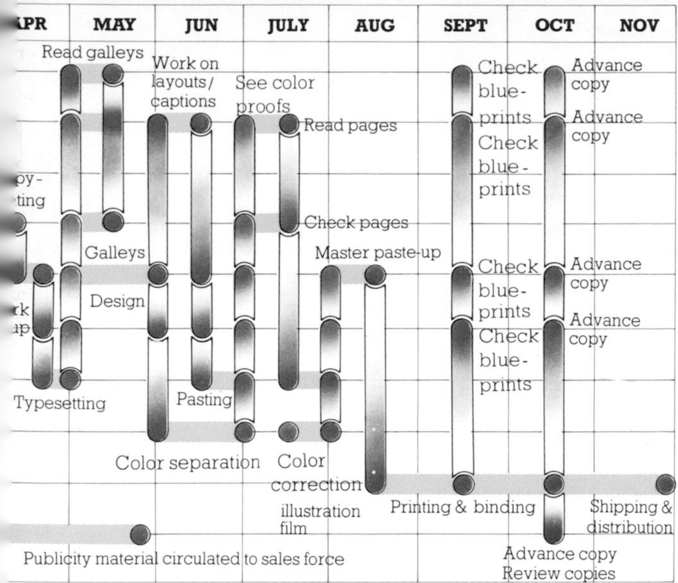

exactly what he or she is doing and when it has to be done within the overall schedule. On a large magazine this may have to take the form of a detailed memo to ensure all the details are officially recorded and that nothing has been overlooked.

Any features that are to be prepared by freelance writers should be commissioned as soon as possible, finding the best writer for the job and checking that he or she agrees and is available to do it. The art department too will need to know what the pattern of their workload for the coming issue will be so they can make sure it is compatible with that of the editorial team. Photography also must be booked and prepared well in advance to meet the deadline and time should be scheduled for any special artwork that needs to be commissioned. The production department and typesetters should be kept fully informed as the magazine progresses.

As soon as copy arrives in-house, it should be photocopied and given out to the picture researcher and to the fact-checking/ research department. The picture researcher will need a headstart in getting pictures and illustrations together for the project. The fact-checking department must verify all facts wherever possible in order to maintain the reputation of the magazine as an accurate information source, and also to prevent lawsuits. Some magazines employ an on-staff lawyer who reads each article for possible legal complications.

Equally important in the scheme of the management plan is the business arm of the magazine. The publisher controls business aspects of the magazine such as advertising, production costs and promotion. Each individual in the business departments of the publication must be kept informed of the magazine's editorial policies and the themes of forthcoming editions. Similarly, the business arm of the magazine also provides the art and editorial departments with valuable information about the magazine's target audience.

The advertising director performs a daily function of keeping abreast of branch-office operations and of the activities of out-of-town representatives at their offices. The advertising director will

A house style sheet (below) is a useful and essential editorial guide, ensuring that rules on punctuation, spelling, capitalization etc follow a given standard throughout the publication.

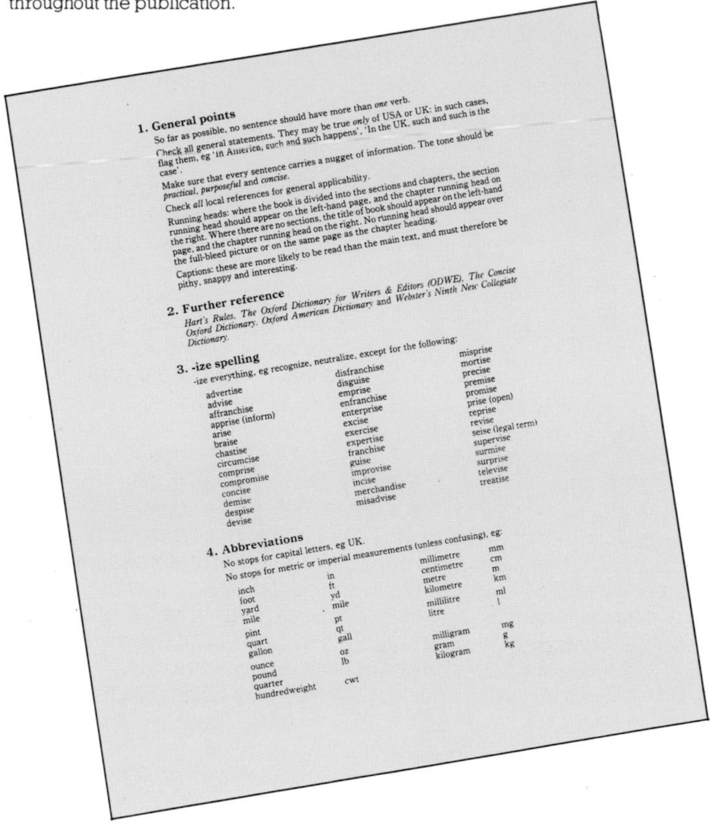

1. General points

So far as possible, no sentence should have more than *one* verb.

Check all general statements. They may be true *only* of USA or UK: in such cases, flag them, eg 'in America, such and such happens', 'In the UK, such and such is the case'.

Make sure that every sentence carries a nugget of information. The tone should be *practical, purposeful* and *concise*.

Check *all* local references for general applicability.

Running heads: where the book is divided into the sections and chapters, the section running head should appear on the left-hand page, and the chapter running head on the right. Where there are no sections, the title of book should appear on the left-hand page, and the chapter running head on the right. No running head should appear over the full-bleed picture or on the same page as the chapter heading.

Captions: these are more likely to be read than the main text, and must therefore be pithy, snappy and interesting.

2. Further reference

Hart's Rules, The Oxford Dictionary for Writers & Editors (ODWE), The Concise Oxford Dictionary, Oxford American Dictionary and *Webster's Ninth New Collegiate Dictionary.*

3. -ize spelling

-ize everything, eg recognize, neutralize, except for the following:

advertise	disfranchise	misprise
advise	disguise	mortise
affranchise	emprise	precise
apprise (inform)	enfranchise	premise
arise	enterprise	promise
braise	excise	prise (open)
chastise	exercise	reprise
circumcise	expertise	revise
comprise	franchise	seise (legal term)
compromise	guise	supervise
concise	improvise	surmise
demise	incise	surprise
despise	merchandise	televise
devise	misadvise	treatise

4. Abbreviations

No stops for capital letters, eg UK.

No stops for metric or imperial measurements (unless confusing), eg:

inch	in	millimetre	mm
foot	ft	centimetre	cm
yard	yd	metre	m
mile	mile	kilometre	km
pint	pt	millilitre	ml
quart	qt	litre	l
gallon	gall	milligram	mg
ounce	oz	gram	g
pound	lb	kilogram	kg
quarter			
hundredweight	cwt		

A house style sheet (below) is a useful and essential editorial guide, ensuring that rules on punctuation, spelling, capitalization etc follow a given standard throughout the publication.

create ads to attract advertising clients to the magazine. This individual, usually in conjunction with the sales promotion manager, will oversee the research done to gather information on the readership for the magazine. The sales promotion manager will also be aware of manufacturer's conventions that he or she can attend to speak to prospective advertisers.

The research director, in turn, provides specific information to the magazine with demographic and geographic criteria on the audience of the magazine and what kind of material the readership would like to see in future issues. The sales staff sells the product, the circulation director attempts to push sales, the promotion director produces an awareness campaign to sell the look and the feel of the magazine, and the public relations manager authors tightly written press releases for the media.

For these business staff members to perform their jobs optimally, there must be a regular interaction between them and editorial. For example, if a forthcoming issue will feature a timely and newsworthy story, the promotion director might want to orchestrate a campaign to highlight this issue and its article.

Copy-tasting
When the first batch of an author's manuscript arrives, some crucial decisions need to be made. 'Copy-tasting' the initial ten percent of the main text reveals at once if the author has produced a manuscript that is up to standard, or not.

It is important to react quickly to the first chapter for two main reasons:

- This is likely to be the last opportunity you have to decide whether or not to proceed with this author.
- Whether your reactions are positive or negative, the author will be planning or writing the following sections to follow the schedule you have given him or her and needs to have your comments as soon as possible.

A rapid scan of the text is usually sufficient to make your eyes light up or confirm your fears. Concise, perceptive but sympathetic comments may successfully steer an errant author back onto the right track. In which case, return the section to the author, together with separate sheets of notes and queries referring to points numbered in the text.

This is not only a neat way of dealing with the problem but it is also psychologically less disturbing for the author than returning pages of typescript covered with editorial criticisms.

If the text is beyond redemption — something that should have been apparent at the sample chapter stage but sometimes only becomes clear in the actual manuscript — then you must reject the manuscript and the author. Although this will entail a hold-up in the schedule and a settlement of a proportion of the contracted fee, it is much better for all concerned to make the decision at this point than to struggle on with manuscript that is totally unsuitable.

Style sheets
There are two principle types of style sheets: your own editorial style sheet and the house style sheet.

In your early reading on a new subject you will come across technical terms, foreign words, jargon and other words associated with the subject. Jot these down as you see them, recording the various ways in which other publications use and spell them. This is the beginning of what we might call an 'editorial style sheet'. When the author's manuscript arrives, this list of words will grow and you should know enough about the subject to decide between alternative spellings and applications of the words.

Further 'styling' changes are made by the content editor and the copy-editor according to the house style sheet (if there is one). Arguments about hyphenation of certain words, capital letters and so on often rage right up to page proof stage.

Well established magazines frequently have house style sheets to standardize editorial presentation in the same way that book publishers do.

The needs of the manuscript will determine the formality of the editorial style sheet. An article using many defined terms, unusual words, italics, references, cross-references, capitalization, abbreviations, charts, graphs and footnotes will no doubt require an extensive, typed document. By contrast, a general article that only needs to be styled on standard points like spelling, hyphenation and use of italics may require only a few handwritten notes.

While going through the manuscript and jotting down notes, the copy-editor is creating a working style sheet (see page 51).

The copy-editor may find that additional discussion is needed with the author and more research must be done on the topic before a definitive style can be decided upon. If the manuscript is in need of heavy styling, the working style sheet evolves into a preliminary style sheet. It illustrates the manuscript's style in one column and the proposed or recommended style changes in another column.

To create the final style sheet the copy-editor will make changes in or additions to the preliminary style sheet or the working style sheet. At this point, decisions are based on the copy-editor's thorough reading of the manuscript and the final queries answered by the author.

Content editing

When at least 50 percent of the text is available then content editing can begin. The content editor works on the heart of the text, striving to clarify the essential logic of the piece and the expression of the ideas it contains. Strong-sounding, perhaps, but it is important to distinguish the usual effect of content editing from the expected results of copy editing. At one extreme, the content editor's function can be equivalent to rewriting; in its most restrained form, copy editing adds the final patina of editorial style.

As a book editor, concerned as much with administration as with purely editorial pursuits, you will need to delegate major content editing to in-house colleagues or to trusted freelancers. If you have the opportunity to substantially reconstruct a chapter then you may find it helpful to separate the pages and attach them in sequence to a bulletin board. You can then see the whole section at a glance, without having to turn pages backward and forward to follow the chain of thought from paragraph to paragraph.

Although different in kind, the line between content editing and copy editing may become very fine. Some copy editors manipulate the style of a piece so strongly as virtually to content edit it; many content editors take care of 'fine-tuning' copy editing as they work miracles with the basic structure.

Book publishers vary enormously in the amount of structural editing they carry out, based primarily on the type of books they produce. A paragraph on the life cycle of the common snail, for example, may receive only a superficial level of copy editing, whereas the text for a full-color, international edition of the complete book of house plants may be content edited substantially so that it follows a rigid house style and then be 'shoe-horned' into a predetermined layout.

Content and copy-editing for magazines The process of content editing, sometimes referred to as substantative editing, not only involves rewriting and reorganizing, but also requires an ability to suggest more effective ways of presenting the material in a manuscript. When dealing with each manuscript, the content editor will have to exercise keen judgement and instinct. If the result is to convey the information effectively.

The content editor, who may also be the editor for the magazine, must also practice tact when dealing with the author. Often, it is the content editor who will have to query the author and work out extensive changes that have not been previously agreed to by the author. Following a preliminary letter suggesting certain changes, the manuscript may be sent to the author with a diplomatic letter explaining certain changes and asking for further suggestions from the author. A list of queries may also be sent, or a copy of the manuscript may be sent with gummed slips attached to the pages that require further elaboration. In this case, the author should be instructed not to remove the tags even after the queries have been answered.

Copy-editing may commence after content editing has been completed, and the copy-editor may still have further queries for the author. On some occasions, the copy-editor may find that not enough content editing has been done and need to return the manuscript for further work.

Copy-editing: principles and practice

Copy-editing is a 'hidden' skill. When it has been done well, the reader is unaware of the hours of work that have gone into eliminating errors. The text is a pleasure to read; the information is easy to absorb.

Unfortunately, the reverse can also be true. If the copy-editing has been done poorly, the reader is distracted by errors in much the same way that a filmgoer is distracted by poor continuity: the very best of films is spoiled when the hero's moustache appears and disappears between shots!

The importance of copy-editing Copy-editing makes a vital contribution to the quality of the final text by making it clear and accurate for the reader. It also helps to maintain the publisher's reputation as a producer of high-quality texts. A large part of a copy-editor's work is concerned with making sure that the text adheres completely to the publisher's house style. This means that the copy-editor must work to a set of rules compiled by the publisher that encompasses preferences for spellings, hyphenation, use of capitals, and so on.

The more meticulous the copy-editing, the less likelihood there is that problems will arise during the production process. Anything that causes the typesetter to pause in his or her work — illegible handwriting or a relocated passage — adds to his or her time and, in turn, increases typesetting costs. Similarly, if the designer has to query, for example, the positioning of halftones or line drawings, delays occur and costs increase.

Another potential strain on budgets is the cost of corrections at proof stage. Again, these can be kept to a minimum by making sure that the typscript is complete and accurate before it is passed on to production. This requires extreme vigilance on the part of the copy-editor as he or she works on the typescript. However, keeping in mind that the insertion of a single comma at proof stage is extremely expensive helps the copy-editor to stay alert to the finer details.

Good copy-editing eases the work of both the typesetter and designer, which in turn helps to maintain the kind of cooperative working relationships essential for efficient production. Problems are bound to arise from time to time in the best of systems, but they are much easier to resolve when the copy-editor, editor, typesetter and designer work together as a team.

The role of the copy-editor The copy-editor not only helps to ease the work of production but also provides a link between the author and the rest of the production team. It is the copy-editor's job to help the author to say what he or she wants to say. This involves pointing out and discussing with the author any ambiguities or contradictions in the manuscript, and conveying to the typesetter and designer specific instructions on setting and layout that will clarify the text. This may mean, for example, indicating on the typescript that certain passages should be set in bold type for emphasis or that others should be expressed as tables, graphs or flow charts. Or, say, in a natural history text the author may choose to capitalize the common names of plants and animals, such as 'Paper Flower' and 'Yellow-faced Angelfish' to avoid confusion with other terms used in the book. If any of these instructions create problems during the production process, again it is the copy-editor's job to discuss them with the typesetter and designer and, if necessary, the author in order to find mutually satisfactory solutions.

By solving problems quickly and efficiently the copy-editor can keep the production process on schedule. At proof stage delays can be prevented by making sure that the author receives, corrects and returns the proofs in the shortest possible time. This will allow the maximum amount of time for correction and page make up so that if any unavoidable hold-ups do occur, there is time on hand to overcome them and still remain on schedule. The copy-editor's own reading and correcting of galley and page proofs must be equally swift in order to meet the print deadline. Publishers' marketing and promotional activities are planned with a particular publication date in mind, so it is vital that all deadlines are met.

What makes a good copy-editor? This is a question that many excellent, experienced copy-editors ask themselves as they struggle with particularly difficult typescripts! There is no one answer. Many qualities and skills combine to make a good copy-editor. The two most fundamental points are first, good copy-editors are most definitely *made*, not born. It takes a lot of experience and practice to develop the personal qualities and skills necessary to do the job well. Second, once a copy-editor has reached a high level of competence it takes a lot more hard work to stay at that level! Most copy-editors would agree that they continue to learn from every typescript they handle. This is

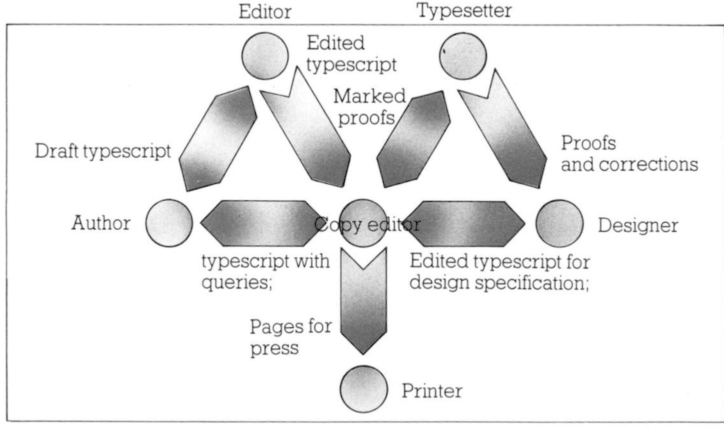

As the arbiter of style and, in some companies, the focus of activity on all detailed aspects of the text, the copy-editor must cope with many important elements of the publishing process.

a very healthy attitude as it keeps complacency at bay and complacency leads to errors.

The most important quality a copy-editor can possess is commitment to his or her work. This leads him or her to strive for high standards and seek ways to develop all the other qualities and skills the job demands.

The golden rule of copy-editing is: *be consistent*. If, for example, the copy-editor decides that 'cat-breeder' is hyphenated, it must be hyphenated consistently throughout the typescript. However, not all decisions are easy to make. It is not always possible to be absolutely sure what is right in a particular instance (even copy-editing experts disagree on some points). This is the time when a copy-editor needs to stick to his or her decision and avoid the temptation to change that decision halfway through the typescript. It is often said that, for the sake of a consistent typescript, it is better to be consistently wrong, than inconsistently right.

A copy-editor also needs endless patience. Every typescript presents problems, large and small, which the copy-editor has to make decisions about, sometimes with the editor's and/or author's assistance. It takes patience to follow up each one.

Many of the problems that confront a copy-editor have common-sense solutions. For example, if the text fails to read on correctly from one page to the next, even though the folios are numbered consecutively, it is more likely that they were numbered while in the wrong order than that one is missing. Similarly, if a cross-reference to a chapter is inaccurate, it is likely that the author changed the order of the chapters at some point but failed to alter the cross-references accordingly. In both cases, common-sense 'detective work' is called for. It is also common sense not to reverse authors' decisions that are consistent throughout the manuscript. The copy-editor would introduce errors in trying to change each occurrence.

The negative-sounding quality of 'suspicion' does, in fact, have very positive results for a copy-editor. By cultivating a policy of never taking anything for granted in a typescript, the copy-editor can home in on, and correct, the subtle errors that occur: a simple typing error, for instance, can change the events of Henry VI's reign into those of Henry VII. Authors often send their work to the publisher without checking the typing, so it pays for the copy-editor to be 'suspicious'.

A copy-editor must never assume that an author is infallible. However eminent they may be, authors are human and therefore make mistakes. So, if the meaning of a passage is unclear, the copy-editor must not think that it is his or her own power of understanding that is at fault. The copy-editor must have faith in his or her judgment, point out the passage to the editor or author, and, if possible, suggest a way to clarify it. Authors are generally very happy to receive any suggestions that will enhance their work.

Tact is vital when it is necessary to point out to an author that he or she appears to be contradicting another point in the manuscript. There may be, for example, a statement in Chapter One that is contradicted in Chapter Three. In a case like this the copy-editor needs to find a way to point out the discrepancy without appearing over critical.

At any one time a copy-editor may be working on many titles, all in different stages of production. Some will still be at the typescript stage, some at proof stage. Some may be on or even a little ahead of schedule; others may be lagging behind. If proofs come through that are needed urgently the copy-editor must be flexible enough to put aside whatever he or she is currently working on and read the proofs as quickly and accurately as possible. A flexible attitude will allow the copy-editor to do this without feeling annoyed: seething annoyance does not provide a good background to accurate proof-reading!

Tenacity is the quality a copy-editor needs in order to work steadily through the kind of typescript that is every copy-editor's nightmare — one that has been reworked several times, has numerous additions in the margins and incomplete directions for the reorganization of the text.

Concentration is a 'must' for the job and something that has to be worked at continuously. Distractions are inevitable in any publishing office — telephones ring; people walk in and out — and a copy-editor needs to be able to maintain a high level of concentration in order to prevent errors slipping through. Obviously, everyone's level of concentration drops after a certain length of time. This varies from one individual to another. Each copy-editor must therefore judge the length of their own concentration span and take small breaks as necessary.

A good copy-editor is organized. There are two reasons why a copy-editor needs good organizational skills. First, in order to draw up working plans that will help him or her meet schedules. Effective plans not only help to ensure that work is done to schedule but also that the author or typesetter is contacted if they fail to send text or proofs on time.

Second, it is important to be able to organize the content of the typescript. The typescript needs to be read critically to judge whether the subject matter is arranged in a logical sequence or whether the order of chapters, or sections within chapters, needs to be changed.

If a copy-editor has an academic knowledge of language structure, that is all the better. Even more useful, though, is the kind of instinctive 'feel' for language that alerts him or her to clumsy sentences or misused words. Then the ability to rephrase or reword the text, to clarify meaning and improve the flow, is vital.

From what has been said already it almost goes without saying that a copy-editor must have a keen eye for detail. However, this is something that cannot be emphasized enough. It is all too easy to fail to notice that a word such as 'specialty' has, because of a typing error, become 'speciality'.

In publishing, schedules are tight and production costs high. A copy-editor must therefore be able to produce work of a high standard, even when time is limited.

Having 'multiple awareness' is an advanced skill that enables a copy-editor to work on several aspects of copy-editing at the same time; for example, reading for sense; looking for errors; implementing decisions on spelling, hyphenation and other points, and effecting the publisher's house style. Obviously, it takes time to acquire this skill to a high degree, and a new copy-editor is more likely to read through a typescript once for sense and errors and then go through a second time to make changes of a more mechanical nature.

In conclusion, probably no copy-editor ever possesses all these qualities and skills in full measure, but is strong in some and weak

COPY-EDITING — A CHECKLIST

A few of the things that a copy-editor looks for have been touched on already. There are many more, so many in fact that they can be covered only briefly here. However, in the Reading list on page 156 are some books that describe in detail the areas a copy-editor must cover and the rules that should be followed.

The copy-editor's work on a typescript focuses on five areas:

1 Completeness
2 Sense
3 The needs of the reader
4 Detail
5 Final checks

Completeness
As soon as a copy-editor receives a typescript he or she looks through it and its accompanying correspondence to check its completeness, so that:

- no pages are missing;
- any illustrations to be provided by the author are complete;
- the preliminary matter (prelims) is complete, including acknowledgements and preface;
- lists are made, for the copy-editor's own reference, of any material still to come and the date by which it should be received.

Sense
The copy-editor also checks for sense, looking for any:

- chapters or parts of chapters that need reorganizing to facilitate the flow of the author's ideas;
- over- or under-use of headings or subheadings;
- contradictions;
- ambiguities;
- faults in grammar;
- misused words.

The interests and needs of the reader The copy-editor looks for:

- passages where the meaning is unclear;
- references to people, places or things that may be obscure to readers in countries other than the one in which the book is published. These should be changed, if possible, to make the book accessible to readers everywhere;
- parochialisms;
- abbreviations or terms that would not be understood internationally;
- dates that may be misunderstood, for example 3.9.85 would mean 9 March, 1985 in the United States, but 3 September 1985 in the United Kingdom.

Detail
In matters of detail, the copy-editor looks for errors and inconsistencies in:

- spelling;
- punctuation;
- capitalization;
- spacing between, or indentation of, paragraphs;
- abbreviations;
- contractions;
- the use of italics;
- the style for use of periods in, for example, UK, US;
- the use of en dashes;
- the use of single and/or double quotation marks;
- dates;
- the entries for the bibliography, glossary or index.

Final checks
Before passing on the typescript for typesetting, the copy-editor makes a final check, looking for any omissions or inconsistencies in the:

- preliminary pages;
- cross-references;
- coding of headings;
- coding of illustrations into the text;
- jacket/cover copy.

in others. This is fine as long as he or she is fully aware where the strengths and weaknesses lie. Then the strengths can be consolidated and attempts can be made to overcome the weaknesses. This is not easy, but as a copy-editor takes full responsibility for the accuracy of the typescript, it is well worth the effort.

How a copy-editor approaches a typescript When a typescript arrives on a copy-editor's desk, his or her initial approach is an investigative one designed to determine its subject, the level at which it is written, and the kind of readership at which it is aimed. These features are common to all typescripts and must be kept in mind when changes are made to the text. However, what largely determines the way in which a copy-editor approaches a particular typescript stems from the type of publication it is for. If it is a straightforward publication of simple design — mostly textual matter with a low illustrative content — the copy-editor's work will also be straightforward and relatively undemanding. But if, for example, the publication is a magazine or a highly illustrated work, the approach must be tailored to the demands of each one, as shown above.

• **Highly illustrated books** The copy-editor's approach to a typescript that will be highly illustrated must differ considerably from that toward a typescript of lower illustrative content. The copy-editor needs to adopt a highly organized approach to the quantity of illustrative material. Some may have been supplied by the author as prints or transparencies; some as finished line drawings; some as hasty sketches. He or she will need to liaise closely with the designer to arrange for any further halftones or line drawings to be commissioned, and work out a schedule for their receipt. He or she will also need to devise an error-proof identification system to make sure that all the illustrations are inserted correctly into the text.
• **Magazines** Speed is the essence of magazine work and so it follows that the copy-editor's approach must be one that acknowledges the need for accuracy while working under the pressure of very tight deadlines.

Any one issue of a magazine has many contributors, so the copy-editor's main task is to make each contribution consistent with the style set for the magazine. Each writer will have their own idiosyncrasies so the copy-editor must be alert to a wide range of possible errors and inconsistencies.

Among these are nonuniformity of heads, lack of agreement between subject and predicate, overuse of certain pet words and phrases, sexist and racist connotations, unclear antecedents and accuracy of dates and quoted matter. The copy-editor must also ensure that the manuscript is reading logically and smoothly. When styling for a specialty or trade magazine, a copy-editor should keep in mind that certain unfamiliar terms may be well-known in the author's field or business, hence it is unnecessary to define them.

Helpful hints *All* decisions on spelling, capitalization, hyphenation, and so on need to be listed alphabetically as they are made in order to avoid having to hunt back through the typescript to find out, for example, whether 'summer' was spelled with a capital or lower case 's'. The most systematic way to do this is to divide a sheet of paper into six 'boxes' (see right) and as the decisions are made, enter them in the appropriate box. It is then quick and easy to check any decision made earlier and make the final book consistent.

Very long typescripts are much less dismaying if each chapter is paper-clipped separately. From a psychological point of view the prospect of working on twenty chapters seems a great deal better than working on two thousand pages. It is also easier to check a cross-reference if the chapter in question can be picked out quickly. A lot of time can be wasted hunting through a large pile of paper to find the chapter required.

A pristine typescript should be regarded with suspicion. If a manuscript has the appearance of being typed and presented to perfection, a copy-editor can be lulled into believing that it will be an easy typescript to work on and need little editing. However, the author might well have written several drafts and compiled the final typescript from the best of them. This does not always make for a succinct and smooth-flowing text. Also, the final typing may have affected its accuracy. Some authors' handwriting is almost illegible, which leads to problems for the typist who may type what he or she *thinks* the word is, for example, the word 'discrimination' being typed as 'dissemination'. Typing errors can also affect the sense: an apparent contradiction can be caused, for instance, by the omission of the word 'no' from a

Keeping track of textual style decisions on a particular publishing project is an important part of the copy-editor's role. A useful way of doing this is to divide a sheet of paper into boxes, one for each letter the alphabet (**below**) and to jot words down in the appropriate box as they arise in the text. Such a sheet enables the copy-editor to check on style decisions made earlier when the same word or construction comes up again rather than having to rely on memory.

a b c d	e f g h
cat-breeder (hyphen) autumn (l.c) Cream (breed) cat litter (no hyphen) dual purpose (adj)	house-trained (adj)(hyphen) hookworm (one word) Egyptian Mau Exotic Shorthair
i j k l	**m n o p**
long-haired (adj) (hyphen) litter-tray (hyphen) incoordination	mother–kitten relationship Piperazine Ocicat
q r s t	**u v w x y z**
Spring (l.c) summer (l.c) Red Tabby (breed) queen (l.c) Self-colored Persian tapeworm (one word) roundworm (one word)	winter (l.c.) Van Wong man (ital)

sentence.

Interruptions, such as telephone calls, can cause inaccuracies. To avoid the danger of leaving a word half-written or part of a line uncorrected, it is a good idea to mark the typescript at the point where the interruption occurred. Then, later, work can be resumed easily and accurately.

How to mark changes to a manuscript The way in which typescripts are marked is relatively standard. The marks used are listed on pages 68-7. The mechanical skills needed are as follows:

- **Precise marking**

All copy-editing marks must be made with precision so that the typesetter can follow them easily and accurately.

- **Legible handwriting**

When a copy-editor makes additions to a typescript these must be written neatly and legibly so that there is no possibility that they will be misread by the typesetter.

- **Accurate coding of headings**

Each heading will usually have the letter A, B, or C written against it in the left-hand margin of the typescript to indicate to the typesetter whether it is a main heading, A; a subheading, B; or a sub-subheading, C. These are referred to as first-, second-and third-level headings, respectively. Before the typescript is passed to the typesetter, the designer indicates on the typescript the required typeface and typesize for each level of heading. The typesetter then sets each heading accordingly.

- **Accurate coding of halftones and line drawings**

Halftones or line drawings must be coded into the typescript to indicate to the designer the required position of each. One hundred percent accuracy is necessary to prevent any being misplaced. Each halftone or line drawing is therefore numbered on the back and the same number written in the left-hand margin of the typescript together with an instruction as to its required position, such as 'Figure 1 here'. These and all other instructions must be circled in pen to indicate that they are not part of the final book material and so must not be set (see the example of a marked typescript on page 62).

Tools of the trade Reference books are invaluable for looking up the many rules a copy-editor must follow and a good dictionary is essential. *The Chicago Manual of Style*, *The Oxford Dictionary for Writers and Editors* and Judith Butcher's *Copy-editing* have all become standard sources of reference (see page 156).

Pens are other fundamental tools. Some publishers stipulate the use of a red pen for all corrections, additions to the text and instructions to the typesetter or designer. However, other publishers prefer the somewhat clearer system whereby insertion or deletion marks and written instructions are made in red; additions to the text in blue (see the example of a marked galley on page 62). This is easier for the typesetter to follow since all new portions of text and substituted letters stand out clearly. Whatever the color, pens with fine points are recommended for precise marking.

Any of the author's handwritten corrections or additions, which the typesetter may find difficult to read, must be blotted out with correction fluid and rewritten. The clearer the typescript, the less likelihood there is of typesetting errors. Care must be taken, however, to remember to rewrite the blotted-out word (or words) after waiting for the correction fluid to dry.

Typography

Typography is a fascinating blend of history, art and science. Its history goes back hundreds of years to the work of Johann Gutenberg in Germany. In about 1437 he devised the system of 'movable type'. This consisted of separate pieces of metal for each letter, which could be arranged into words and printed as lines of text. Art has permeated typography from its inception. Not content with using one style of typeface, artists and designers have influenced the look of the printed word to an almost unimaginable degree. Science too has been an important element in the whole development of typography, from the practical limitations of hand-crafted typefaces to the speed and sophistication of modern computer typesetting. With such an ancestry, it is easy to lose sight of the fundamental purpose that typography serves — to put the message across with clarity and with style.

As an editor, the conversion of your author's manuscript into type is one of the most fundamental processes within your control. Here we look at the basic characteristics of type, the styles of typefaces, casting off and marking up a manuscript for setting.

Besides the style of the typeface, the main, noticeable features of a page of typeset text are all concerned with size and measurement: the size of the letters; the space between the lines; the length of the lines; and whether both edges are vertically aligned down the page, or just one, or neither. Closer inspection reveals finer details of the setting, such as how close together the individual letters are and how much space there is between the words. All these individual variables together contribute to the overall appearance of the page and the legibility of the text.

Type size and line spacing The height of individual letters in typeset copy is traditionally expressed in terms of units called 'points', a straightforward and relatively simple measurement system that has been in use since the 1700s. It was initially developed in France but the Continental point (or more correctly, Didot point) is slightly larger than the point subsequently developed in America and the United Kingdom, which unfortunately hampers international compatibility. An inch contains approximately 67.5 Continental points and approximately 72 Anglo-American points. Using the Anglo-American system, therefore, a 72 point (written 72pt) 'A' would be about an inch (2.5cm) high and a 12pt 'A' would be six times smaller. The word 'high', however, is somewhat misleading for two reasons:

- The measurement is made from the top of the ascenders (the 'up strokes' — the top part of an 'h' for example) to the bottom of the descenders (the 'down strokes' — the lower part of a 'y' for example) of the lower case letters, or characters, and so letters without ascenders or descenders look smaller.
- The point size is based not on individual letters but on an invisible 'strip' which holds all the letters in any one sentence. This has its origin in handsetting where the individual pieces of metal used, each of which carried a raised letter on its face, were placed in rows — the width of metal needed to hold the letter then gives the point size of the letter. Since the design of the letters varies from one typeface to another, their actual size also varies depending on how completely the letters fill the 'strip' (or 'body').

The spaces between lines are also measured in points. If one

Point sizes
The units used to measure characters in typeset copy are called 'points'. The measuring system was first introduced in France and developed into a Continental standard. However the Continental, or Didot, point differs from the point used in the US and the UK: an inch contains 67.5 Continental points but 72 Anglo-American points. Letters are measured from the top of the ascenders to the bottom of the descenders of lower case letters. The point size is thus based on an invisible 'strip' which holds all the letters in a sentence. This originates from handsetting when individual pieces of metal, each carrying a raised letter on its face, were placed in rows..

In the metric system, type size is determined by the height of the capital letters — 'cap height' (CH). The spacing between lines of type is called 'line feed' (LF) — both are measured in millimeters. A 'pica em' is a unit which is 12 points wide (approximately 4mm or 1/6in). It is used to measure the length of lines. The pica is an Anglo-American term, in France and Germany it is called a *cicero*, in Italy *a riga* and in Holland, an *aug*.

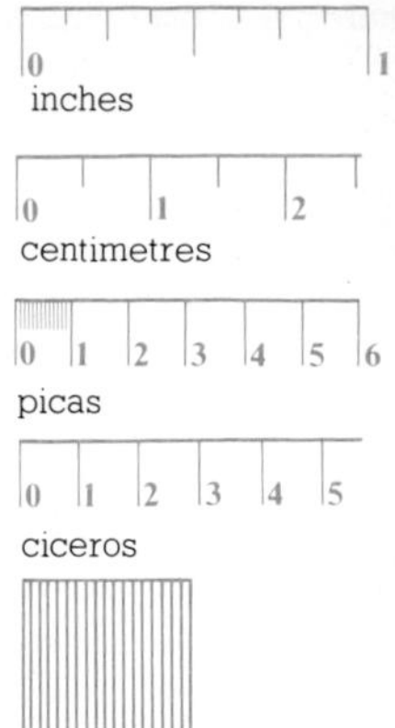

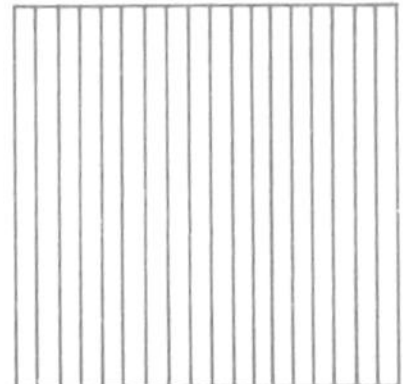

72pt em divided into 18 units

36pt em divided into 18 units

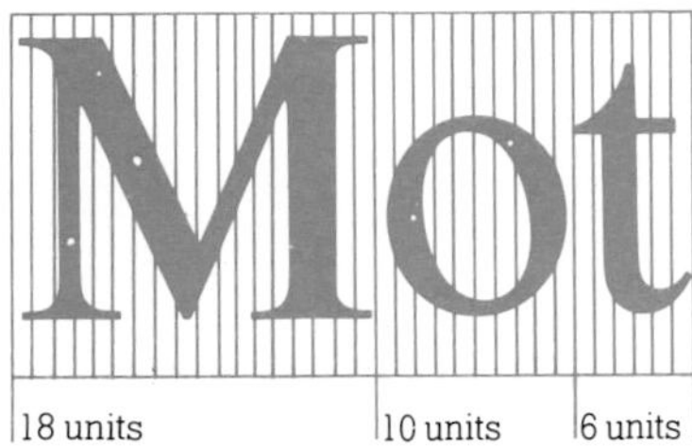

Loose
The form typography is to take

Normal
The form typography is to take

Tight
The form typography is to take

Very tight
The form typography is to take

Overlapping
The form typography is to take

Letterspacing can be specified to suit the designer's requirements. The type of spacing is usually specified as normal, loose, tight or very tight. In phototypesetting letterspacing is defined in terms of units or half units, depending on the system. The latter system is very flexible and letterspacing can be altered by fractions of a millimeter.

The point or body size of type is measured from the top of the ascender to the bottom of the descender. This distance varies from typeface to typeface as well as from one point size to another. Type can be measured from base line to base line (**right**) to establish the point size if there is no leading between the lines.

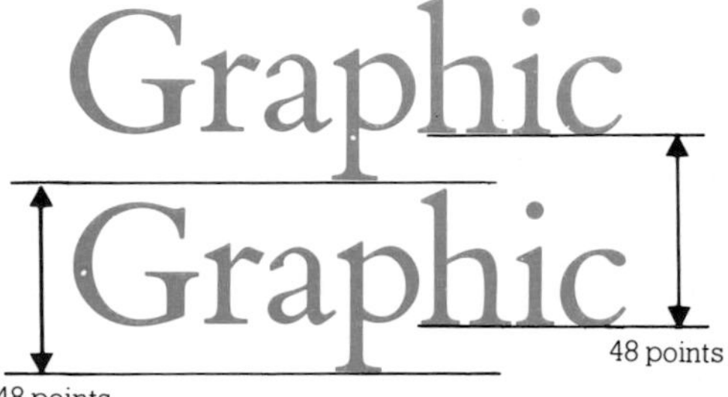

There are so many different typefaces available today, making a choice can be confusing. The most obvious difference between one typeface and another is whether they have serifs or not. Serif faces were the first to be developed. Faces without serifs are called *sans-serif* and are a relatively recent development.

SANS SERIF

Ut einim ad minim veniam, quis nostrud exercitation ullamcorpo laboris nisi ut aliquip ex ea commodo consequet. Duis autem

SERIF

Nimirum quia terra locis ex ordine certis lumine priuatur quod liquimus, eius, propterea fit uti uideatur, quae fuit

---

The examples here are all 36pt. A face with a large x-height is called a large appearing face and one with a small x-height a small appearing face.

abc	abc	abc
Bembo	Times	Rockwell

The x-height of small caps is the same as that of lowercase characters. Designed small caps are of even weight. Photographically reduced small caps tend to look lighter when set with normal type.

Designed SMALL CAPS

Reduced SMALL CAPS

A variation on SMALL CAPS

When two or more characters are joined and set as a single unit, they are termed ligatures. Common examples are ff, fi, fl and ffl. They should not be used when letterspacing is tight, as the result may look gappy.

fi fl ff ffi ffl

fi fl ff ffi ffl

When the spacing between specified characters is deliberately reduced, leaving the rest of the setting the same, the result is called kerning. The technique is frequently used with certain letter combinations, such as Yo, Te, LY and la. When these are set, there is often too much space between them, compared to the rest of the setting. Kerning solves this problem. If used properly, it can greatly improve letter-fit, legibility and the evenness of a line of typesetting — it is particularly useful with large display type.

VAULT VAULT

AT AY AV AW Ay Av Aw

FA TO TA Ta Te To Ti

Tr Tu Ty Tw Ts Tc LT

LY LV LW Ly PA VA Va

Ve Vo Vi Vr Vu Vy RT

RV RW RY Ry WA Wa We

Wo Wi Wr Wu Wy YA Ya

Ye Yo Yi Yp Yq Yu Yv

line of, say, 10pt type is followed immediately below by another line of 10pt type, the result is called 10pt solid or 10 'on' 10pt setting — usually written 10/10pt. In many typefaces this produces a very dense effect, with the descenders on one line almost touching the ascenders of the line below. Putting in a 1pt space between each line (known as 'leading' from the practice of putting strips of metal, with a high lead content, between rows of metal type) creates a much more legible result. This setting is then described as 10 'on' 11pt or 10/11pt. Putting in a 2pt space between lines produces 10/12pt, and so on.

The difference between Continental and Anglo-American point sizes is being cast aside gradually by a unifying influence entering the world of typesetting which is based on the metric system of measurement. The type sizes are expressed not in points but in terms of the height of the capital letters, or 'cap height' (CH), and the spaces between lines are referred to as 'line feed' (LF) — both measurements are given in millimeters. The use of metric units is inextricably tied up with modern forms of typesetting, such as computer setting.

Line length Traditionally the measurement of typeset lines across the page is also based on points, but expressed through the agency of another unit, the pica (or pica em), which is 12pts long (approximately 4 millimeters or 1/6 of an inch). The pica is the Anglo-American unit; the equivalent term for 12 European points varies from country to country — it is a *cicero* in France and Germany, a *riga* in Italy and an *aug* in Holland.

The word 'em' originally referred to the capital letter 'M', which in traditional typesetting systems occupied the full width of a square body of type (the 'body' being the piece of metal carrying the raised letter for letterpress). Thus, a 12pt 'M' is 12 points high and 12 points wide. In the same way, an 18pt em refers to the square of an 18pt body, and so on for all type sizes. In practice, however, editors, designers and typesetters usually (but incorrectly) drop the 'pica' from 'pica em' and use the word 'em' on its own to mean a 12pt em. Thus, a piece of text to be set to a maximum line length of 24 pica ems may be marked up as '24 ems'. However it is marked up and regardless of the typeface, a block of justified text with a measure of 24 ems is approximately 10 centimeters (4in) wide.

Margins In the days when type was set by hand, both left- and right-hand margins were aligned vertically down the page. This was because the individual pieces of type, letters and spaces, were packed into a metal frame (a form) for printing. The frame needed to be completely full to prevent pieces falling out. Therefore spaces were added between words to ensure that all the lines were the same length. The result is called 'justified setting', from the word 'just', which originally meant close-fitting. Although justified setting is still widely used, it is no longer obligatory. It is possible to have the left-hand margin aligned ('ranged left') and the right-hand margin unjustified ('ragged right'). 'Ranged right, ragged left' setting produces the opposite effect, although this rarely makes for easy reading and is therefore usually restricted to display setting or advertisements. It is also possible to set copy centerd about a vertical midline and to a maximum width.

Word and character spacing Look closely at a page of justified setting and you will see that the space between the words varies from line to line. In some lines the words may be crammed close together and in other lines there may be large gaps. Occasionally these spaces form distracting areas of white running down and across the page, which are called 'rivers' (see page 71). It is the typesetter's skill or the complexity of the computer program that determines how well balanced the result looks. Unjustifed setting, with a constant space between each word, is less likely to suffer from rivers.

The spaces between words and characters are measured by using another unit of measurement, one that is used not only to measure spaces, but also the width of individual characters in any given typeface. It is arrived at by subdividing an em into still smaller units called 'set points' or, in phototypesetting and computer typesetting systems, simply 'units'. The number of units per em varies between typesetting systems: 18 units per em is the most common. This applies to an em of any point size. Thus a 6pt em and a 72pt em would both be divided into 18 units, but the latter unit would be twelve times bigger than the former, although both would be in the same relative proportion.

The width of each character in any particular typeface is expressed as a number of units — the set width of that character. The same units are also used to register the spaces between characters and between words. In phototypesetting and computer typesetting systems it is possible to increase or decrease the set width of characters in extremely fine steps to vary the appearance and spacing of the final setting.

Typefaces The most obvious difference between one typeface and another is the presence or absence of serifs (the cross-lines at the ends of the main strokes in each letter). Typefaces without serifs are called, quite logically, *sans serif* faces. In the historical development of typefaces, serif faces came first; the *sans serif* faces are a relatively recent development. They were initially devised for posters and other display purposes but are now accepted for all types of printing.

The variety of typefaces available today is staggering. And the flexibility offered by modern typesetting systems has only added to the possible confusion for editors and designers. Thankfully, book publishers tend to select from a fairly restricted range of typefaces for the main body of the text. Like book sizes, the typestyles may fit into prearranged formats for books of a certain kind or books in a series. This provides some immediate pointers in what would otherwise be a bewildering situation.

Many traditional serif typefaces are classic designs that have survived alongside more modern typefaces with dignity and style. Typefaces such as Bembo, Baskerville, Bodoni, Century and Times are all tried and tested favorites. Among typefaces with slab serifs, where the letter does not curve into the serif but is straight, Rockwell (the typeface used in this book) has achieved great popularity, and the leaders of the *sans serif* typefaces must be Helvetica and Univers.

Most typefaces are available in a wide range of 'weights', or thickness of line: extra light, light, medium, bold and extra bold, the exact weight varying with the face and the typesetting system. Faces can also be condensed (compressed laterally) and italic (sloping to the right). To distinguish it from italic type, ordinary upright characters are called 'roman'. These stylistic variations to the basic typeface are extremely useful devices for editorial and design emphasis.

Each complete set of characters available in a typeface in any one weight or 'style' is called a font or fount, (from 'found' meaning to cast in a mold). Helvetica medium, therefore, is one font, while Helvetica bold italic is another, and so on.

Using type Having reviewed the basic characteristics of type, there are certain guidelines that should be considered when choosing and using type.

Legibility is an obvious starting point. Legibility is a product not only of the basic shape and size of the letters, but also of the measure (width of the setting) and the leading (space) between the lines. Serif faces are easier to read than *sans serif* faces and so they are widely used for the main text in books, magazines and newspapers. Type sizes between 8pt and 12pt are the most suitable for adults to read, usually set with 1 or 2pt leading — for instance 8/9pt, 9/10pt, 10/12pt, 11/13pt and 12/14pt. *Sans serif* faces are ideal for tables, charts, annotation and captions, and can be read at sizes down to 6pt if there is limited space on the page. In larger sizes *sans serif* faces are excellent for children's books.

If the lines are set to too wide a measure and too close together, the eye loses its way when it reaches the end of one line and tries to locate the beginning of the next. One formula suggested for easy reading is that each line should not exceed one-and-a-half alphabets (39 characters) in measure.

Gauging the suitability of a typeface by looking at only a specimen alphabet can give a misleading impression. You really need to see a sample block of copy set to your specifications to judge the overall effect. How dark or light a page of set text looks is called its 'color'. One important aspect that contributes to the color of a typeface is the x-height. This is the height of the main part of a lower case character. In some typefaces, such as Bembo, the x-height is small in relation to the extent of the ascenders and descenders, known as 'small appearing' faces. 'Large appearing' faces, such as Rockwell, have relatively large x-heights.

Successfully combining different typefaces and weights on the same page is largely a question of aesthetic taste and experiment. The designer will probably have some strong ideas about the typography that would best suit a new project and will ask the typesetter to provide samples of copy set in different typefaces before discussing and making a final choice. The combination of a serif face for the main text and a clean-looking *sans serif* face for captions is usually a very effective combination.

Typography for magazines

A magazine relies on effective typography to provide style and interest as well as making it pleasant and easy to read. Fashions change in the presentation of magazines and a good art editor or designer should always be keen to update and improve the look of the issue. He or she should take a keen interest in other magazines on the market and work closely with typesetters to make the most of the services available and any new technology that may have been introduced. Many magazines are charged a set rate per page and will be restricted to whatever typefaces and headline faces (a large typeface, usually above 36pt) their typesetter has available (some can offer a wider selection than others). Anything not available has to be charged separately and will add to the magazine's budget.

However, most magazines keep their main, or body, text to a set style of one or two typefaces and rely on a variety of headings, crossheadings, tints and boxes to change the pace and look of a page. The most important thing is that the copy should be easy to read and follow a logical sequence, so anything less than 8 or 9pt is too tiring to read in large quantities and badly positioned pictures can make a nonsense of the text if they have not been checked carefully at layout stage.

Crossheads are useful for breaking up text that has no illustrations and tend to have one or two line-width spaces either side (anything more can look as though you are trying to fill space unless you use rules). Dots or squares, or 'bullets', can be used effectively to indicate separate points. Charts, colored areas (tints) and boxes add variety to an all-text page. If you have a one-color page in a color printed area, small patches of color can sometimes look remarkably effective and cost relatively little compared with four-color printing.

Sometimes it is not always obvious where a feature starts or finishes: effective and well-sized headlines with a 'blurb' or 'sell' are essential, but a capital letter at the beginning of a piece occupying a space two or three lines deep (a dropped cap) and a device such as a small square, dot or other motif at the end can be used to reinforce the effect if necessary.

Casting off

Before sending off the edited manuscript for setting you may need to estimate how much space it will take up when set in the chosen typeface. This estimation process is called 'casting off'. The first stage involves counting the number of characters in the piece. If the text is neatly typed to a constant width, it is fairly easy to count the number of characters on a typical line (remembering to also count each space as one character) and then multiply this by the total number of lines. If the lines are uneven, it is helpful to draw a pencil line down the page to divide off the main part of the text from the straggly line endings, and then count these separately.

Always add on five or ten percent to your estimate of the number of characters as a margin of error. Knowing the total number of characters that are to be set (known as 'ens' in typesetting terms because each is equivalent to a lower case 'n') will enable you to establish the amount of space the set text will take up and also act as a guide to the cost; many typesetters charge per 1,000 ens. ('En' is also used to mean half a pica em, or em, and in this context is six points long.)

The most accurate way of working out how much space the copy will fill is to have some text set by the typesetter and simply count the characters in several lines and take an average figure. Typesetters usually supply text samples set at various leadings (or line feeds). These are useful for general reference, but a 'real' sample is the most reliable guide. It is also possible to work out how long a text will be once it is set by using suitable reference tables. These may list the number of characters per pica em for several typefaces, the number of lower case letters per line for each face and size over a given length, or generate a code number that you can 'decode' in a copyfitting table (see pages 60-61). A copyfitting table lists the number of characters per pica em according to the length in points of a complete alphabet and the number of characters for the respective point sizes per pica em.

Copyfitting tables
Special tables, which enable an estimate to be made of the amount of space copy will fill, are included in many type specimen books or sheets. The tables usually give the number of characters per pica for each size of every typeface, or the number of characters for each size of a variety of given measures. The table shown here has been devised to cover any typeface at any size on any typesetting system, however, it can work accurately only if the length of the lowercase alphabet of the face to be used is known. To use the table, first measure the length of the lowercase alphabet in points. The alphabet must be in the desired size and unit spacing, and the type produced on the typesetting system that will eventually be used for the actual job. Look at the lefthand column of the chart and select the number nearest to the alphabet length of the typeface to be used. The figure immediately to the right of this gives the number of characters per pica for the typeface that has been selected — at the correct size and on the correct system — and the number of characters in any measure can be calculated simply by multiplying the characters per pica figure by the length of line to be set (in picas). In other words, an alphabet length of 113 points gives a reading of 3.05 characters per pica (when read off against 114). A line measure of 26 picas will have 79 characters per line (3.05 × 26 = 79). To save having to make this calculation, the table gives the number of characters for a range of measures up to 40 picas.

Length of lower case alphabet (in points)	Number of characters per pica	Length of line to be set (in picas)						
	1	**7**	**8**	**9**	**10**	**11**	**12**	**13**
60	**5.80**	41	46	52	58	64	70	75
62	**5.61**	39	45	51	56	62	67	73
64	**5.44**	38	44	49	54	60	65	71
66	**5.27**	37	42	47	53	58	63	69
68	**5.12**	36	41	46	51	56	61	67
70	**4.97**	35	40	45	50	55	60	65
72	**4.83**	34	39	43	48	53	58	63
74	**4.70**	33	38	42	47	52	56	61
76	**4.58**	32	37	41	46	50	55	60
78	**4.46**	31	36	40	45	49	54	58
80	**4.35**	30	35	39	44	48	52	57
82	**4.24**	30	34	38	42	47	51	55
84	**4.14**	29	33	37	41	46	50	54
86	**4.05**	28	32	36	40	45	49	53
88	**3.95**	28	32	36	40	43	47	51
90	**3.87**	27	31	35	39	43	46	50
92	**3.78**	26	30	34	38	42	45	49
94	**3.70**	26	30	33	37	41	44	48
96	**3.63**	25	29	33	36	40	44	47
98	**3.55**	25	28	32	36	39	43	46
100	**3.48**	24	28	31	35	38	42	45
102	**3.41**	24	27	31	34	38	41	44
104	**3.35**	23	27	30	33	37	40	43
106	**3.28**	23	26	30	33	36	39	43
108	**3.22**	23	26	29	32	35	39	42
110	**3.16**	22	25	28	32	35	38	41
112	**3.11**	22	25	28	31	34	37	40
114	**3.05**	21	24	27	31	34	37	40
116	**3.00**	21	24	27	30	33	36	39
118	**2.95**	21	24	27	29	32	35	38
120	**2.90**	20	23	26	29	32	35	38
122	**2.85**	20	23	26	29	31	34	37
124	**2.81**	20	22	25	28	31	34	36
126	**2.76**	19	22	25	28	30	33	36
128	**2.72**	19	22	24	27	30	33	35
130	**2.68**	19	21	24	27	29	32	35
135	**2.58**	18	21	23	26	28	31	34
140	**2.49**	17	20	22	25	27	30	32
145	**2.40**	17	19	22	24	26	29	31
150	**2.32**	16	19	21	23	26	28	30
155	**2.25**	16	18	20	22	25	27	29
160	**2.18**	15	17	20	22	24	26	28
165	**2.11**	15	17	19	21	23	25	27
170	**2.05**	14	16	18	20	23	25	27
175	**1.99**	14	16	18	20	22	24	26
180	**1.93**	14	15	17	19	21	23	25
185	**1.88**	13	15	17	19	21	23	24
190	**1.83**	13	15	16	18	20	22	24
195	**1.78**	12	14	16	18	20	21	23
200	**1.74**	12	14	16	17	19	21	23

14	15	16	17	18	19	20	22	24	26	28	30	32	34	36	38	40
81	87	93	99	104	110	116	128	139	151	162	174	186	197	209	220	232
79	84	90	95	101	107	112	123	135	146	157	168	180	191	202	213	224
76	82	87	92	98	103	109	120	131	141	152	163	174	185	196	207	218
74	79	84	90	95	100	105	116	126	137	148	158	169	179	190	200	211
72	77	82	87	92	97	102	113	123	133	143	154	164	174	184	195	205
70	75	80	84	89	94	99	109	119	129	139	149	159	169	179	189	199
68	72	77	82	87	92	96	106	116	126	135	145	155	164	174	184	193
66	70	75	80	85	89	94	103	113	122	132	141	150	160	169	179	188
64	69	73	78	82	87	92	101	110	119	128	137	147	156	165	174	183
62	67	71	76	80	85	89	98	107	116	125	134	143	152	161	170	178
61	65	70	74	78	83	87	96	104	113	122	131	139	148	157	165	174
59	64	68	72	76	81	85	93	102	110	119	127	136	144	153	161	170
58	62	66	70	75	79	83	91	99	108	116	124	133	141	149	157	166
57	61	65	69	73	77	81	89	97	105	113	121	129	138	146	154	162
55	59	63	67	71	75	79	87	95	103	111	119	127	134	142	150	158
54	58	62	66	70	73	77	85	93	101	108	116	124	131	139	147	155
53	57	61	64	68	72	76	83	91	98	106	113	121	129	136	144	151
52	56	59	63	67	70	74	81	89	96	104	111	118	126	133	141	148
51	54	58	62	65	69	73	80	87	94	102	109	116	123	131	138	145
50	53	57	60	64	67	71	78	85	92	99	107	114	121	128	135	142
49	52	56	59	63	66	70	77	84	90	97	104	111	118	125	132	139
48	51	55	58	61	65	68	75	82	89	96	102	109	116	123	130	136
47	50	54	57	60	64	67	74	80	87	94	100	107	114	120	127	134
46	49	53	56	59	62	66	72	79	85	92	98	105	112	118	125	131
45	48	52	55	58	61	64	71	77	84	90	97	103	110	116	122	129
44	47	51	54	57	60	63	70	76	82	89	95	101	108	114	120	127
43	47	50	53	56	59	62	68	75	81	87	93	99	106	112	118	124
43	46	49	52	55	58	61	67	73	79	85	92	98	104	110	116	122
42	45	48	51	54	57	60	66	72	78	84	90	96	102	108	114	120
41	44	47	50	53	56	59	65	71	77	83	88	94	100	106	112	118
41	44	46	49	52	55	58	64	70	75	81	87	93	99	104	110	116
40	43	46	48	51	54	57	63	68	74	80	86	91	97	103	108	114
39	42	45	48	51	53	56	62	67	73	79	84	90	95	101	107	112
39	41	44	47	50	52	55	61	66	72	77	83	88	94	99	105	110
38	41	44	46	49	52	54	60	65	71	76	82	87	92	98	103	109
37	40	43	46	48	51	54	59	64	70	75	80	86	91	96	102	107
36	39	41	44	46	49	52	57	62	67	72	77	82	88	93	98	103
35	37	40	42	45	47	50	55	60	65	70	75	80	85	89	94	99
34	36	38	41	43	46	48	53	58	62	67	72	77	82	86	91	96
32	35	37	39	42	44	46	51	56	60	65	70	74	79	84	88	93
31	34	36	38	40	43	45	49	54	58	63	67	72	76	81	85	90
30	33	35	37	39	41	44	48	52	57	61	65	70	74	78	83	87
30	32	34	36	38	40	42	46	51	55	59	63	67	72	76	80	84
29	31	33	35	37	39	41	45	49	53	57	61	66	70	74	78	82
29	30	32	34	36	38	40	44	48	52	56	60	64	68	72	76	80
27	29	31	33	35	37	39	43	46	50	54	58	62	66	70	73	77
26	28	30	32	34	36	38	41	45	49	53	56	60	64	68	71	75
26	27	29	31	33	35	37	40	44	48	51	55	59	62	66	70	73
25	27	29	30	32	34	36	39	43	46	50	54	57	61	64	68	71
24	26	28	30	31	33	35	38	42	45	49	52	56	59	63	66	70

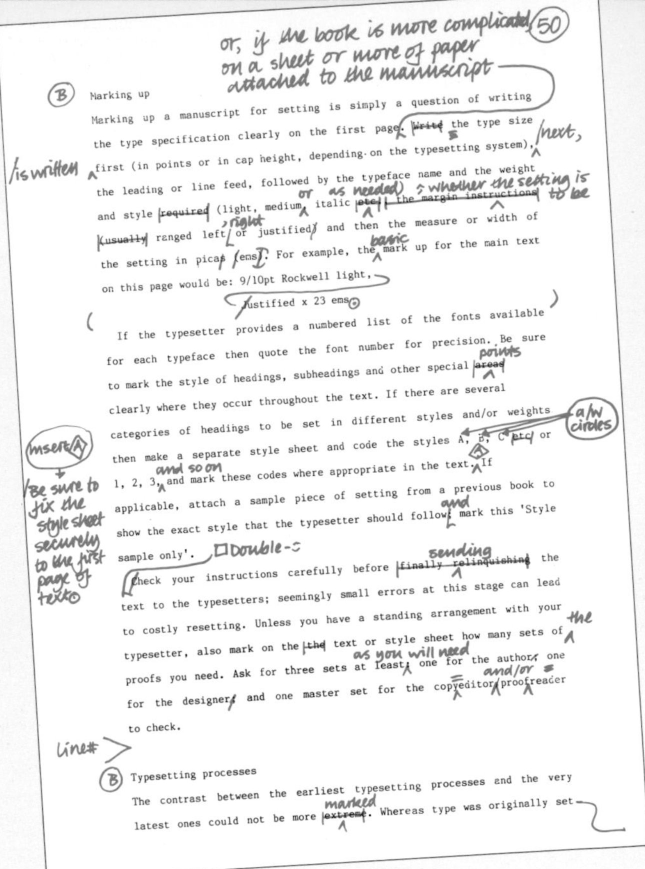

Marking up

Marking up a manuscript for setting is simply a question of writing the type specification clearly on the first page. Write the type size first (in points or in cap height, depending on the typesetting system), the leading or line feed, followed by the typeface name and the weight and style required (light, medium, italic etc), the margin instructions (usually ranged left or justified) and then the measure or width of the setting in picas (ems). For example, the mark up for the main text on this page would be: 9/10pt Rockwell light, justified x 23 ems.

If the typesetter provides a numbered list of the fonts available for each typeface then quote the font number for precision. Be sure to mark the style of headings, subheadings and other special areas clearly where they occur throughout the text. If there are several categories of headings to be set in different styles and/or weights then make a separate style sheet and code the styles A, B, C etc or 1, 2, 3, and mark these codes where appropriate in the text. If applicable, attach a sample piece of setting from a previous book to show the exact style that the typesetter should follow; mark this 'Style sample only'. Check your instructions carefully before finally relinquishing the text to the typesetters; seemingly small errors at this stage can lead to costly resetting. Unless you have a standing arrangement with your typesetter, also mark on the the text or style sheet how many sets of proofs you need. Ask for three sets at least; one for the author, one for the designer, and one master set for the copyeditor proofreader to check.

Typesetting processes

The contrast between the earliest typesetting processes and the very latest ones could not be more extreme. Whereas type was originally set

Marking up

Marking up a manuscript for setting is simply a question of writing the type specification clearly on the first page or, if the book is more complicated, on a sheet or more of paper attached to the manuscript. The type size is written first (in points or in cap height, depending on the typesetting system), next, the leading or line feed, followed by the typeface name and the weight and style (light, medium or italic as needed), whether the setting is to be ranged left, right or justified and then the measure or width of the setting in pica ems. For example, the basic mark up for the main text on this page would be: 9/10pt Rockwell light, justified × 23 pica ems.

If the typesetter provides a numbered list of fonts available for each typeface then quote the font number for precision. Be sure to mark the style of headings, subheadings and other special points clearly where they occur throughout the text. If there are several categories of headings to be set in different styles and/or weights then make a separate style sheet and code the styles A, B, C or 1, 2, 3 and so on and mark these codes where appropriate in the text. Be sure to fix the style sheet securely to the first page of text. If applicable, attach a sample piece of setting from a previous book to show the exact style that the typesetter should follow and mark this 'Style sample only'.

Double-check your instructions carefully before sending the

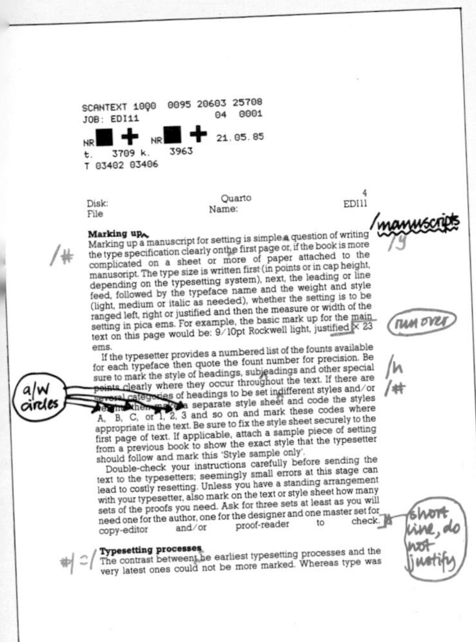
SCANTEXT 1000 0095 20603 25708
JOB: EDI11 04 0001
NR ■ + NR ■ + 21.05.85
t. 3709 k. 3963
T 03402 03406

Disk: Quarto 4
File Name: EDI11

Marking up
Marking up a manuscript for setting is simple a question of writing the type specification clearly onthe first page or, if the book is more complicated on a sheet or more of paper attached to the manusoript. The type size is written first (in points or in cap height, depending on the typesetting system), next, the leading or line feed, followed by the typeface name and the weight and style (light, medium or italic as needed), whether the setting is to be ranged left, right or justified and then the measure or width of the setting in pica ems. For example, the basic mark up for the main text on this page would be: 9/10pt Rockwell light, justified × 23 ems.

If the typesetter provides a numbered list of the founts available for each typeface then quote the fount number for precision. Be sure to mark the style of headings, subjeadings and other special points clearly where they occur throughout the text. If there are several categories of headings to be set indifferent styles and/or [illegible] them make a separate style sheet and code the styles A, B, C, or 1, 2, 3 and so on and mark these codes where appropriate in the text. Be sure to fix the style sheet securely to the first page of text. If applicable, attach a sample piece of setting from a previous book to show the exact style that the typesetter should follow and mark this 'Style sample only'.

Double-check your instructions carefully before sending the text to the typesetters; seemingly small errors at this stage can lead to costly resetting. Unless you have a standing arrangement with your typesetter, also mark on the text or style sheet how many sets of the proofs you need. Ask for three sets at least as you will need one for the author, one for the designer and one master set for copy-editor and/or proof-reader to check.

Typesetting processes
The contrast betweenthe earliest typesetting processes and the very latest ones could not be more marked. Whereas type was

When a manuscript is sent to the typesetters (**left**) it must always include specifications as to typeface, weight (bold, medium, light, etc) measure and may require other instructions for headings or areas of text to be set to a different measure or in a different weight, for example. This is returned as a proof which has to be carefully checked line for line against the original manuscript to ensure that the typesetter has set it as requested. Any errors on the proof have to be marked clearly, using the proof-reading marks (**left** and 68-71). The reader uses red when the typesetter has made an error and blue or black to indicate alterations made by the author or editor. Some typesetters have their own reader who will have checked the proof and marked any typographical or literal errors, such as transposition of letters, in green before it is returned.
The reason that different colors are used is to aid the allocation of correction costs.

text to the typesetters; seemingly small errors at this stage can lead to costly resetting. Unless you have a standing arrangement with your typesetter, also mark on the text or style sheet how many sets of the proofs you need. Ask for three sets at least as you will need one for the author, one for the designer and one master set for the copy-editor and/or proof-reader to check.

Typesetting processes

The contrast between the earliest typesetting processes and the very latest ones could not be more marked. Whereas type was originally set by hand, using individual characters cast or punched in metal, the computer typesetting systems of today contain no literal representation of the characters at all, only electronic pulses that 'hold' the information necessary to recreate the characters as and when they are needed. As with so many other mechanical processes, the power and subtlety of electricity have revolutionized typesetting to an extraordinary degree. Contact with the original methods has not been lost, however, for some handsetting is still carried out today for special editions and display titles.

Computer-oriented typesetting processes dominate the publishing world today. Only two other basic approaches still survive as intermediate steps in the evolutionary process — hot metal and photomechanical typesetting.

Hot metal typesetting

Hot metal typesetting machines are precision engineered to mechanize the handsetting process. The various types of machines are known universally by their manufacturer's names.

The Monotype machine, as the name suggests, casts the letters individually and assembles them into lines. The operator uses a separate keyboard unit to generate a perforated paper tape about 9 centimeters (3.5 inches wide) that the caster unit decodes it into a complex series of mechanical functions. In short, a case containing separate molds of each letter (the matrix case) is moved into position so that the correct letter mold receives a measured amount of molten metal. Once it has been cooled by water, each individual piece of type is moved up to take its correct place on the line. Since this operation is achieved by compressed air and a great deal of metal-to-metal contact, such machines generate a large amount of mechanical bustle.

The Linotype machine generates hot metal type a line at a time. The molds, or matrices, for each letter are not held together in a case but are individual pieces stored in magazines at the top of the combined keyboard/caster unit. When a key is pressed on the keyboard the appropriate matrix drops down and joins others to make up a complete line of type. As the line is completed it is moved sideways to receive the hot metal. Once the solid bar of type is trimmed and moved into position on the galley case, the individual matrices are conveyed back to the top of the machine and re-sorted into their respective magazines.

Although hot metal setting is becoming increasingly rare, it has provided an example of excellence in terms of the quality of the typeset characters — a quality that, for all their speed, some of the modern computer systems have failed to match completely.

Photomechanical setting

The term 'photomechanical' is also relevant for some of the computer-oriented systems in use (described below), but used specifically it applies to machines, such as the Monophoto, that are direct developments of hot metal technology. Using a perforated tape generated on a keyboard, machines such as the Monophoto employ a complex system of lenses, prisms and mirrors to direct light through individual negatives of the characters held rigidly in a matrix case. The light exposed through each negative produces a positive image directly onto a length of film fed into the machine. Film is commonly used, although it is possible to use photographic paper (bromide).

Such systems are slow and noisy but they do produce very clear and well-formed characters, a virtue that many publishers exploit even though most computer typesetting is faster and quieter.

Computer typesetting systems

Several different typesetting systems make use of computers at some stage in their operation. They can all be described loosely as phototypesetting processes because the eventual image of the characters is formed on photosensitive film or paper. They differ, however, in the way in which this image is generated and can be divided on that basis into the following categories:

- Photomechanical systems
- Digitized Cathode Ray Tube (CRT) systems
- Laser systems

The hot metal Monotype typesetting machine (**left**) and the computer typesetting machine (**below**) reflect the traditional and the modern aspects of typesetting techniques respectively. The often excellent image produced by hot metal setting is still used today although more and more rarely as in most cases, the greater speed and flexibility of computer setting will usually prove to be too advantageous to resist.

Photomechanical systems In the realm of complex typesetting systems these are perhaps the easiest to comprehend. Quite simply, the text is exposed onto photosensitive film or paper by light shining through negatives of the individual type characters in turn, in a similar way to the Monophoto machine. But the use of computer controls enables the process to take place much more quickly. Thus, the coded text information that has been keyed in by the operator onto a magnetic disk can coordinate the very fast movements of the typeface negative and the light source to create the text. The light source may move relative to the master set or the characters may move relative to the light. In one system, for example, the master set consists of a spinning disc illuminated by a timed, high-intensity flash tube. Lenses, mirrors and prisms direct and bend the light to project characters of the required size onto the film or photosensitive paper. The negative images of the characters — the master set — may be carried on strips of film, on discs or segments of discs, depending on the system. Such phototypesetting systems produce clean-edged characters but are not as fast or flexible as most digitized systems.

Digitized CRT systems The systems described below represent the mainstream of digital typesetting techniques used for a wide range of published material.

The fundamental innovation of digital typesetting is that the shape of the typeset character is not stored in any recognizable form (like the negative in phototypesetting). In any modern typesetting company using this type of system the moving mechanical parts are restricted mainly to the keyboard, the disk drives and the paper or film transport mechanism; everything else moves incredibly fast and quietly.

Although digital systems vary in their capacity, complexity and method of image formation, they all have an input unit and an output unit. In some systems these units may be physically combined, in others they are separate, free-standing boxes.

The input unit, more correctly called a workstation, consists of the familiar QWERTY keyboard plus a number of command and function keys, a visual display terminal (VDT), a computer, and a number of data storage devices (usually disk drives). The output unit, or phototypesetting unit, contains the image-forming mechanism, a computer and a number of disk drives (some also have paper tape readers). The other essential item is a photographic processing unit that develops the final image on the exposed paper or film.

These are the sophisticated devices that are immediately apparent, but it is the unseen workings of the computer programs, or software, that provide the power, flexibility and speed common to all digital typesetting systems. In a typical sequence, the operator keys in the text at the keyboard having first selected the basic setting parameters of the job. The options available may be displayed in a set of boxes displayed on the VDT. At the touch of a key, therefore, the operator can select (and possibly see confirmed) the typeface; the type size (in mm of body size or cap height, in Didot points or pica points — see page 53-56); line feed (leading); the style of setting (justified, ranged left or otherwise); the letter spacing and word spacing (both variable in very small steps) and modification of the character (such as condensing or slanting); horizontal and vertical tabs; and many other specifications that affect the appearance of the final setting. The VDT can also show useful parameters related to the job, such as the number of lines in the job, the job name, the page number, and other details.

One of the most important aspects of the computer's activity in digital typesetting is the hyphenation and justification (H&J) program. This performs the decisions about where to break words or end a line that traditionally lie in the hands of human typesetters. Such a program will normally perform word breaks at the ends of lines based on a specific logic together with an 'exception dictionary'. This is a list of words — complete with hyphenation details — that would not be hyphenated correctly following the computer's set of rules. Less commonly, the program may contain a 'true dictionary' detailing precise hyphenation rules for all the words likely to be encountered. Without an H&J program the machine will not break words at all but carry them over to the next line. And most systems allow the operator to overrule the computer's logic if necessary.

Having keyed in and stored on disk the text and appropriate format codes, the operator inserts this disk and a disk containing the font details into two separate disk drives in the output unit. Drawing on the information stored on both disks, or in the memory, the computer in this unit sends appropriate signals to the imaging device and the transport mechanism moving the roll of photosensitive paper or film across the screen or CRT face plate. In some systems, the image of the typeset characters is formed by a cathode ray tube (CRT) (rather like a very small television tube) that scans up and down as it moves across from left to right, building up the image as it goes. The emissions from the CRT pass through a lens onto a glass screen over which the photosensitive paper or film is moved in precise steps. Alternatively, the image can be formed by the scanning activity of a larger CRT, its patterns of light being transferred to the image screen by millions of optical fibers. The net result in both systems is that the characters are built up in a series of vertical lines, visible only through a powerful magnifying glass.

The flexibility offered by digital and phototypesetting is evident not only in the fact that a large number of different typefaces are available at the touch of a button, but also in the manipulation of the text that is possible once it is stored on disk. In fact, the text can be typed in before any format decisions are made. To this end, 'off-line' (portable keyboards) are available on which the text can be typed and stored quite separately from the typesetting unit. Once transferred into the system, such 'remotely captured' text can be edited and then set in the conventional way.

A further sophistication possible with digital typesetting systems is a graphic display unit that shows on the VDT screen not only the layout of the text, but also reproduces it in its real style and proportion. Such terminals are excellent for laying out advertisements, magazine pages and other such structured items.

Laser systems Laser typesetting systems combine the solid state technology of the previous digital systems but produce the image on paper or film by means of a laser beam. The laser beam is deflected by a complex series of devices, such as a spinning, mirrored polygon and a lens system. One of the features of laser and certain CRT typesetting is that they can expose whole pages (up to 305mm wide by 655mm deep (approximately 12 by 26 inches) deep) at a time.

Galley proofs

Galley proofs are usually photocopies of the continuous setting bromide (strip of photographic paper that has been exposed by the typesetting machine according to the keys pressed by the typesetter). At this stage there are no gaps for the insertion of illustrations, or divisions into pages. It is not until the galley proofs have been corrected that the designer divides the continuous setting into pages and inserts the illustrations.

Reading galley proofs In most cases the author and the proof-reader each read a set of proofs. However, if the text has been accepted by a foreign publisher it is usual to send a set of proofs to the foreign editor so that any translation can begin immediately and promotion of the book can be planned.

The copy-editor reads the galley proofs against the original typescript to check that the typesetter has set exactly what was typed. To do this the copy-editor reads a few words from the proof, then looks across to the typescript to check their accuracy. This requires intense concentration because every letter of every word must be noted and compared, as opposed to the usual reading technique of absorbing several words or even a complete sentence at one time. It is, of course, time-consuming, but essential if the final text is to be as error-free as possible. Frequent breaks are often necessary to maintain concentration.

To correct the galley proofs the proof-reader uses a system of proof-reading marks (see pages 68-71). If an error is found to the left of an imaginary line drawn down the middle of the proof, the correction is written in the left-hand margin; if more than one error occurs in a line, the corrections are separated by an oblique stroke. They must read in the order that the errors appear from left to right in each margin.

When the proof-reader receives the galley proofs there may be some errors that have been marked already. This will have been done by the typesetter's reader. These marks may have been made in green to identify them as errors made by the typesetter. If the typesetter has queries for the author or proof-reader, these too will be marked in green. When the copy-editor reads the proofs, he or she marks typesetter's errors in red. The author also marks typesetter's errors in red, but if he or she decides to make changes or additions, they are marked in blue or black.

Three colors are used so that when correction costs are allocated it is easy to see the percentage of corrections due to typesetter's errors (red and green marks) and the percentage of author's or editor's corrections (blue or black marks).

Compiling a master proof When the proof-reader receives the author's marked proofs each correction is looked at and, if it is one that has already been noticed it can be ignored. If it corrects an error that has been missed the correction can be marked on his or her own proof. This compilation becomes the master proof. As to any changes or additions that the author wishes to make, the proof-reader first looks for those that affect factual accuracy and transfers them to the master proof. Of the remainder, only those changes that involve minimal resetting should be marked. The proof-reader then sends the master proof back to the typesetter for the corrections to be made.

PROOF CORRECTION MARKS

Proofs that are being corrected should be marked up in the margin as well as in the text. This is because the printer always looks down the margin to see where the corrections occur. Proof correction marks are standard, but those shown (**below**) were only recently introduced. These are now being adopted although many people still use the old systems.

Instruction to printer	Textual mark	Marginal mark
Correction is concluded	None	
Leave unchanged	typeface groups	STET
Remove unwanted marks	typeface groups	X
Push down risen spacing material	typeface groups	lower
Refer to appropriate authority	typeface groups	?
Insert new matter	^ groups	typeface
Insert additional matter	type groups	A
Delete	typeface groups	
Delete and close up	typeface groups	
Substitute character or part of one or more words	tipeface groops	y/ u/
Wrong fount, replace with correct fount	typeface groups	wf/fix
Correct damaged characters	typeface groups	X

Instruction to printer	Textual mark	Marginal mark
Set in or change to italics	typeface groups	ital
Set in or change to capitals	typeface groups	cap
Set in or change to small capitals	typeface groups	sc
Capitals for initials small caps for rest of word	typeface groups	cap+sc
Set in or change to bold type	typeface groups	bf
Set in or change to bold italic type	typeface groups	bf+ital
Change capitals to lower case	typeFACE groups	lc
Change small capitals to lower case	typeFACE groups	lc
Change italic to roman	*typeface* groups	rom
Invert type	typəface groups	9
Insert ligature	filmsetter	fi
Substitute separate letters for ligature	filmsetter	fi
Insert full point	typeface groups	⊙
Insert colon	typeface groups	⊙
Insert semi-colon	typeface groups	;
Insert comma	typeface groups	,
Insert quotation marks	typeface groups	' / '
Insert double quotation marks	typeface groups	" / "
Substitute character in superior position	typeface groups	sup
Substitute character in inferior position	typeface groups	sub
Insert apostrophe	typeface groups	'
Insert ellipsis	typeface groups	⊙⊙⊙
Insert leader dots	typeface groups	⊙⊙⊙
Substitute or insert hyphen	typeface groups	=
Insert rule	typeface groups	2pt rule
Insert oblique	typeface groups	/
Start new paragraph	are called set points. The dimension of	¶
No fresh paragraph, run on	are called set points. The dimension of	no ¶

Instruction to printer	Textual mark	Marginal mark
Transpose characters or word	groups typeface	tr
Transpose characters (2)	tpeyface groups	tr
Transpose lines	The dimensions of are called set points.	tr
Transpose lines (2)	The dimension of are called set points.	tr
Centre type	typeface groups	center
Indent 1 em	typeface groups	indent 1em
Delete indent	typeface groups	flush left
Set line justified	typeface groups	justify
Set column justified		justify col
Move matter to right	typeface groups	
Move matter to left	typeface groups	
Take over to next line	typeface groups	run over
Take back to previous line	typeface groups	move up
Raise matter	typeface groups	
Lower matter	typeface groups	
Correct vertical alignment	typeface groups	||
Correct horizontal alignment	typeface groups	align
Close up space	type face groups	
Insert space between words	typefacegroups	#
Reduce space between words	typeface groups	reduce #
Reduce or insert space between letters	ty pe f a c e groups	/#
Make space appear equal	typeface groups	equal #
Close up to normal line spacing	typeface groups	normal spacing
Insert space between paragraphs	are called set points. The dimension of	#
Reduce space between paragraphs	are called set points. The dimension of	reduce #
Insert parentheses or square brackets	typeface groups	( )/[ ]
Figure or abbreviation to be spelt out in full	12 point twelve pt	sp
Move matter to position indicated	are called The set points. dimensional	tr

Types of errors
Shown here are some of the types of errors that a copy-editor looks for in galley proofs.

Omission of one or more lines when the typesetter 'drops' from a word in the line being set to the identical word one or more lines below. This is a frequent, major error and one which can destroy the author's argument.

Omission of punctuation marks

Omission of closing parenthesis or quotation mark

'Literals', the setting of a wrong letter in a word

Incorrect word breaks at the ends of lincs

Headings set in the wrong size or weight of type or font

'Rivers' – when the spaces between the words in successive lines form a meandering line of white space

Disk: Quarto 4

File Name: EDI9

Title Editing for Print

(the fundamentals).

At this stage three basic plas are set into operation: a production schedule, a budget and a flat plan (a page-by-page 'story-board of the whole book). These plans are discussed and monitoring each stage.

The editor usually maintains regular contact with the author throughout the manuscript development period discussing and monitoring each stage.

Once the author's manuscript starts to arrive, and it often comes in batches, the whole process moves ahead with some urgency in order to meet the publication date set by the production schedule. As batches of text arrive, the editor will sub edit it for content and logic or arrange for this to be done, elicit the expert reactions of any suitable consulents, and then organize detailed copy-editing for style and consistency. The editor, designers and sometimes an author, will generate a list of the photographs and illustrations that will be required throughout the book.

Having originated or fine-tuned an idea, engaged an author, planned the general approach of the book and edited the text, the editor's initial push is now over and the impetus passes to the design department.

Design The designer's first task is to decide on the typestyle for the text and send sections of text for sample typesetting. When the designer has decided on the fonts to be used he or she will style the whole manuscript and send it to be set. In some companies the editor will do this. In the meantime, attention turns toward designing the layout grids that will serve as the working 'blueprint' for all departments during the rest of the production period. Picture research, photography and illustration are usually commissioned by the designer, but always in close association with the editor. Using the typeset text (in galley form), photographs chosen from those provided by the author or picture researcher and ideas for il- ustrations, the designer produces the layouts – a full-size visual record of the whole book in the form of flat 'double-page spreads' (sheets showing the left- and right-hand pages in a book). Now the editor becomes actively involved again, writing captions, cutting or extending the text to make it fit the design exactly, inserting headings and other elements

At this point in the sequence the boundary between design and production becomes a little blurred. In companies without a production department, the design will send the photographs and illustration artwork off for speaation into the coloru films needed for printing and will also check the colour proofs.

Production Traditionally, the production department is concerned with all the mechanical aspects of the production process rather than with the artistic ones. This may include sending the styled text for typesetting and certainly involves desparching photographs and artwork for origination and separation. It is the production manager's job to secure the highest quality work for the time and money available.

When all the material for the book is assembled (in the form of text and ilustration films), the production manager 'chaperones' it through the printing, binding, delivery and warehousing stages. Where a distinct production department does not exist, the designer will perform these roles. It is rare for an editor to become involved with the printing stage itself, although checking the final imposed proof (ozalid before the book is passed for press and printing starts is an important editorial task.

Sales/Marketing having published the book in advance, based on the synopsis and other information from the editor, the promotion side of the sales/marketing department oversees the distribution of the book to bookshops and also sells the rights to book clubs, foreign publishers and others. A company engaged in international publishing may have foreign rights staff who will be responsible for selling language rights to different areas of the world. The various book fairs held throughout the year are focal points for this selling activity.

At this stage the author or editor may be asked to champion the the book sales conferences and book fairs, and will certainly be required to write penetrating blurbs for catalogues and other publicity material.

Too much or too little space between words or paragraphs

Substitution of a word that is very close in spelling to the original

A word at the end of one line repeated at the beginning of the next

Computers and the editor

People have been saying for some time that the invention of the microchip is going to revolutionize our lives. And, in many ways, the revolution is already with us: we watch videos, have digital watches, use calculators, use a card to get money from the bank. In publishing the revolution has proceeded as far as accounts and stock control but it has taken a long time to come to editorial departments. Now that it is finally here, what does it mean?

For editors the first evidence of the revolution has been the word processor. A word processor is a microcomputer that has a special facility, either built in or inserted in the form of a program on a floppy disk for processing words. That is, it lets you type (or 'key' in) text, which appears not on a piece of paper but on a screen (visual display terminal, or, more commonly, VDT). Once the text is there, you can alter it as much as you like – without crossing out, using correction fluid, retyping sections or cutting up bits of paper – you can correct mistakes, move whole passages of text from place to place, add bits or delete them. If you have consistently misspelled a word, you can program the word processor to check your spelling and to help make an index. And when you are ready, you can either print out what you have done on paper or store it electronically on a disk. Undoubtedly a word processor is a marvelous tool for editors and authors, but what effect does it have on publishing as a whole?

The most basic way you can use a word processor is to make it produce a near perfect manuscript. An author, for example, can submit virtually error-free copy to the editor, which is useful in itself. The editor can use a word processor to work from this manuscript and, once the editor is satisfied with it, he or she can print out a perfect copy for the typesetter to work from. Doing this

The impact of computers on the editor's environment and work usually takes the form of advantages, such as the swift and easy manipualtion of text made possible with word processors and the peripherals, such as disk drives and printers, used to store and print out the result.

makes the author's and the editor's lives a lot easier and it saves editor and typesetter the problems of reading messy manuscripts. But using the computer solely in this way is to treat it like a glorified typewriter when it can do very much more.

Instead of printing out and sending the manuscript to the editor, the author can simply send the disk on which the manuscript has been stored. Provided the editor's word processor can 'read' the disk, the editor can put the author's disk into his or her word processor and work on it directly. (Like many things in computing, however, this is not always as simple as it sounds, see page 76.)

When the editor has finished with the disk, it can be sent to the typesetter, who, if the typesetting machine can 'read' the disk, (if there is no in-house typesetting terminal), can put the disk straight into the machine and start to work on the text. There is no need for retyping at any stage so both author and editor have the reassurance of knowing that accidental errors are less likely to creep in. For the editor there is the added advantage that, because what comes back from the typesetter is, as far as the words are concerned, exactly what was sent off, there is no real need to check the galleys line for line against the original text and that saves time – either on the schedule, or in giving the editor more time for the broadly 'creative' functions that should be the most important part of the job. Things can still go wrong, of course – the computer can malfunction or refuse to work – but by and large the mistakes that computers tend to make are so obvious (they will miss or repeat large chunks of text, or just print gobbledygook) that they will be obvious. However, it is a wise precaution to proof-read the copy.

This technique, or 'single stroke key capture', to give it its proper name, is something about which the print unions have been

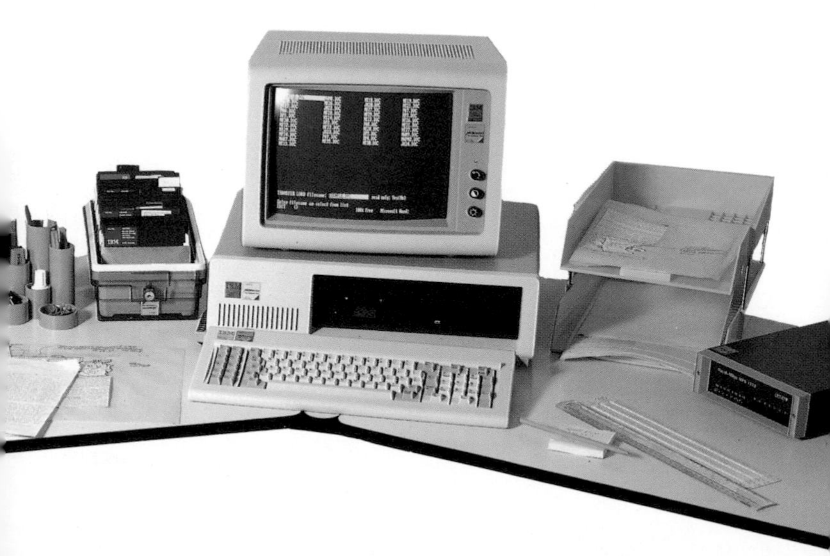

concerned for some time. For editors, it saves a great deal of time and drudgery. But it is not all computers are capable of.

Until now, computer typesetting has been done on specialized machines that are not much good at anything else. But, as it becomes easier to design more power into smaller and smaller computers, it is becoming possible – at reasonable cost – to have a microcomputer that will do two jobs. The editor may be able to use the machine first to edit the text – and then to typeset it. That will give complete control: the editor will know where word breaks are going to be, where column endings are and exactly how text and captions fit. When he or she is satisfied it is right, the disk can simply be sent to the typesetter, who does nothing more than put it into the setting machine, press a button, run the galleys out and paste them up into page proofs. What the editor gets back is exactly what was sent off so there is no need for cutting and filling at page proof stage. That, in turn, means a saving of time on

The keyboard of a microcomputer is more than just a keyboard – it actually contains the computer itself. It looks like an ordinary QWERTY typewriter keyboard (**1**) flanked by some specialized keys (**2**) by which the cursor can be moved to any part of the screen; insert and delete keys (**3**) that allow characters to be added or removed (these often appear on a single, shifted key); a group of function keys (**4**) that can be programmed to carry out complicated instructions at the touch of a button; and possibly a separate pad of numeric keys (**5**) (here the numeric pad also houses the cursor control keys).

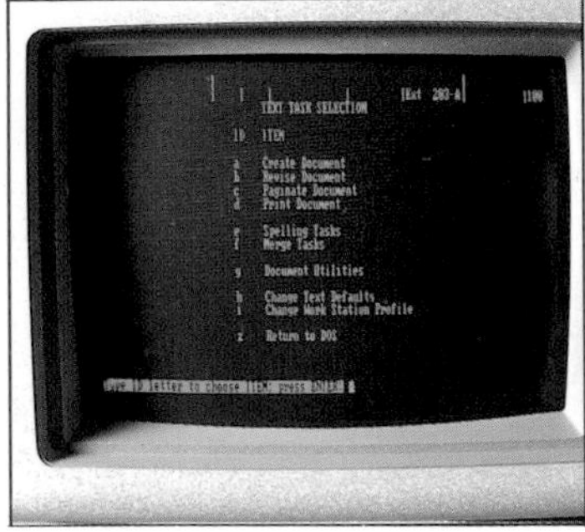

Turn on your micro, insert the program disk into the disk drive and load. Wait a minute or two and the screen will display a 'menu' – a list of options. Here we want to start a new piece of work, so the option to select is 'A' – create document.

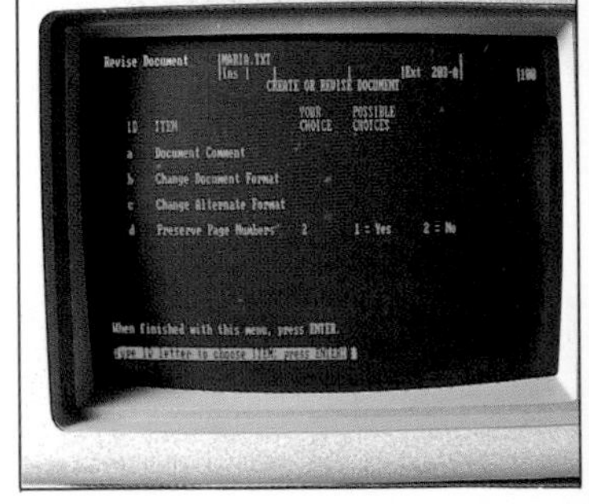

The screen will display an information or status line at the top. Start typing. When you have finished, remember to transfer the first draft on to a file disk to store it (this program does it automatically).

the schedule.

The layout stage in book production is the area that future developments will change the most. Ultimately, the designer will be able to work out layouts on a computer screen. He or she will be able to pass the disk over to the editor, who will be able to feed in the typeset text and see exactly how it looks on the page – and make any necessary cuts and fills on screen. It will be like working on paper page proofs and seeing immediately what effect alterations will have on the page. The disk the typesetter receives will contain *all* the information about how the page will look.

From all this it is clear that understanding and using the power of computers is an important part of the modern editor's armory of skills. But an editor does not need to become a computer programmer or interpret everything in computer terms. The basic skills of vision, caring diplomacy and patience are still of

If you want to edit something that is already on disk, go back to the menu and select the relevant option – here it is option 'B'. The screen will display another menu. Here we want to change the margins. Select option 'C' – change alternate format.

The machine allows you to make alterations. When you have made your alterations, you will see the text displayed according to your instructions. You can then print out the copy or take your disk to a typesetter.

paramount importance, for publishing is still essentially a human endeavor.

As for the future, computers offer publishers two possibilites: to streamline the process of transforming raw text into print, and to go beyond print into the realms of publishing material on disks specifically for use with computers. Such material is called software (as opposed to 'hardware', which refers to the machines themselves) and includes word processing programs. There is a lot of computer software available already – computer games, educational programs, business programs and 'on-line databases' (systems whereby people can subscribe and gain access to a central bank of information via a link to their own computer). Most of what is available now is not put out by publishers – and much of it is not sold in traditional bookstores, but in computer stores or department stores. It is a big step for traditional publishers to contemplate. But the market is wide open and publishing will have to change radically to meet the challenge. The future is already here.

Briefing authors who use word processors

More and more authors are using word processors. And more and more publishers are using word processors in editorial offices. The author can simply use his or her word processor to produce a perfect manuscript, which the editor can type into his or her word processor – but doing this involves two keying-in operations. In principle, it is possible to ask the author to supply not the manuscript, but a disk on which the manuscript is electronically stored, thus eliminating the need for retyping.

In practice, this depends on the compatibility of the author's and editor's machines, and on the word processing programs they use. If machines and programs are compatible, the author can send the disk through the post and the editor sets to work straight away. There are however, many different types of computer and program available and, even if the manufacturers say that two machines and word processing programs are compatible, it may not work perfectly in practice. If it does not work satisfactorily, you may as well work from manuscript. Ask the author to supply a test disk and see how well it works before the deadline draws too close.

More often than not, however, the machines are not compatible. In that case, there are three choices: the author and editor can both instal 'modems' – pieces of equipment that allow their computers to 'talk' to each other over an ordinary telephone line; or the author can use a text-retrieval terminal, or 'milking machine', to convert the manuscript into a form that can be read by the editor's machine; or the editor can send the author's disk to a multi-disk reader that can take the information on the author's disk and put it onto a disk that can be read by the editor's machine.

In the United States, many publishers ask their authors to submit their copy on disks that the editor's machine can read. If not, or if they submit ordinary typescripts, they may be expected to meet the cost of having their disk 'translated' or having the typescript keyed into a word processing terminal. It may be a brutal way of treating one's authors, but it is bound to create strong consumer demand for more compatible machines.

Marking up on a word processor If an editor wants to send a disk containing a manuscript for typesetting the procedure is a little different to that of marking up a manuscript on paper.

Generally, word processors display all text in the same typeface.

They do not show bold or italic text – and they cannot indicate changes in typeface. Neither is it possible to show accurate indents – of one pica em or en, for example. There are many symbols used in print that just do not appear on an ordinary word processor's keyboard. And it is not easy to make marginal notes, as can be done with ordinary manuscripts. So marking up can be problematical.

The British Printing Industries Federation has proposed a system of marking up computer manuscripts that it recommends as a standard for use by everyone involved in editing and typesetting – it is one way of cutting out the possibility of misunderstanding. The system is called ASPIC, which stands for Authors' Symbolic Prepress Interfacing Codes.

The idea behind ASPIC is to code the various instructions needed in marking up, put them in square brackets to pick them out from the general text, and use them to flag the text in the relevant places. Typesetting instructions for text and headings, for example are numbered [h1], [h2]; [t1] [t2], and the detailed instructions given to a key so they need not be repeated every time; [i] indicates italics, and [b] bold; there are other codes for symbols that do not appear on a word processor keybord – co, for instance, indicates a copyright sign.

Office practices when using computers

Computers can 'lose' passages of work. When this happens it is difficult to maintain confidence in word processors and disks over typewriters and paper. It is not easy, after all, to lose or destroy pieces of paper while they are actually in your typewriter. Unfortunately, the equivalent *is* possible on a computer, as any one who has used one will testify.

Computers have two distinct ways of storing information – two different memories: what is in the machine, and what is stored on the disk. It is possible to lose either or, in particularly unfortunate circumstances, both.

The computer can have its power interrupted by a power failure, during a thunderstorm or someone can simply switch it off by mistake. If that happens everything that was in the memory will have gone; and if you are very unlucky (and particularly if the cause of the power failure was a thunderstorm) you may have lost what was on the disk, too.

Every word processing program has its weaknesses – and generally one of these is the propensity to 'lose' part or all of the information you have stored on the disk if you do not use the program exactly as instructed. When you are getting to know a new program you will be likely to experiment with all sorts of ways of doing things that are not in the instruction book, and you may well lose text. You will soon get to know the program, however and you will be unlikely to make the same mistake too often – the fear of losing a chunk of your own work is enough of a deterrent.

More often than not, whether it is the computer or the program that is at fault, there will be nothing you can do to retrieve the information you have lost — except to use a special retrieval program, if one is available for your machine. But if you use a little forethought you can minimize the damage.

As you are working, make a habit of storing what you have done on disk – 'saving' it or 'writing it to disk' – every half hour or so. That way, if you do lose everything that is in the memory, but the disk stays intact, all you will have lost is the work you have done in the past half hour. And whenever you have finished a significant amount of work, copy what you have done onto another disk – even if you lose *all* the information on your working disk, you still have your back-up copy and a day's work is the maximum amount you can lose.

It is inconvenient enough in an editorial office if you lose a piece of paper but it is even worse if you lose a disk. Many word processors use floppy disks that can store up to 100,000 words each. It is a wonderfully convenient way of storing a lot of information in a very small space – the equivalent number of words on paper would take up at least a drawer. However, it is just as easy to mislay a disk as it is a piece of paper. And it is also alarmingly easy to damage a disk badly enough to make it impossible to get at the information you have stored on it. And if you damage or lose a disk, you have lost an awful lot of work.

Floppy disks can be damaged by having cigarette ash or coffee spilled on them. Also, if they are placed near a magnet, all the information on them will be lost. And if you use them intensively, they may simply wear out, preventing you from recalling the work that is on them.

There are some rules that should become office practice anywhere that floppy disks are used. Make sure they are kept in a clean plastic (magnet- and dust-proof) filing cabinet. Disks come with paper sleeves and they need to be kept in these whenever they are not actually in the computer. They must not be handled roughly, and should be kept well away from anywhere where anything could be spilled on them.

Computers and health There is a great deal of concern about how microcomputers may affect the health of people who use them. Generally speaking, unions have drawn attention to health hazards while management and manufacturers have been concerned to play them down. But the problems are not merely political. The difficulties are not with microcomputers as such, but with the screens, or VDTs, on which they display their information. Using a VDT all day is rather like sitting two feet from a television screen for eight hours since, like televisions, VDTs produce their images by using electrons. Although electrons are a form of radiation that, in sufficiently large doses, are known carcinogens, radiation from VDTs is well below the permitted maximum levels and there is at present absolutely no evidence that VDTs cause cancer. What nobody knows, however, is what the effects of long-term exposure to low — and permitted — levels of radiation are likely to be. It is not as if we are not exposed to considerable amounts of low-level radiation all the time, but the effects of adding that little bit of extra radiation to the daily dose are unknown. This is not reason enough for banning the use of VDTs, but it makes it important to monitor the effects of their long-term use.

The other major risk concerns women in particular. There is some evidence that pregnant women who work intensively with VDTs increase the risks of miscarriage or having babies that are deformed in some way, but the evidence is not conclusive, and it certainly is not understood why this should be the case. There is no evidence that working with VDTs has any effect at all on fertility in women. Most reasonable employers allow women who work with VDTs to cease doing so during pregnancy.

Other health problems are better documented and have more to do with day-to-day work. In finding out how to prevent them, it is worth bearing in mind that many are stress-related symptoms. The introduction of computers in an office requires a new way of working, which always cause some stress, but the particular adaptations required with computers can cause difficulties.

There is always the uncertainty, for example, as to how the introduction of computers is going to affect jobs. And no one knows, at the beginning, how good he or she is going to be at computer work. There is a rule in computing that says that your results can only be as good as what is put into the machine — in computer speak, this is known as GIGO, or 'garbage in, garbage out'. This means that any shortcomings in the person operating the computer are going to be obvious in the computer's output. The early days in learning to use a computer, therefore, are always stressful and anything that can be done to reduce this pressure is a good idea. That is why good, structured and formal training is so valuable.

Physical problems of eye strain and headaches are induced by glare and flickers from the screen and by the fact that the user's eyes are focused on the same spot for several hours in succession. Flickers can also bring on attacks of migraine. It is possible to reduce glare and flickers considerably by choosing the right VDT. Choose one where it is possible to turn down the brightness of both characters and background. (Most people find it best to work with green or amber characters against a dark background, or with black characters on a white background.)

Your surroundings, too, are important. Make sure that light from lamps and windows is not reflected in the screen — it helps if the screen is matte rather than shiny. Do not use overhead fluorescent light — or, if it is unavoidable, make sure the light is fitted with a diffuser. If the flickers of the VDT irritate you, you will find it is exacerbated when it is combined with the flickers of ordinary fluorescent lighting. Low general lighting, with adjustable, directional sources of light (100 watt lights, for example) are the best choice. Pay attention, too, to the general level of glare in the office: bright, shiny surfaces in light colors make the problem worse. And if you have more than one VDT in the office, make sure that when you sit at the screen of one, you cannot see the other screens, even out of the corner of your eye, as flickers from another screen can be very distracting (in people who suffer from epilepsy, it can even bring on fits).

Using a computer demands a curiously intense kind of concentration, and it is easy to find that you have been working for hours hardly lifting your eyes from the screen — and hardly shifting your position. The combination is sure to cause both eye strain and backache.

It is important to make sure you *do not* spend hours without a break in front of the VDT. Try to work so that your job takes you away from the computer without you having to think about it. Failing that, make sure you take frequent rest breaks. There has been a lot of discussion about how often, and for how long, rest breaks should be taken. The important thing is that you should do it *before* you begin to feel tired — and spend the time right away from the computer.

While you are working on the VDT, it is worth cultivating a habit of looking up every few minutes to vary your vision. Make sure, therefore, that you do not face straight on to a wall as the difference in the focusing distance will be so small that it will not rest your eyes at all. Give yourself something to focus on — a window, or a painting hanging on the other side of the room, is ideal. Beware of facing onto a space where there is a lot of movement, however, as you will find that your eyes are involuntarily attracted to it, and you will find it difficult to concentrate.

If you wear glasses or contact lenses, you may find you have extra problems with glare. If your lenses are scratched, light will be refracted off the scratches and you will not see so well. And you may find that all the close work you are doing causes changes in your vision. If you do find you are not seeing as well as you were, go to your optician at once as he or she will be able to advise you on polishing or replacing your lenses. Some unions in fact recommend that everyone should have an eye test before starting to work with VDTs, and that their sight should be checked at regular intervals thereafter.

There are certain kinds of mild sedative or tranquilizing drugs that slow eye movement. If you are taking one of these, you may find difficulty in using VDTs. This is not serious, even if it is inconvenient, and will disappear when you stop taking the drug.

Backache can be reduced by positioning your chair and desk properly. Make sure that you can adjust your chair *yourself* to suit you — and make sure that it has some support for your back, which is also adjustable. You may find a footrest helpful too. Make sure you can read the copy or reference books you are working from without craning your neck. You can buy special copy holders that may help. And make sure you can adjust the lighting to suit you.

Some people find they suffer from dry skin or facial rashes when they are working with VDTs. It is difficult to know exactly what causes this — stress may play some part, but it is certainly true that visual display terminals generate static electricity and, as this tends to dry the air, it may be a contributory factor. Central heating is likely to make the problem worse. It is worth installing an anti-static carpet, and you may even consider using humidifiers.

COMPUTERS: HEALTH AND SAFETY

Desk lighting
Use a source of light that you can direct – an ordinary adjustable lamp is ideal – to give you good illumination and no glare

Printer
These can be noisy. Have it as far from your desk – and other people's – as you can. And buy an acoustic hood

VDT
Choose the kind that you can swivel to slant away from you when you are copy-typing

Copy holder
You can buy these from computer supply stores. Adjust them so that you can work from your reference material *without* getting a crick in the neck!

Carpets and heating
Use anti-static carpets. Central heating makes the air dry – think about using humidifiers

Overhead lighting
Use ordinary tungsten lighting, or fluorescent light fitted with a diffuser

Windows
Make sure you do not back onto a window so light is not reflected off your screen. And have some way of reducing glare on bright days – light curtains or Venetian blinds

Walls and surfaces
Avoid light, shiny surfaces. Choose restful colors and matt finishes. Make sure you do not directly face a wall – when you lift your eyes you should have to change their focus quite a bit. It is useful to have something to focus on – a painting or poster on the opposite wall, for instance

Chair and desk height
Adjust these so that they are comfortable. Your elbows should be at roughly the level of the computer keyboard. Make sure that you have an adjustable chair that *works* – you need to be able to change the height yourself. You may find a footstool useful

3
THE DESIGN PHASE

Working with designers/Design grids/Preparing layouts/Commissioning artwork illustrations/Commissioning photographs/Picture research/Working on a layout

The emphasis in this section moves from purely editorial aspects to the collaboration between designers and editors in the design phase of books and magazines.

Working with designers

As a book editor, your involvement with the designer or the design department starts at the earliest stages of the project. When the author's text is in first galleys and the flat plan has been agreed – at least in broad terms – the working relationship between you and the designer becomes much closer. Together you will organize and discuss artwork references, picture research, location photography, captions, annotation and all the other elements that go to make up the design.

Working successfully with designers depends as much on your personality and how you get on with others as on your creative flair or your administrative skills. Designing a book is not a purely mechanical process and in the atmosphere of a pressing design schedule disagreements are not uncommon and tempers may flare. Being overbearing rarely wins the day. If the designer has read the text and considered the options and possibilities, then what he or she needs from you is helpful advice rather than instruction. It is absolutely essential that you and the designer agree on the general approach as well as on fine detail. A good working rapport can be a catalyst for true innovation; a bad one can produce books nobody wants to buy.

Working with magazine designers Every magazine relies on a happy balance between good visual design and interesting, informative text. The editor and designer or art department must therefore work closely together right from the early planning stages to make sure these two parts jell. While the editor has final overall say on every aspect of the magazine, the art editor or designer is responsible for the general 'look' and presentation. It is essential for the designer to contribute to the early ideas meetings, translating feature ideas and suggestions into visual layouts for the approval of the editor.

At flat plan stage the designer's advice is useful for assessing the suitable length for a feature, how much color it merits and whether it should encompass left- or right-hand pages or even a double page spread. It is at this point that editors and designers will start to form a rough idea of how the individual features will look, making it easier to commission writers and photographers.

The page layouts when completed (see pages 94-97) give a clearer impression and should be carefully scrutinized and agreed by the editor: galleys should be correctly positioned, photography or artwork traced and headlines mocked up with full setting instructions. You may wish to change the style of a layout to suit the copy or feel that it is too confusing. This will have to be discussed between you and the designer until you reach agreement. It is useful for the editor to keep an eye open for points of house style, whether captions are in the right place, arrows indicating that a feature continues on the next page or that a page reference is given if it continues several pages on, and that picture credits are correctly given.

Once agreed, the layout can go to the typesetters for making up, if it is not done in-house, and it will then be largely the designer's responsibility to ensure the instructions are followed accurately.

The art department should also be involved directly in the commissioning of artwork (using references supplied by the editorial department and approved by the editor) and in any specially commissioned photography – editorial staff are usually responsible for selecting and arranging the props; the designer should be present at the shoot to supervise the angle and lighting and to make sure it fits the proposed layout, all very much a matter of teamwork. Another aspect of the job shared by both designer and editor is examining the portfolios of prospective artists and photographers; the decision to use a new person should be a joint one, each respecting the other's tastes and experience.

The role of the designer is therefore monumental for it is this individual who must create much of the visual interest of the magazine. The designer's job begins when he or she 'specs' the material for the layouts in order to ensure that everything will fit. The designer will dispatch the final mechanicals to the printer and they will return as black-and-white photoprinted page proofs. Color proofs are then made of the corrected pages. The designer, with the production manager and perhaps an editor, will color correct the proofs.

Editor and designer must decide on the way copy will be organized. The use of subheads and headlines must complement the structure of the article and the arrangement of the illustrations. Good layouts reflect an appreciation of spatial relationships and also an understanding of how to reflect a magazine's image. For example, a business magazine tends to thrive on clear, crisp layouts, while consumer and specialty magazines will often need more vibrant, eye-catching spreads with shocking, bold color usage. A designer must know when to employ a conventional format and when to break it up with various devices.

There are many things that a designer must watch for in order to create a cohesive layout. Overall, commonsense and understanding of the context of the material are essential to the successful designer.

Design grids

The integration of words and pictures takes place on the design 'grid' (see also page 84). This is a visual organization of the design and editorial parameters for a particular book or magazine. Each grid is a life-size plan of a double page spread, showing the position and extent of the text and illustration areas, the location of headings and page numbers, the trim size of the page, and so on. In fact, all the positional information that everybody needs, from the editor and designer right through to the typesetter and printer.

Since the grids pass through so many hands and convey vital information for so many people, they must be robust and meticulously accurate. The designer usually prepares the original of the grid by drawing out the areas and dimensions with exactitude as a master artwork. This is best prepared on some professional quality tracing paper so that it can be placed over the printed versions to check their accuracy. It is also possible to draw up a grid using a computer typesetting system.

However it is produced, the master grid is used to print two versions for everyday use: one on tracing or 'layout' paper and one on stiff paper or thin card. The tracing grids are ideal for sketching in illustrations using the viewing screen of a visualizing camera to project a reduced or enlarged image of the correct size. The more substantial card grid sheets are used for the final paste-up of the text with positional and size indications for the illustrations, if the company follows conventional paste-up procedure. The lines are usually printed in pale blue ink on a white background so that they can be used as 'camera-ready' artwork if necessary as the blue lines do not show up on film.

Preparing layouts

The design process literally converts the empty grids into layouts that show how the text and illustrations fit together on each spread. This is not an instant operation, for the designer may well make several rough layouts before arriving at the finished design for any particular page. Assembling the raw materials for the layouts – text proofs, artwork ideas and sketches, photographs, tables, charts, maps, display titles (larger, heading typeface), chapter headings, captions, and so on – goes hand in hand with the preparation of the layouts themselves. The final layout is not finished until the last element is ready; the lack of one photograph can delay a whole book that is otherwise complete.

During the design phase, layouts in various stages of completion pass to and from the editor and designer. Later sections in this chapter will look at the specific tasks that face an editor on the layouts. First we shall look briefly at the important search for artwork illustrations and photographs.

Commissioning artwork illustrations

The author's original synopsis for a book is usually the first indication you receive of the type of artwork illustrations that will be needed. Since these usually take longer to plan and prepare than finding photographs, always start to think about them as early as possible. Read the text and see if you agree with the author's choice of illustration subjects (you may well have quite different views) and prepare a list for the designer. After reading the text, the designer may come up with variations on the ideas that you and the author have put forward.

Ideas are vital, but converting them into finished illustrations requires two steps. First, finding suitable references to make them accurate; and, second, visualizing them in a style suitable for the book. Broadly speaking, it is your task as the editor to amass the reference material and the designer's task to visualize the illustrations.

Where do you find reference material? It depends on the

Printed grids are a vital element in the design process. They not only help to reduce the number of errors that would occur if every double page was drawn up separately, but they also minimize the time spent on page layout. The grid must show all the essential information needed by the designer — column depths, type measure, text and illustration area and the exact positioning of folios, running heads and crossheads. These elements are combined into a more permanent form which will provide a reference not only for the designer but for all the specialists involved in the various stages of production. In most cases two sets of grids are printed. The first set are often transparent and are used for the rough paste-up as they enable illustrations to be traced and checked for size and positioning. The other set, printed on thin card, are used for the final paste-up. The grids are printed in a pale blue ink which does not show up when being photographed to produce final text film.

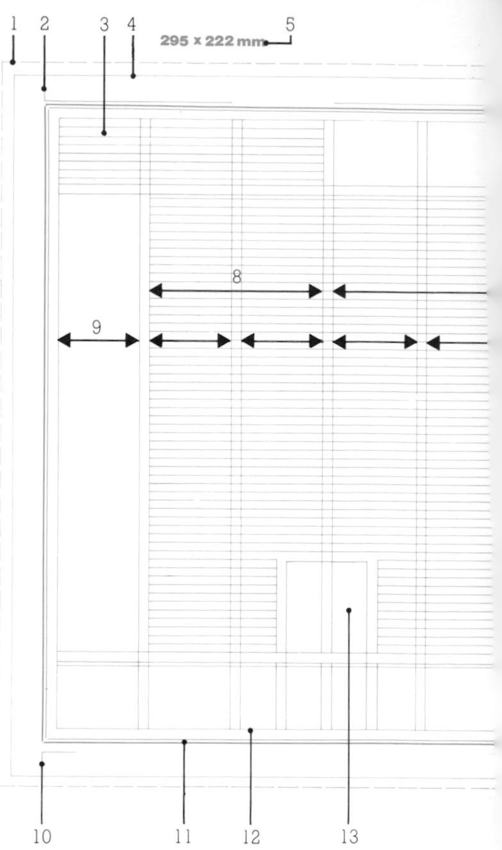

illustration idea. If it is a fairly straightforward concept, such as the orientation of the planets in relation to the sun, then the task is not so much where to look but which one to choose. Naturally, thousands of illustration concepts have been used in other books on the subject and these are the first sources of reference. To select a suitable illustration of the planets from an astronomy book should not be difficult. The onus then lies with the designer to mold that basic information into a different shape to avoid conflict with the copyright of the original illustration. Although it is not possible to copyright an idea or knowledge as such, the *presentation* of that idea or knowledge can be copyrighted.

If the illustration is a little more obscure, such as the osmotic regulation of a freshwater fish as opposed to a marine fish, then you will need to open the pages of more authoritative, specialized books or scientific papers. Here the task may be to draw out from complex and perhaps 'dry' diagrams the essence of the concept that will fire the designer's imagination. In some cases, no illustration exists and you will need to piece together the elements into a simple sketch to show the designer. The most difficult step is moving from a blank piece of paper to one with at least some intelligible marks on it.

If the illustration is to depict a commercial process, writing to relevant companies is often very fruitful. Public relations or marketing departments are only too happy to send brochures of

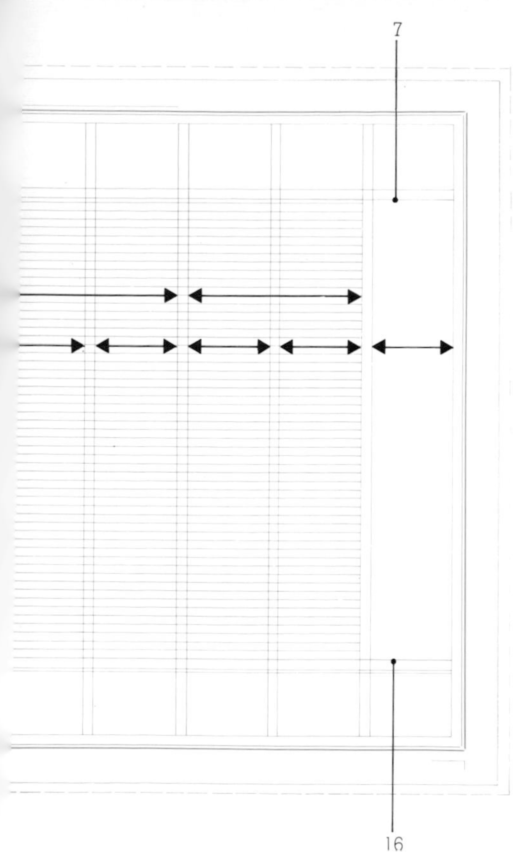

their products and processes – especially if you promise to credit their help in the book. Unfortunately, the more impressive the brochure, the less likely it is to show the actual working principle you are seeking in a clear way. If you have engaged a consultant, he or she might also be a good source of reference, especially if his or her connections range wider than those of your author.

In the designer's hands your sketches and accumulated references will be turned into an accurate illustration brief. Sometimes, however, a visual *looks* very good but misses the editorial reason for including it. This is where tact and sensitivity are needed. It is best to suggest ways in which the design concept can be altered to show the exact point in question, rather than discarding it altogether. You may also suggest other approaches that suit the subject. Naturally, designers and editors vary in their skills and temperaments and once you have worked with a designer on several projects then you will probably know how best to work through these design/editorial decision processes.

When the illustration brief has met with everyone's approval, the designer will call in a suitable artist to prepare the finished artwork. In many cases, it is the artist rather than the designer who will visualize the illustration. He or she prepares a pencil sketch, or 'rough', to show the designer and editor before moving ahead with the artwork itself. This is especially important when there are several different ways of approaching the subjects, such as in

Commissioning an artwork illustration usually begins with reference material which is supplied to the designer by the author or editor (**1**). The designer will work out a rough layout on the book or magazine grid and use this to give the artist as accurate a brief for the illustration as possible – indicating possible colors, techniques and whether the artwork should be produced half up (one and a half times larger than the illustration will appear when it is printed) or given a percentage enlargement to work to so that it will fit the grid (**2**). The artist will produce one or more 'visuals' and discuss possible changes with the designer. Once these decisions have been made, the artist will produce the finished artwork (**3**) with five overlays, one with annotation in position, one indicating the key line and three for different tints. The designer will specify to the origination house and printers the percentage reduction and colors required to produce the desired effect on the printed page (see page 18).

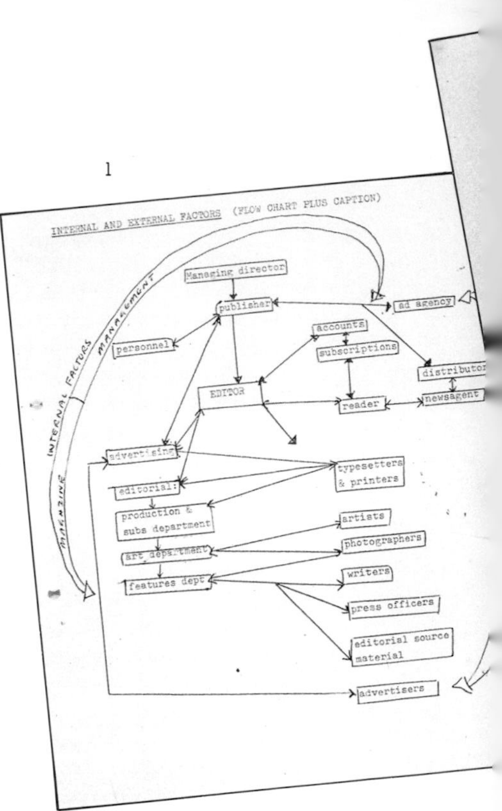

natural history.

The finished artwork can be prepared in a number of ways, depending on the type and content of the illustration and the printing method to be used. A flow chart for a chemical process, for example, might be prepared as a black line drawing of the hardware with different tones of color, (laid down as mechanical tints (tints consisting of colored dot or line patterns) by the color separators, printer or designer, as necessary within the various shapes. Alternatively the artwork may be in the form of a full-color painting or a simpler line illustration with no color at all. The designer will specify the final size the illustration is to appear in the book and ask the artist to prepare the artwork the same size (S/S) or larger (usually one-and-a-half times or twice the final size) as any looseness in the drawing disappears upon reduction.

Commissioning artwork illustration for magazines Wherever something can be treated visually in a magazine it usually is. If there is no photograph available, or if it would be better conveyed by an illustration, an artwork is used. Artwork is almost always specially commissioned for a feature — whether it be step-by-step diagrams, drawings or cartoons. Whatever form it may take, it needs to refer directly to the text and fit in with the design of the page, so careful research and a clear briefing are required. If step-by-step illustrations are to be commissioned, the writer of the feature should be asked to provide a sufficient number of artwork references in the form of rough sketches or copies of existing

diagrams. A copy of the text is usually sufficient for a cartoonist to work from, but more general illustrations will need a selection of picture references. These can be magazine or catalog clippings, photographs or even samples of the products to be drawn or painted. If the illustrations are very technical, they will call for a full briefing of the artist if the finished artwork is to fulfil its purpose.

The freelance artist is briefed in much the same way as the freelance writer. Someone from the art department, either an artwork visualizer or the art director, and sometimes an editor for the project will talk to the artist about several topics: where the rights are to be sold (national or worldwide), in what areas the project will be sold, the complexity of the project; the turnaround time for the artist, the artist's budget and how expenses will be handled. When an artist sells rights to a work the copyright falls into the magazine's domain. Otherwise, such works are considered the possession of the copyright owner, who is the 'author'. An artist's release is much like an agreement with a writer.

When the artwork is brought in, the artwork visualizer or the art director will examine it for style and accuracy, and if necessary, specify alterations. If the illustration is not used, the artist is paid a kill fee, a sum which is either the original fee or a percentage of it. Otherwise, the artist is paid upon approval of the material.

The art and editorial departments will then work together to determine the most effective use of the illustration.

Commissioning photographs
Publishers usually commission new photographs for practical 'how-to' sequences. These apply to many subjects, from bricklaying to flower arranging. Although paying a photographer on a daily basis seems expensive at the time, the photographs usually work out cheaper than paying copyright fees to an agency, with the added bonus that the publisher can use them again in future books without further payment.

As the editor, you should involve yourself in any studio or location photography for your book. In most publishing companies the designer takes the initiative in setting up the session, but he or she will value your help and advice on the editorial content of the photographs. With your designer draw up a list of the shots to be taken during the session and send this to the photographer well in advance of the day. This will enable the photographer to bring along or set up the most suitable camera and lenses, film, lighting and other equipment for the session.

Studio photography can take much longer than you might imagine. Actually arranging the objects or people to be photographed takes the most time; actually clicking the shutter takes a matter of moments. If the shots include close-ups of hands, make sure that the model or author has clean fingers and trimmed finger-nails. These seemingly small considerations become quite obvious in the finished prints and spoil the entire set of pictures.

The advantage of commissioned photography is that you can 'engineer' the pictures to suit your design grid. This is particularly effective for 'set pieces' that will take up a whole double page spread in the finished book. For pinpoint accuracy using large format studio cameras, your designer can prepare a miniature version of the grid for the photographer to place over the glass viewing screen. You can then arrange the objects in precise positions according to the page margins and center line of the spread and allow room for any overprinted text or captions.

Commissioning photographs for magazines Once a feature is considered to have sufficient illustrative material, whether it be press photographs, plans, artwork or photographs requested from a picture agency, go through it thoroughly to make sure they are all relevant and give the designer an adequate selection of good quality pictures. You may wish to make a few recommendations – that there should be the widest range of products possible featured, or a certain picture given priority, for example. These will then be passed to the art department for final selection.

Sometimes, however, it is worth commissioning photographs specially. For instance if the right photographs are not available, or if the photographs are to fit the design in some special way – for example, if the text is to run round the objects in a picture. As always, however, this has to be justified in terms of cost. If the pictures are likely to be needed again (in relaunches or spin-offs — reusing some of the material in one magazine in another later magazine) or if they can be used by the publisher in unrelated publications, commissioning photographs is very worthwhile from editorial and financial viewpoints. Indeed, in such instances it can even be cheaper to use commissioned rather than agency photographs.

The publisher generally makes special arrangements with the

photographer. Instead of paying by individual picture, the publisher pays the photographer an agreed amount (known as a flat rate) per day, however many pictures are taken. The editor selects the pictures he or she wishes to use; the rights of any that are rejected revert to the photographer, who undertakes, however, not to sell them to anyone else for an agreed number of years (usually three or four).

Specially commissioned photographs are tailor-made for the magazine and have been planned to fit a feature down to the last detail. With location or studio work, it is the job of the picture researcher, in conjunction with the editor and photographer, to fix up the session and ensure that the results are satisfactory. A stylist may be hired to 'dress' the picture – or the picture researcher may be required to do it and find all the props needed. The art editor may be present at the 'shoot' itself – or it may be up to the picture researcher to direct it. If fully equipped, studio work generally presents no problems unless you are working with an unpredictable subject, such as a small child or an animal.

In order to ensure that you are getting the right photographer for the job, it is a good idea to get to know a number of photographers specializing in different areas: food, fashion and still life, require different talents. If you become familiar with a variety of individuals' work, you will be better able to match photographer to job — and the more familiar the photographer becomes with the look of the magazine, the less lengthy your briefing will have to be.

When dealing in highly conceptual photography, there should be a greater dialogue between the art department, the photographer, and the editorial department to achieve a desired effect.

Among the many expenses that will have to be taken into account are film and processing, hire of models and renting of props and stylists, and the studio fee. Find out how much is included in the photographer's rate, and what are considered extras. Make sure everything is spelled out in the contract, particularly in the area of rights. Recent laws have made it easier for photographers and artists to retain rights on their photos for second-time usage. Sometimes, a magazine will claim ownership of all material, and other times only of those pictures that are used.

Commissioned photography can be exorbitant, but there are ways to get around it. Finding and nurturing a young talent who will not charge as much as an established professional can save you money, as can using a large volume of a photographer's work over a period of time.

You might even trim costs by using yourself or staff members as models, particularly since many articles do not necessarily call for professionals. Do not schedule the time for the models to arrive until you are sure that everything will be set up and in order. Someone from the art department can act as stylist for the session, and some manufacturers or antique shops will lend you props in exchange for a credit line.

Picture research

The search for suitable existing photographs proceeds in tandem with artwork visualization. In fact, picture research normally begins well before the design phase gets fully underway.

Although it may at first sight seem a simple matter to 'dial around' for a few photographs to illustrate a chapter, there are pitfalls that may trap the unwary, particularly the problems that may be encountered when dealing with professional picture agencies. If the project requires a wide range of photographs, it is best to engage the services of a picture researcher as he or she speaks the same 'language' as the picture agencies and can save you from the situation of paying unnecessarily high fees for pictures that are not exactly what you wanted.

Most picture researchers are engaged on a freelance basis for one project at a time, although some publishing companies have staff picture researchers. Their help can be invaluable, particularly if the subject is new to you and you employ them early on in the project. Using their services to the full, you can expect the competent picture researcher to perform the following functions:

- prepare a picture list from the author's text;
- advise you on the general illustration strategy for the book;
- suggest the most suitable sources for your subject and budget;
- obtain a wide selection of pictures for you and the designer to view;
- if necessary, make a preliminary selection before showing them to you;
- catalog and safeguard the pictures against damage or loss;
- negotiate the most favorable copyright fees;
- clear copyright on the used pictures;
- remind you about possible holding fees on overdue pictures;
- return used and unused pictures to their sources;
- check captions and adjacent text, particularly to avoid legal problems;
- prepare a detailed picture credit list for the book;
- handle any queries raised during the picture research period.

If you have ever had to sort through a large number of pictures from a wide variety of sources, you will know how valuable these services can be.

Many of the possible problems in picture research revolve around the physical nature of the pictures themselves. 'Pictures' usually means color transparencies or slides, for these are the most common type of photographs used in illustrated publishing. For the truest color reproduction it is advisable to use the original transparencies rather than photographic copies or duplicates. The problem is that original transparencies are not only extremely vulnerable to damage but also expensive to replace. Professional picture agencies may charge several hundred dollars per lost or damaged transparency, but will usually refund a percentage of the fee if a lost transparency is subsequently returned undamaged. The publisher's insurance policy protects the picture researcher from any personal liability for lost transparencies but, with care, such compensation payments can be kept to a minimum.

The most palpable benefit to be gained by using picture researchers is that they save you valuable time by going straight to the best sources for each request. This is because, with experience, they become familiar with thousands of picture sources across the world and can often match mental images of actual pictures they recall from existing collections to your requests. Professional agencies are usually the best sources for many pictures, but they are also the most expensive because they must cover their operating expenses and split the copyright fee with their contributing photographers. Many picture agencies specialize in one area, such as sports, art or natural history. If time and top quality are not at a premium there are countless other sources that might suffice — from museums and private institutions to commercial companies and amateur photographers. Your picture researcher will always advise you on the best strategy for your particular budget, schedule and project.

When the pictures have been selected, the picture researcher will clear the copyright with the owners and negotiate appropriate fees. In some companies, the designer or editor will handle the financial aspects. As we have seen in the Principles of budgeting (see page 15), the fee depends on whether the picture is to be used in color or black-and-white, on the size and position in the book, the rights required, the print run and on the total number used from one source.

Picture research for magazines The picture researcher's job is to obtain all the photographs that will be used in the magazine. Because magazines rely so much on the quality of their visual content, and it is the photographs that give them their visual impact, the picture researcher's role is a very important one. The picture researcher must also ensure that pictures are in on time.

Picture researchers work closely with the editorial department of a magazine. Procedures vary for different magazines but, generally, the picture researcher reads the copy as soon as it arrives, which may be some time before the content editor starts to work on it. The picture researcher makes a picture list immediately, and starts to work on getting pictures in. As soon as the article has been allocated to and read by a content editor, the content editor discusses the picture list with the picture researcher and editor. There may even be a formal picture meeting which the art editor and/or designer also attends.

Illustrations come from three main sources: commissioned artwork and photography; photographers and picture agencies; and companies' publicity material.

The picture researcher should know how to obtain high-quality pictures without paying premium prices. There is an abundance of copyright-free illustrations in the public domain available to the magazine. These low-priced pictures can be used effectively with good design and typography. Museums, galleries, and private collectors are often happy to lend transparencies at low rates. Press agents and public relations firms also often give away free photographs in exchange for a credit line in the magazine.

The picture researcher can place an advertisement specifying the amount to be paid, the format desired, the subject matter, and reproduction rights and deadline details. Then, the photographers make submissions directly to the magazine. This process saves a lot of time sorting through photographers' portfolios.

As a result of the recent copyright laws, it is also possible to buy the second rights on materials seen in other magazines. This is particularly applicable if you read through regional magazines that are not widely available in your area. You can probably obtain second rights to the material at a cheaper cost, but the material will not have been seen by the readers in your region.

Procedures vary for different magazines but, generally, the picture researcher reads author's material when it arrives and draws up picture lists. Sometimes, an author will supply a detailed, ready-made list saving the picture researcher time.

When choosing photographs there are a number of points to consider. The pictures must be expressive of the main thrust of the article. They must carry an amount of attention-grabbing potential, and form a logical relationship with the text. Some picture researchers make their own selection and simply present that to the editorial staff for approval. The final decision as to what pictures are to be used, however, must lie with the editorial and design departments, since it is the editor and the content editor who know exactly how the picture should relate to the article and the designer who must assess the picture's visual impact. Pictures must be chosen that will help give life to an exciting caption.

After the final pictures are selected, the remainder of the picture researcher's job is largely administrative. Transparencies are both valuable and easily lost or damaged. It is the picture researcher's job to keep track of them: to catalog them when they come in, keep them safe and make sure that the right pictures are returned to their owners when they are no longer needed. Finally, the important jobs of recording which pictures were actually used in the magazine, where they came from, and the name of the photographer, are also the picture researcher's responsibility.

CHOOSING PHOTOGRAPHS

However strongly you express your editorial motive for choosing a particular photograph, the designer is unlikely to be persuaded to use it if it is not of an acceptable aesthetic standard or is of poor quality. Although there can be some conflict between editors and designers when choosing photographs there are a number of clear-cut reasons for rejecting photographs, usually because they are:

- **Out of focus** A surprising number of photographs are 'fuzzy' when you look at them through a lens. Naturally, action shots and documentary material can be excused on these grounds.

- **Underexposed** A common failing, particularly with amateur photographs. For modern processing techniques the fully saturated colors produced by slight underexposure are to be preferred, but frequently slides are just too opaque to use. A quick and approximate test of correct exposure is to hold the transparency a little way above a well-lit white sheet of paper; if you can see the image properly then it will probably be suitable for processing. If the transparency is too bright and the colors washed out then it will be unsuitable for reproduction.

Picture research using computer databases Word processors are of two kinds – 'dedicated' and 'non-dedicated'. Dedicated word processors are computers that are designed to do one thing, and one thing only: processing words. Non-dedicated word processors, on the other hand, are microcomputers that can do a range of things by being given different programs.

It is sometimes argued that dedicated word processors do the job they are designed for best. With more and more sophisticated computer software, however, it is also arguable that non-dedicated micros can do just as well. For normal editorial purposes, they are fine. And they do have the great advantage that you can take out the disk that makes them into word processors, replace it with another one, and, in effect, get a completely different computer.

In an editorial office, and particularly for the picture researcher,

• **Unbalanced in color** Some transparencies, particularly among those supplied by agencies, are several years old and some are beginning to show their age. The dyes used in transparencies will take on an unacceptable color cast if continually exposed to light for long periods. Duplicates may suffer from the same drawback. If possible view the transparencies on a light box with the correct light source for color film.

• **Scratched** The emulsion of well-used transparencies may show signs of wear. Retouching, although expensive, can compensate for this in most cases.

• **Aesthetic qualities** Frequently photographs are badly composed so that, for example, the eye is not drawn to the subject of the picture, or, simply, the arrangement of objects or color combination is unappealing. Cropping or masking off backgrounds can sometimes improve otherwise unusable pictures.

• **Too well known** This is 'overexposure' of another kind. When a publisher has prepared several books on the same or very similar subjects, you will begin to see the same selection of pictures reappear. Quite naturally, every publisher wishes to retain a certain exclusivity on the photographs it publishes. The only effective way of doing this is to commission new photographs.

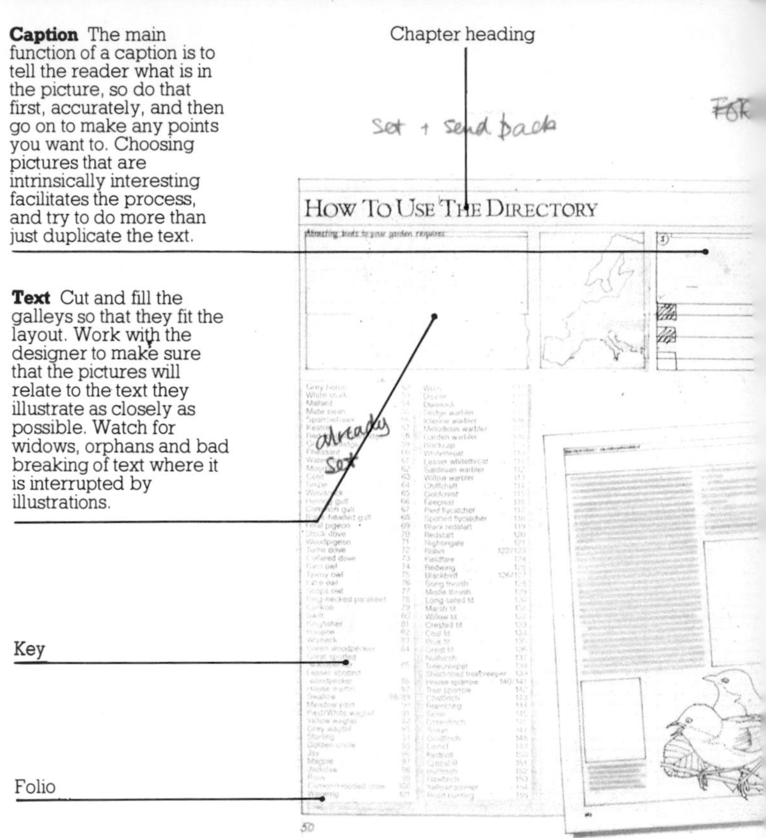

this can be a great advantage. If you get a database system for your micro, you can use it to catalog anything you want and use it to keep track of your pictures by entering where the picture is in your files, what agency or photographer it came from, when it came into the office and when it is due back, the serial number, the subject and the kind of details that helped you to choose it originally. Then you can use the computer to rearrange the information you have given it in any way you find useful – for instance asking it to make a list of all the pictures of a certain subject or a particular detail. When it comes to picture credit lists, the page numbers on which the pictures appear are entered into the computer and it can then print out the credit list. The computer can arrange the pictures in the list alphabetically by source or numerically by the page number on which they were used. The database is also very useful for picture returns. It can be asked to produce a list of all the pictures that are due back by a certain date, with serial numbers and sources. The computer can then arrange the list by source, leaving you with the much simplified task of using the index of where the pictures are in your files, locating them and sending them back.

Caption The main function of a caption is to tell the reader what is in the picture, so do that first, accurately, and then go on to make any points you want to. Choosing pictures that are intrinsically interesting facilitates the process, and try to do more than just duplicate the text.
Chapter heading
Set + send back
HOW TO USE THE DIRECTORY
Text Cut and fill the galleys so that they fit the layout. Work with the designer to make sure that the pictures will relate to the text they illustrate as closely as possible. Watch for widows, orphans and bad breaking of text where it is interrupted by illustrations.
already set
Key
Folio
50

Working on a layout

The first set of layouts, or rough paste-ups, the editor receives from the designer usually has the first galleys of text pasted down

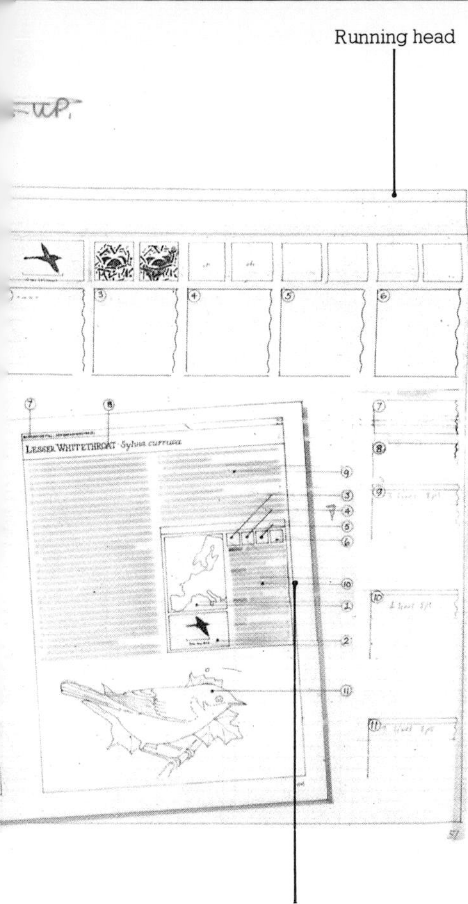

WORKING ON A BOOK LAYOUT
A layout needs to be checked very carefully when it is returned by the designer. Firstly, check that you *like* the design of it, that it is clear and easy to read and that no sections of galley are missing or have been incorrectly positioned. Often copy will need to be cut or extra words or sentences needed to fill space — these marks should be added to the master set of galleys. Pictures will be indicated on the layout by a rough tracing to scale and will usually require appropriate captioning. Captions should be typed out on a separate sheet to be sent for typesetting. It must be remembered that typesetters follow the *given* instructions so carefully check all the seemingly minor details (page numbers, rules and crossheads) that can be overlooked very easily. As computerized word processors and typesetting machines offering automatic layout facilities are more widely used, this stage should eventually be reduced to checking an almost complete page proof and keying in the corrections directly.

in the correct position; the display headings, running heads, folios and caption areas marked in; and the illustrations and photographs sketched in the appropriate places. First, the text proofs should be checked to make sure they have been pasted down in the correct order. This is done by checking the beginnings and endings of paragraphs with your master galleys, paying particular attention to the top and bottom of columns and where separate pieces of galley have been pasted down (run your fingernail lightly down the text to find the cut).

Invariably, there are places on the layout where the text is either too long or too short. Adjusting these is called working on the 'cuts and fills'. Designers may leave any excess galley hanging over the edge of the layout or cut it off where it should end and paste down the extra piece on one side, indicating quite clearly how many lines you should cut. If possible, the lines should be cut from the ends of paragraphs to save excessive resetting. Often it is quite difficult to determine what effect complicated cuts will have on the run of the text. In these cases, when the page proofs come in you will see if the text fits exactly.

Adding text to fill empty areas on the layout is usually much more difficult than cutting. The need to add lines may arise because, in laying the text down, the designer discovers that a subheading falls at the bottom of a column. Since, aesthetically, a subheading should have at least two lines of text directly below it, the designer will take the heading up to the top of the next column and indicate that the two or three lines at the bottom of the previous column will need to be filled in. To save unnecessary disruption, try to add the extra lines to that column rather than earlier on in the text.

Dealing with 'widows' (single words left on a line at the end of a paragraph) resembles a scaled down version of 'cut and fills'. The designer will indicate whether you should cut a widow to reduce the text by one line or fill out the line to improve its appearance, or the editor will decide on the treatment of widows. A widow at the top of a column is called an 'orphan'.

If you have the use of a word processor, however, the whole process can be simplified: it can be set to work to any margins, so typing to a measure is completely accurate and very easy. Also, the effects of any changes of measure or character count can be seen at the press of a button. That means that when writing to length there is no need to retype heavily edited text or count characters in order to cast it off accurately. In essence it is helping you do what you would be doing anyway and, although this may not *sound* much, it does take some of the effort out of working on layouts – and allows the editor to concentrate on thinking creatively about the words.

A typesetting terminal furthers this process by giving the editor the complete accuracy and confidence of going straight to final

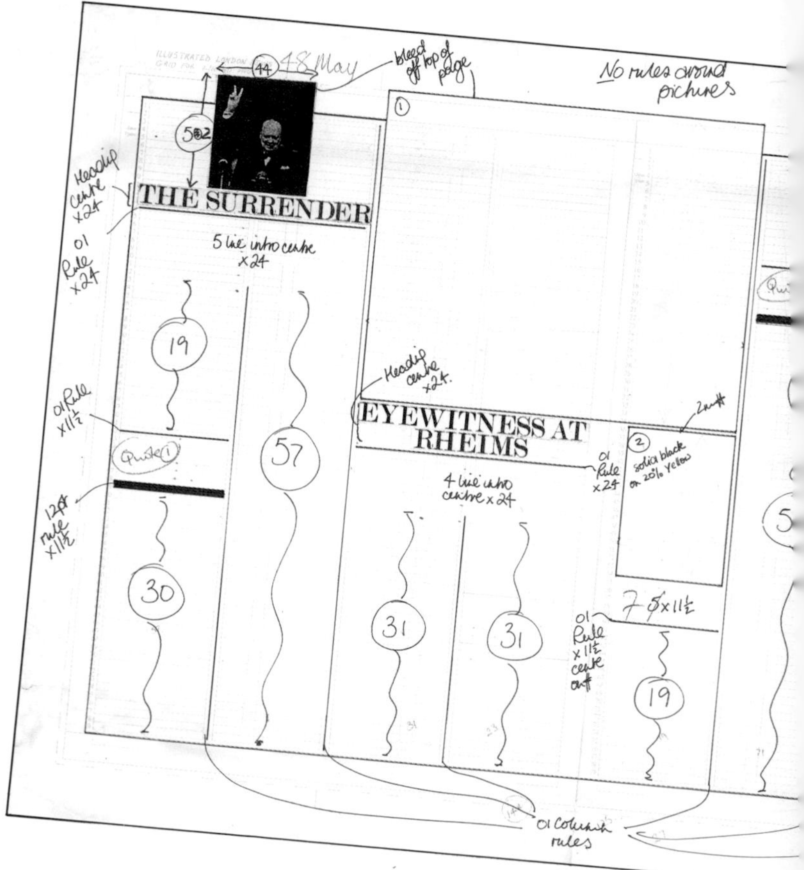

page layout. He or she knows exactly where all line and page endings will fall and can deal with word breaks, widows and orphans immediately rather than waiting for page proofs. Captions can be written to length with complete accuracy; with intros and titles the editor knows exactly how words are going to fall on the page, which can be significant. The editor has complete control of how pages are going to look. And a very fluid interplay can be achieved between the presentation of information in the text and in captions.

Writing captions In illustrated general market books and magazines — particularly on practical subjects such as cooking, gardening and do-it-yourself — captions to the artwork, illustrations and photographs are a key element on each page. They tie the separate elements of text and pictures together, both visually and editorially. Research shows that most readers scan the pictures and their accompanying captions before they read the text. To be effective, therefore, the captions must receive as much editorial attention from you as any other part of the book.

When choosing typefaces for text and captions, bear in mind how they will look together on the page. On a crowded layout, for example, where text and captions are positioned close together, it is almost essential to distinguish the two quite clearly in terms of measure, type size, face and/or weight. Captions invariably look

THE SURRENDER

Five years, eight months and seven days after the outbreak of war on September 1, 1939, Hitler's successor, Grand-Admiral Karl Dönitz, finally accepted defeat. **Max Hastings** describes the Germans' last doomed efforts to split the Alliance.

Eisenhower declined to meet the German delegation until their unconditional surrender had been signed.

EYEWITNESS AT RHEIMS

Charles Collingwood, CBS war correspondent, attended the German surrender 40 years ago. He recalls the historic, nocturnal ceremony held in a nondescript schoolroom.

We were asked to give our solemn word that we would not break the news of the surrender.

COUNTDOWN TO VICTORY

WORKING ON A MAGAZINE LAYOUT
All the checks detailed on the previous page under Working on a book layout apply to magazines but the different nature of the publication introduces some other factors. Box copy may have been supplied by the writer and typeset with the rest of the copy or you may leave it until now. Make sure you know how much you can write before you request space from the designer – you will not be popular if you want to change the design later on. Crossheads are there to break up the text and make the page look livelier; generally chosen for position on the page rather than because they help make sense of the text. Make sure, however, that the crosshead does not impede the flow of the text and that the text beneath the crosshead stands by itself. The intro is often set in a larger, bolder type than the text. Its function is to get the reader interested in the article. The galleys of the text will need to be cut and filled so that they fit the layout, and check that photographs and illustrations work well with the text.
Illustrated are the rough layout (**left**) and the finished printed page (**above**).

better and can be used in a more flexible way around illustrations or photographs if they are set to a narrower measure than the main text. They are also usually set a point or two smaller. For example, a main text set in 10/11 pt × 15 pica ems would be complemented very well by captions set in 8/9 pt × 7 pica ems. Italic captions are also particularly effective, as are captions set in a *sans serif* face to distinguish them from a main text set in a serif face. And if the main text is set justified, then captions set in a ranged left style also stand out well — the combinations are almost limitless.

Since the role of captions is to describe the pictures, they should be positioned as closely as possible to the illustrations to which they refer. Given the complexity of layouts in highly illustrated books, this is not always possible and linking captions and pictures logically can sometimes be a design compromise. Use clear directional indications such as 'above', 'below', or 'above right', but try to avoid tortuous and misleading constructions such as 'opposite far left'. Arrowheads in ones, two and threes pointing in various directions can also be confusing.

In their simplest form, captions are one-line descriptions of illustrations. At their most effective, they are a little more complicated – the best being 'microcosms' of their subject, which not only describe illustrations in the context of the main text but also take the story a little further by introducing new concepts. The style and content of captions should, therefore, be considered as seriously as the main text.

In mapping out the general approach of captions, the most important editorial decision for you to make is whether they should immediately identify the subject of the illustration and then go on to relate that to the main theme of the chapter or spread, or, alternatively, open with a general statement and then highlight the illustration in particular. Naturally, the appropriate strategy depends on the subject and type of illustration. The position of the directional is also important. If a caption opens with 'Above', you then need to say what is in the picture. If the caption opens with a scene-setting explanation, then the directional can be placed in parentheses close to the key word (such as the name of the plant in the photograph) in the depth of the caption. Both strategies are effective. The 'immediate' approach seems more appropriate for crisp, down-to-earth subjects and the 'indirect' angle generally suits more discursive themes. It is possible to mix the two approaches, using a more expansive style for pictures that open an article or section and an incisive phrase for the working illustrations in the body of the piece.

It is fair to say that most authors do not make good caption writers, perhaps because they are too close to their subject or they are simply mentally exhausted by the task of writing the text. Since captions are 'word engineering' exercises that need to be completed quickly at the layout stage, it is usually more efficient for the editor to write them. As a compromise you can ask your author to encapsulate the editorial point of the illustrations, leaving you to reshape this information into captions that fit the layout exactly.

Actually getting down to writing captions can either be a refreshing experience or one filled with indecision. It depends not only on your state of mind and the time available, but also on the material you have to work with. Always try to have the original photographs or color proofs on hand when you are writing on captions; black-and-white photocopies are better than nothing, but you may need to comment on the colors in the picture and will need to see the original.

Quite often the original transparencies are at the color separation house when you want to write the captions. It is best, therefore, to try to make some notes before they go. It is all too easy to find yourself trying to write captions based on indistinct tracings on a photocopy with little idea as to their true content.

Since captions must fit exact spaces, it is essential to consult the design layouts. The layouts not only indicate the length and position of the captions but also show how the photographs and illustrations are to be used, that is, how they are cropped, which way up or around they are to be printed, and how they interrelate. Although it is possible to write captions to pictures alone, this rarely produces ideal results. The layouts also give you the context within which they will be seen, which helps you to write the final captions with conviction.

Always double-check the character count required for captions and make sure that you set the margins on your typewriter or word processor accordingly. It is both irritating and time-consuming to discover that captions marked up as 30 characters wide on a layout should really have been typed to 36 characters as those few missing characters may mean adding one extra line for every five or so lines of the finished caption.

You should not despair if the first caption seems to take forever to write — the next one will take half the time, and after you have completed ten or so the others will come much more fluently. If you are having difficulty getting into the 'mood' of the captions, it can be helpful to take one subject and write something about it, even if it appears to be total gibberish, then reconstruct it until you are happy. It is much easier to criticize something already there than to be faced with a completely blank page.

The temptation to start every caption with 'This' must be resisted. It is good to look back every now and again at the captions you have written to check that you have not fallen into a stylistic rut. And also scanning the main copy and then covering it up while you write the caption can help you to avoid repeating the text. Above all, try to enjoy writing captions; it is after all the last opportunity the editor has to weld the text and pictures together into an effective layout that is more than the sum of its parts.

Checking page proofs When you have checked and fitted the text, written the captions, typed out any annotation for diagrams, inserted headings and folios, you can then send the rough layouts and the master galleys off to be made into pages. Checking page proofs is a very similar process to checking the first layouts, although it should not take you as long.

The first thing you should check is that the typesetters have made the text corrections (without making new errors) and have positioned the text according to the layout. Read beginnings and endings of paragraphs as a quick way of checking the text is in the right place and make any adjustments necessary by cutting and filling. If you have asked the typesetters to set and position the captions in one operation, check that they have done so accurately and cut and fill as necessary. Make sure that all headings and folios have been inserted correctly. Insert page numbers in the list of contents and cross-references in the text. Mark all your corrections and comments in a bright color on the page proof and initial each spread before you return it for correction.

4 PREPARATION FOR PRINTING

Preparation/The master paste-up/ Film assembly, imposition and platemaking/Checking blueprints/ Print processes/Finishing and binding/Casemaking and stamping

The careful selection and preparation of illustrations prior to reproduction is vital, if good quality is to be achieved at a reasonable cost.

Line illustrations are often specially drawn for the book and commissioned by the publisher, in which case the editor or designer briefing the artist can ensure that they are prepared in the right way. The original should be in black and may be drawn larger than the finished size, as reduction can help to minimize any slight inaccuracies in the artwork. It should be mounted on stable board and should include trim marks and indications of 'bleed' (where a picture or heading extends beyond the trim marks and will be trimmed off). Tints can be laid by the artist or inserted by the separation house. The latter is more expensive, but gives a cleaner result.

The size can be indicated either by a linear measurement or a percentage reduction or enlargement. If the work is to be produced to the same size then just indicate S/S.

Photographs that are to be reproduced as halftones should have good contrast and detail and be free of blemishes. It is possible to retouch photographs, either to remove blemishes or improve contrast or detail, but this is expensive and to be avoided if possible. Marking up the size the photograph is to be printed (sizing) will normally be done by the designer and in the case of photographs, the area to be used (cropping) needs to be indicated, as well as the percentage reduction or enlargement. Cropping is normally indicated on a tracing paper overlay.

Color photographs can be either transparencies or color prints. The original should have good contrast and there should not be an overall color cast. Excessive grain (normally from fast films) should be avoided as this will reproduce, particularly if the picture is enlarged. Original transparencies are preferred to duplicates, as the duplicating process always loses some of the sharpness of the original. Sizing of transparencies follows the same procedure as that used for monochrome halftones.

An important point to note is that the separation house will attempt to reproduce the transparency as it stands, unless instructed otherwise. So, if you want the final result to be different, for instance losing a color cast, the relevant instructions should be given at the outset to avoid expensive correction.

Ideally with color flat artwork, the board used by the artist should be flexible, as most color separation is done on a scanner (see page 102-106) and the artwork will need to be wrapped around its drum. Where rigid board is used, this either has to be reproduced conventionally using a process camera or the top surface of the board will need to be stripped off so that it can be wrapped around the scanner.

Finally, it is important to liaise with the designer, production department or the separation house if anything is not clear. If the number of pictures is changed after the original specification has been drawn up, or the sizes or types of originals change, then inform the production department, so a revised estimate can be done.

Preparation for printing

The phrase 'preparation for printing' is used to describe all the operations in the conversion of original photographs or artwork into the printing surface. As nearly all book and publication work is now printed by offset lithography, this is the preparation process that will be described here.

Preparation can be broken down into three main methods, depending on the type of original supplied. These are line, halftone and color separation.

Line copy Here, the original, which is normally black-and-white, is placed on a process camera, which is essentially a large version of an ordinary camera. This is used to photograph the original, producing a negative where the image area is clear film and the non-image area (background) is black, or vice versa if a positive is produced. From this negative, an offset plate can be made — although for certain work, the negative is contacted to make a positive. Typesetting is, of course, a line original. Although

Converting line illustrations or photographs into printing plates starts with a process camera (**above**). The original is placed on the copy board and its image is focused on to a viewing screen/filmholder by the lens.

Unexposed film (plus a screen for halftones) is placed in the filmholder and a timed exposure made. Usually a negative film is produced for making a positive plate.

some typesetters produce setting in the form of negatives or positives, it is usually supplied in the form of camera-ready copy (bromide) and this has to be photographed as a line original to produce a negative or positive from which a plate can be produced.

Halftone preparation This is the process used to produce a halftone negative or positive from a continuous tone original such as a black-and-white photograph or transparency. A photograph, unlike a line original, does not consist only of areas that are either black or white, but is made up of infinite shades of gray. These cannot be printed as such by the offset process, so the grays are simulated by breaking the picture up into very small dots. These dots are larger in the dark areas and smaller in the pale areas, giving the effect of grays although only printed in black ink.

The dots are produced by placing a screen in the camera between the original and the film. The screen consists of a fine grid of lines on film which break the image up into dots and thus produce a halftone negative.

Screens can be fine or coarse, depending on the eventual printing method and paper being used, but most books and magazines use 133 or 150 screen, whereas newspapers can be as coarse as 65 screen. The figures used to describe screens relate to the number of lines per inch on the screen and can also be classified metrically as lines per centimeter — for example, 133 screen in inches is 54 screen in centimeters. Although most halftones are still produced on cameras, separation houses are beginning to prepare them on scanners (see page 102-106), which can give better results.

A variant of the halftone process is the duotone, which is a two-color halftone printed using two negatives. The first is a conventional black-and-white halftone negative, which prints in black, and the second, which is specially shot to give good middle tones, is printed in a second color. The two combined give a fuller range of tones than an ordinary black-and-white halftone. Duotones can be particularly effective when photographs are printed with a gray or black as the second color and many high-quality photographic books use this technique.

Color separation Color originals have to be separated. This is because the effect of full color is achieved in printing by breaking the picture down into four basic colors — these are magenta, yellow, cyan and black. A wide range of colors can be made up by combining these four colors in varying quantities.

Color originals may be transparencies, which will have light shone through them to produce the negative or positive or 'flat copy', which describes a painting or photographic color print where light is reflected from the surface to produce the positive or negative.

Separation is achieved by using filters (or programs — see below), which isolate those parts of the picture that are to print in each color. For example, a blue filter creates a separation negative that prints in yellow. Again the halftone principle is used, so each color film is made up of different size dots.

Color separation on a camera is done one color at a time, using screens and filters to produce a film for each color, which is subsequently contacted to make a film for platemaking.

Scanners Most color separation is now done using electronic scanners, which use the same principles as conventional separation but work at much higher speeds, some give superior

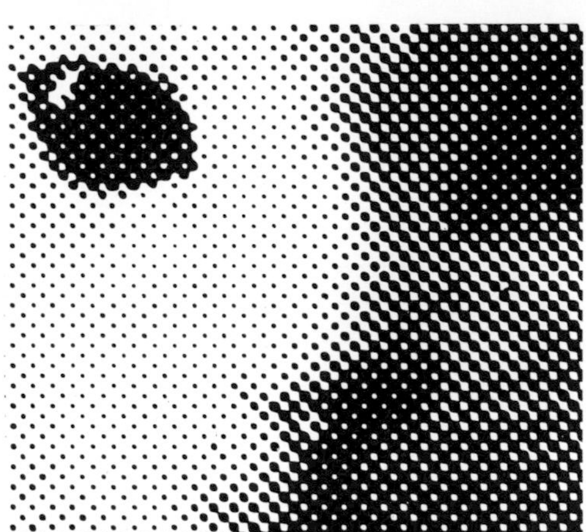

A halftone is reproduced from an original (**above**) by the use of a screen. When this is enlarged (**right**) the dots are visible — the light areas are made up from black halftone dots against white, and the shaded parts are larger black dots.

A screen angled at 90°

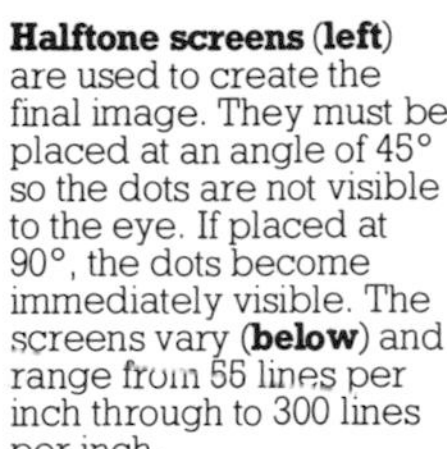

A screen angled at 45°

Halftone screens (left) are used to create the final image. They must be placed at an angle of 45° so the dots are not visible to the eye. If placed at 90°, the dots become immediately visible. The screens vary (**below**) and range from 55 lines per inch through to 300 lines per inch.

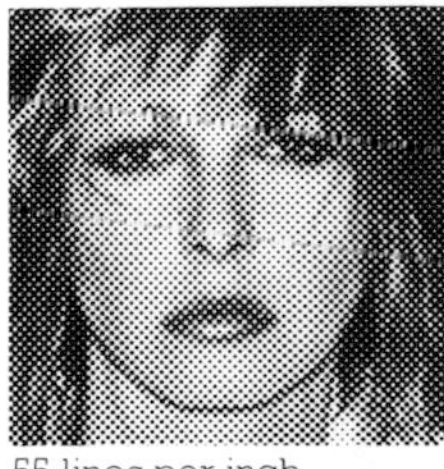

55 lines per inch
20 lines per centimetre

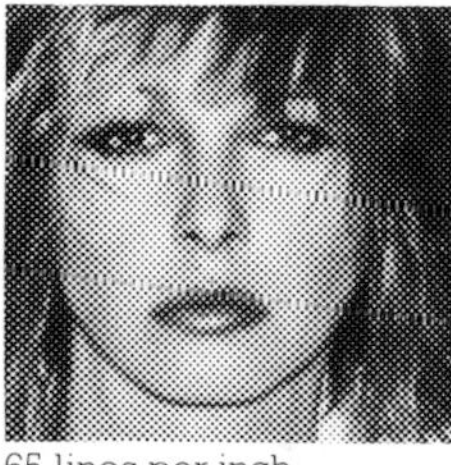

65 lines per inch
26 lines per centimetre

85 lines per inch
35 lines per centimetre

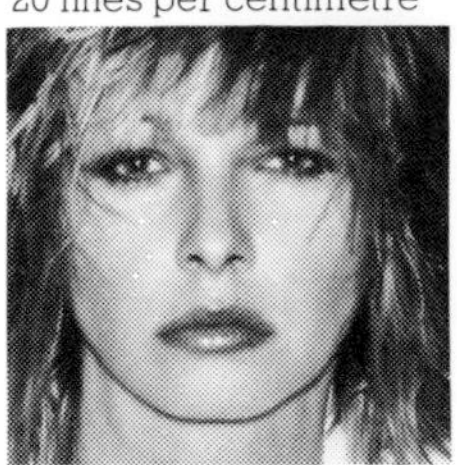

100 lines per inch
40 lines per centimetre

120 lines per inch
48 lines per centimetre

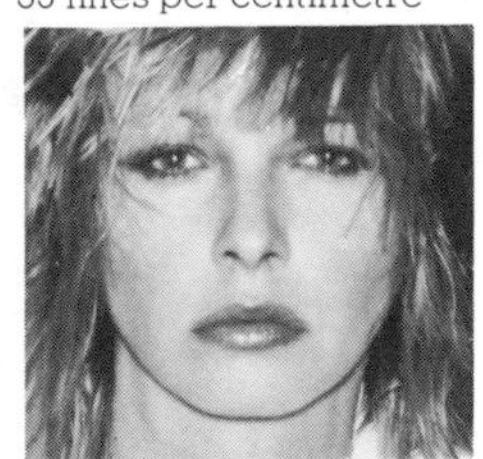

133 lines per inch
54 lines per centimetre

150 lines per inch
60 lines per centimetre

175 lines per inch
70 lines per centimetre

200 lines per inch
80 lines per centimetre

Color scanning is the modern method of reproduction, which will eventually take over completely from the traditional process camera method. It is more accurate, flexible and, in principle, very simple. A laser or high-intensity light beam scans the images, which, by means of color filters and a computer converts them into individual screened films for each color. Depending on the specified requirements, the films can be either positive or negative.

Scanning transparencies The first step is to tape the transparencies to the glass cylinder or drum of the scanner. Since the process is expensive, it is cost-effective for the transparencies to be batched so that the optimum number of whatever size can be fitted to the drum at the same time. Their densities, however, should also be similar, since the scanner will be set to average this out. In addition, the accuracy of a modern scanner means that the slightest flaw or scratch on a transparency will be picked up and magnified. This is a particular risk with 35mm transparencies and, for this reason, it is common for such transparencies to be floated in oil on the surface of the drum if an enlargement of more than 500% is required.

The operator then keys in the percentage reductions or enlargements required on the scanner's computer. These are expressed in two dimensions, or factor numbers, which are calculated from the master chart supplied by the manufacturer. At the same time, the screen percentage is set. This dictates how many lines of dots appear per inch on the final film.

The drum is then fitted to the scanner and rotated at high speed. The light or laser passes through a system of lenses to be angled by a mirror set at 90° to illuminate the images, which are then analysed as the scanning head moves along the surface of the drum. The signals are passed to the computer via the color filters and the computer transmits this in digital form to the film. This is held in 20in (50cm) x 16in (40cm) cassette form of which 19½in (49cm) x 15½in (38cm) is the image area. The

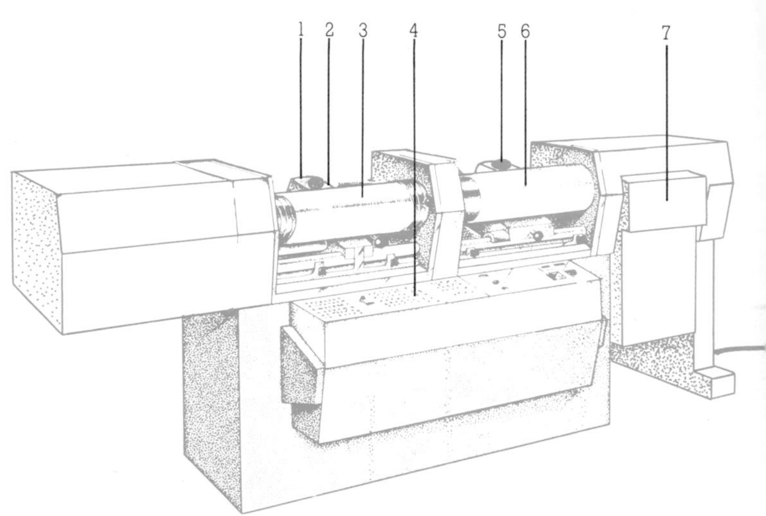

Deliberate programming of the scanner can produce a whole range of different effects. The image of the racing car (**above**) was stretched horizontally to increase the impression of speed. This is done by setting the horizontal enlargement by a greater amount than that of the vertical. They can also be programmed to correct out-of-focus originals (**near right**) to a certain degree (**far right**). The computer modified the signal by increasing the contrast across the adjacent areas of detail.

film used is hard-dot film. Its use means that, if the dots are slightly etched away in color correction, their area remains the same, as opposed to soft dots which become smaller.

The film is removed and processed by rapid access developing. This takes 90 seconds, as opposed to five minutes or more in traditional photolitho processing. Many operators can tell the accuracy of the color by visual examination of the film before proofing. Normally, very little correction is needed, though proofs are correctable up to between 5% and 10% on hard film (20% on soft). The reason why color correction is still necessary – even with this sophisticated system – is simple. With the pigments currently available, it is impossible to produce a perfectly pure printing ink, since each ink absorbs some of the light it should reflect. Color correction compensates for this undesirable absorption of color by the inks.

Often, it is quicker and cheaper to re-run the images than correct. The entire process – from mounting the transparancies to proofing can take as little as five hours, but the normal times is around 10 days.

Scanning artwork The scanning of artwork is carried out in exactly the same way as the scanning of transparencies. However, it is important to remember that the scanner is even more sensitive, because of the amount of light artwork will reflect. Certain colors, too, are difficult or impossible to reproduce. These include turquoise – a slightly warmer color than cyan – and orange-reds. Lemon yellow and fluorescent colors are impossible, while excessive amounts of process white tend to make the color read-out, the basis for computation, inaccurate.

When preparing artwork for the scanner, it is vital to use flexible board as the base, so the artwork can be wrapped around the drum without damaging it. If artwork is incorrectly presented, the operator may try to strip it off so that it can be mounted, with the consequent high risk of tearing. If paint is applied too thickly, it may also crack.

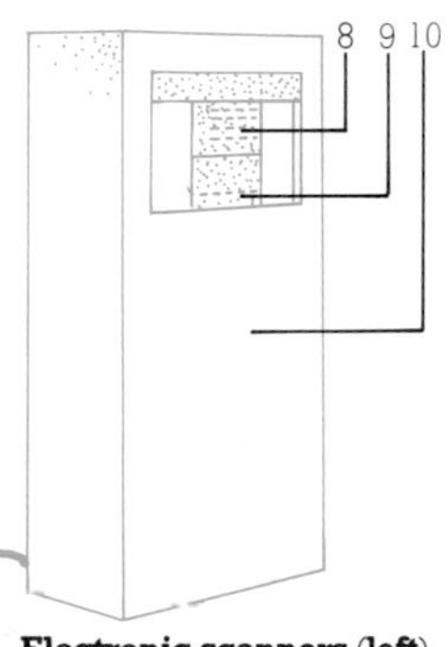

Electronic scanners (left) include a scanning head (**1**), optical color system (**2**), scanning drum (**3**) – seen in action (**right**) – color computer (**4**), recording head (**5**), make up drum (**6**), film cassette (**7**), dimension keys (**8**), screen keys (**9**) and computer shell (**10**).

quality and can produce all four colors at once.

The scanner uses a high intensity light or laser beam to scan the original. Color filters or programs and a computer built into the scanner convert the signals picked up by the beam into screened negatives or positives for each of the four colors.

If a job requires that the originals all be reduced or enlarged by the same percentage, then these can be scanned together, which costs less, although the quality will not be as high. When this is done the originals are described as 'in pro' (in proportion). When the originals need to be enlarged or reduced by different amounts, they are described as 'out of pro'.

On many machines the originals are taped to the drum of the scanner and the operator keys in the percentage reduction or enlargement and the screen ruling. Before scanning begins, the operator uses the scanning head to 'read' the strength of color in different parts of the pictures and adjusts the scanner controls so that they will be reproduced as accurately as possible. The drum then rotates at high speed and the scanning head analyses the image as it moves along the surface of the drum. The signals are often sent to the computer via the color filters and the computer converts this digital information into light signals that are exposed onto the film, carried to a cassette.

Flat color artwork is scanned in the same way, but difficulties can occur with certain strong hues such as turquoise, orange or fluorescent colors. Here the process can approach the color of the original, but cannot reproduce it exactly.

Color correction The introduction of scanners has improved the quality of separation to the extent that, very often, the first scan can be used without correction. However, most batches of separations include a few that need some form of correction. Correction can be done by photographic 'masking', hand retouching to make the dots smaller or larger in the area to be corrected, or rescanning with revised instructions to achieve the desired result.

Electronic page planning Recent developments in scanners have produced machines that can scan as described above, store the separation information on disk in digital form and then use this information to create a complete page, even one consisting of several transparencies. This can be put onto film, in position, so that the page consists of just one piece of film for each color. As well as this, these machines can be used to lay tints, produce shapes and cut-outs and for color correction. All of these machines have a color monitor, so the operator can assess the layout and color before committing it to film.

The capital cost of these machines is very high, but their sophistication means that complex publications such as mail-order catalogs can be produced for less and to a higher standard.

Some of these machines can include type in the layout as well as pictures and even alter typefaces and type sizes at layout stage, which gives the editor and designer tremendous flexibility.

Proofing Once the separations have been made, a proof has to be produced so that the separation house and the publisher can satisfy themselves that the color, quality and sizing are correct and ready for printing. This may be done by making an offset plate (see Platemaking, page 109) and printing from this on a proofing press, which is a slower hand-fed version of an offset printing machine. This method is expensive, but is one way of obtaining several copies of a proof. They are called 'machine proofs'.

At this stage, 'progressives' are produced. These are prints of the

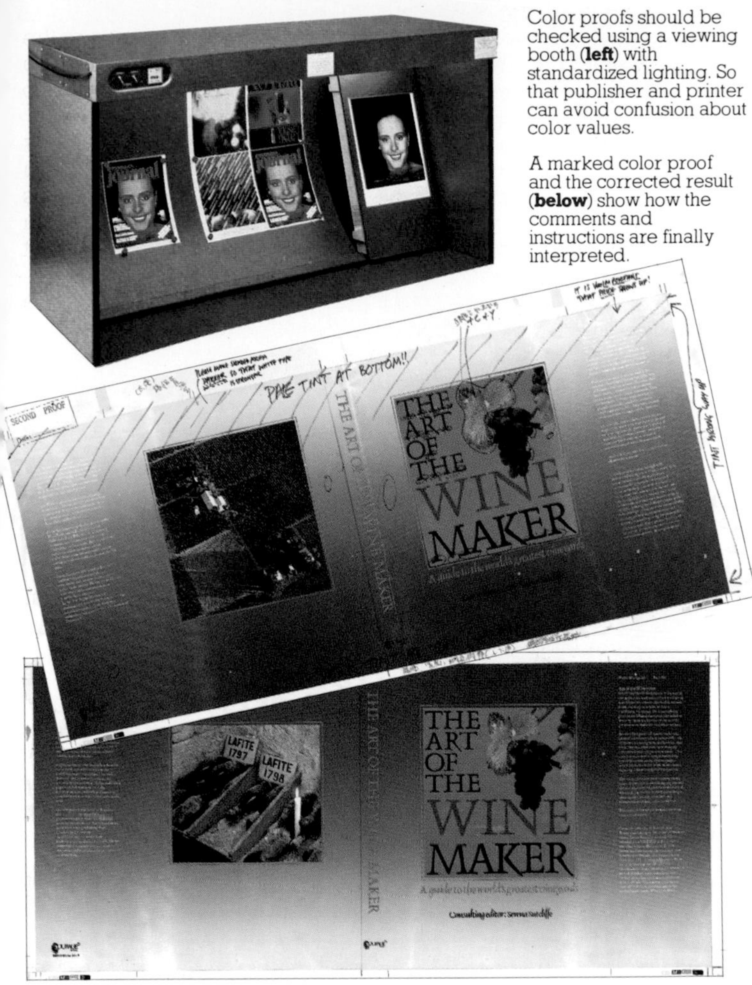

Color proofs should be checked using a viewing booth (**left**) with standardized lighting. So that publisher and printer can avoid confusion about color values.

A marked color proof and the corrected result (**below**) show how the comments and instructions are finally interpreted.

individual colors built up one at a time to show the 'progression' to the eventual four-color result. The printer uses these to set the ink on the printing machine to the correct strength. These are not normally seen by the publisher but are sent with the full color proof.

If only one or two proofs are required, it is cheaper to use some form of photographic proof (Cromalin or Matchprint, for example) where the colors are produced by a combination of photographic and electrostatic methods. These can be very accurate and are cheap and fast to produce.

Checking color proofs When the publisher receives the color proofs, these have to be checked for sizing, which is normally done by the designer, and for color quality and this may be done by either the editorial, design or production departments.

The purpose of this operation is to assess whether the separation house has achieved a result that is faithful to the original. The first requirement is a light box to view the transparencies in correct lighting conditions. If a publisher handles a lot of color work, it is worth investing in a viewing booth, which is specially lit to view the proofs. This light simulates daylight and is standardized, so that the publisher can view the colors under the same lighting conditions as the separation house and the printer.

When checking color proofs, it is best to tell the separation house what result you want to achieve, rather than instructing them as to how it should be achieved. For example, if a darker green is required, it is better to say 'darken green' rather than 'increase blue', because it may be the best way to achieve a darker green is by reducing the yellow, rather than increasing the blue. If in doubt, it is best, if possible, to ask the staff from the separation house to come in and look at the proofs with you.

Where the result is close to the one you want but needs some correction, the separation house may be able to do this without necessitating a further proof; where there is considerable work to be done, however, a reproof should be requested.

Color separation is probably the most complicated area of printing technology and one where a *little* knowledge can be disastrous, so it is best to check with the experts in your production department or at the separation house.

The master paste-up

As a positional guide for the printer all the proofs of the text, headings, captions, artwork illustrations and photographs are pasted down onto a master set of layout grids, forming the 'master paste-up'. It represents the penultimate step in the project's pre-printing schedule. The final step is usually the blueprint (see page 112).

Depending on the system your company uses, the typesetter may supply the text in the form of one-piece page film for you to send to the printer with the master paste-up. Since the text, captions, headings and all other elements of the text are in position, this gives you the reassurance that the printer cannot disturb these elements and that pieces will not fall off in transit. Sometimes, if time is desperately short, you may have to send 'patched positives' of the text. These consist of a backing sheet of clear film with the separate pieces of text stuck in position on it.

Whatever form they are in, the text layouts leave spaces into which the illustrations will be inserted. The designer pastes in color proofs or blueprints of the illustrations and photographs to occupy these spaces on the master paste-up. Each color illustration is in the form of four separate pieces of film that will be used to make the yellow, cyan, magenta and black plates respectively. Your designer will place each complete set in a glassine bag and write the page number or suitable code clearly on it. This 'bagging-up' process usually goes on while the editor is checking through the final text films. (Always place tracing or layout paper between each sheet of film to prevent sticking.)

On some projects the separation house may supply the illustration films as complete spreads, with all the illustrations in the correct positions. This is equivalent to one-piece text film and, likewise, lessens fears about patches of film being lost.

The package you send to the printer will usually contain:

1 The layouts — a precise spread-by-spread positional guide to all the elements involved.

2 The text film or camera-ready boards bearing the text that will be made into film at the printer.

3 The illustration films, bagged-up as separate batches of four films or in paged form.

4 A complete set of the latest color proofs If the paste-up carries only blueprints then this set is vital for the printer as a guide to the color balance required.

5 A complete set of progressive proofs These are supplied by the color separation house and show the effect of printing each of the yellow, cyan, magenta and black illustration films separately and then in combinations leading to the finished four-color result. The printer uses these as a color reference at the printing stage. If necessary, you can delay sending them until after you receive the printer's blueprint.

As a double-check for all concerned, always include a list detailing all the materials enclosed for each page or spread of the master paste-up. Normally the printer signs and returns one copy of this checklist when the materials arrive. Since the color printing may be carried out thousands of miles away from the publishing company, such simple checks save possible confusion later on.

As the parcel leaves the office, it is quite normal under such stressful conditions to feel you have forgotten to include something. If you have left something out or you know further action is necessary, you have one more opportunity to set things straight – when the blueprint, arrives.

Film assembly, imposition and platemaking

Film assembly This is the operation by which all the type and pictorial elements within a page are assembled and placed in their correct positions. Usually, the typesetter will have already assembled the type in page form as camera-ready copy, leaving spaces for any illustrations, and the printer shoots the camera-ready copy (see page 100), makes negative or positive film and then inserts the illustrations in their correct positions to make complete film pages. Sometimes, the typesetter supplies camera-ready copy in galley form and the printer does the complete page make up, rather than just inserting illustrations.

The illustrations may be sent to the printer by the publisher or separation house and take the form of film positives or negatives. The printer will work to the publisher's layout so all the elements will be in the right place. The film assembly is normally done with adhesive tape, although electronic methods are starting to be used (see Electronic page planning page 206).

Imposition This operation involves positioning the pages in the right place on the plate, so that they come out in the right order, in the correct position and with the intended margins.

Most printing machines print 8, 16 or 32 pages or multiples of these numbers and the printer will work out an imposition scheme that will print the required number of pages in the most economical way on the machines. Normally, imposition will not concern the editor if the publication is printed in black, two-color or four-color on every page; however, if the printing is to be planned so that, for example, half the pages are to be in four-color and half in two-color, the publisher must obtain the imposition scheme from the printer at flat plan stage, as discussed earlier. Then the publisher will know which pages will print in four-color and which in two, so the illustrations and layout can be planned accordingly.

Normally, publications are imposed as sheet work, but they can be imposed as 'work and turn'. This means that all the pages are printed on one side of the sheet and the sheet is then turned over to print the other side (see page 110).

Imposition is the term used to describe the organization of the pages on each side of a printed sheet so that they will be in the correct order when they are cut, folded and trimmed. The diagrams (**below**) show the commonly used imposition schemes and the corresponding folding methods (**right**). Margins of about 3-6mm (⅛-¼in) are left when printing and folding for trimming.

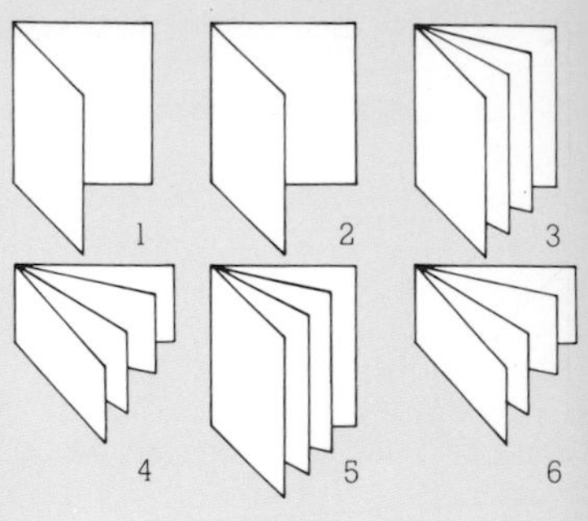

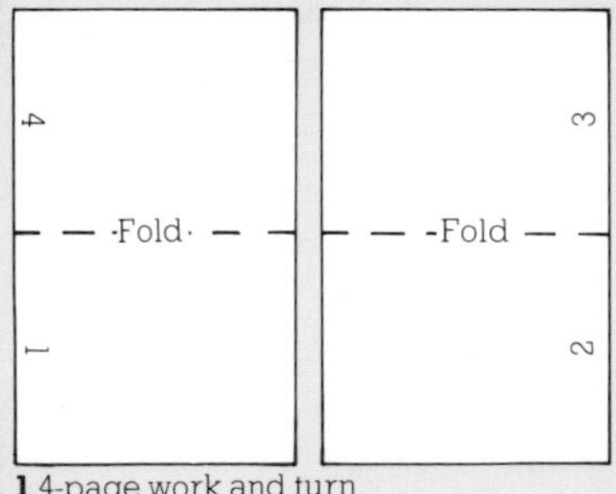

1 4-page work and turn

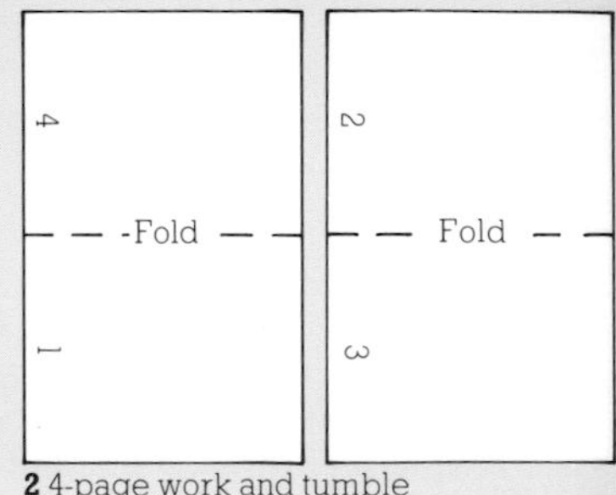

2 4-page work and tumble

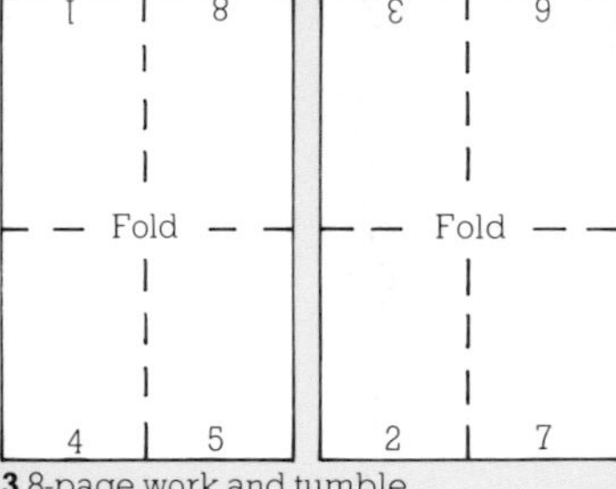

3 8-page work and tumble

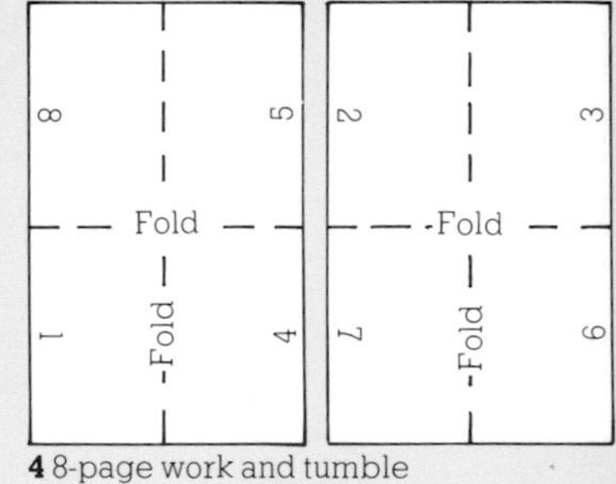

4 8-page work and tumble

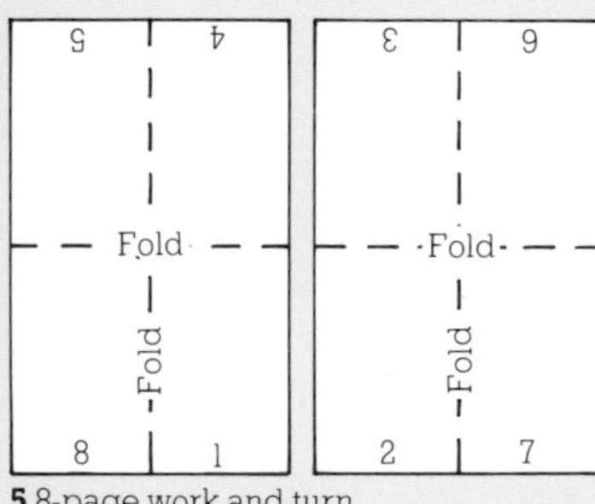

5 8-page work and turn

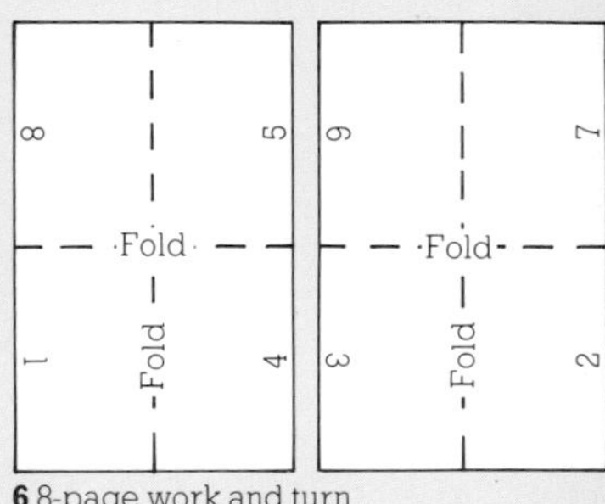

6 8-page work and turn

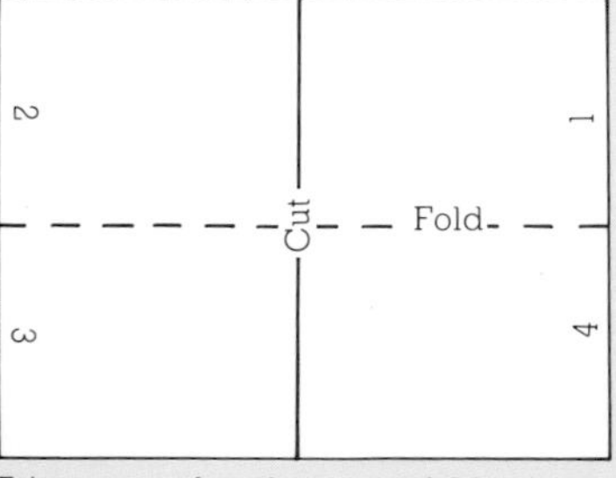

7 4-page work and turn one fold

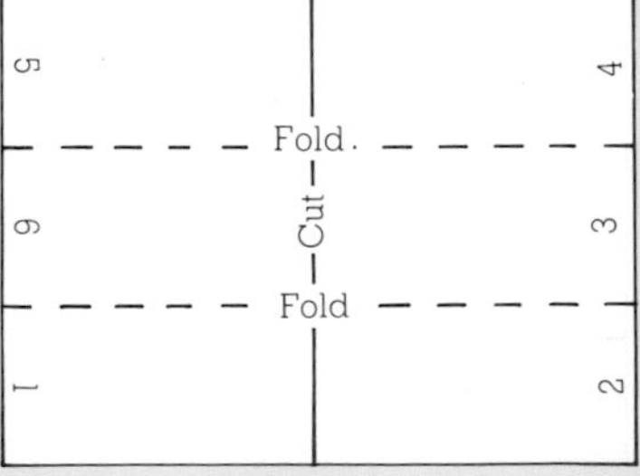

8 6-page work and turn

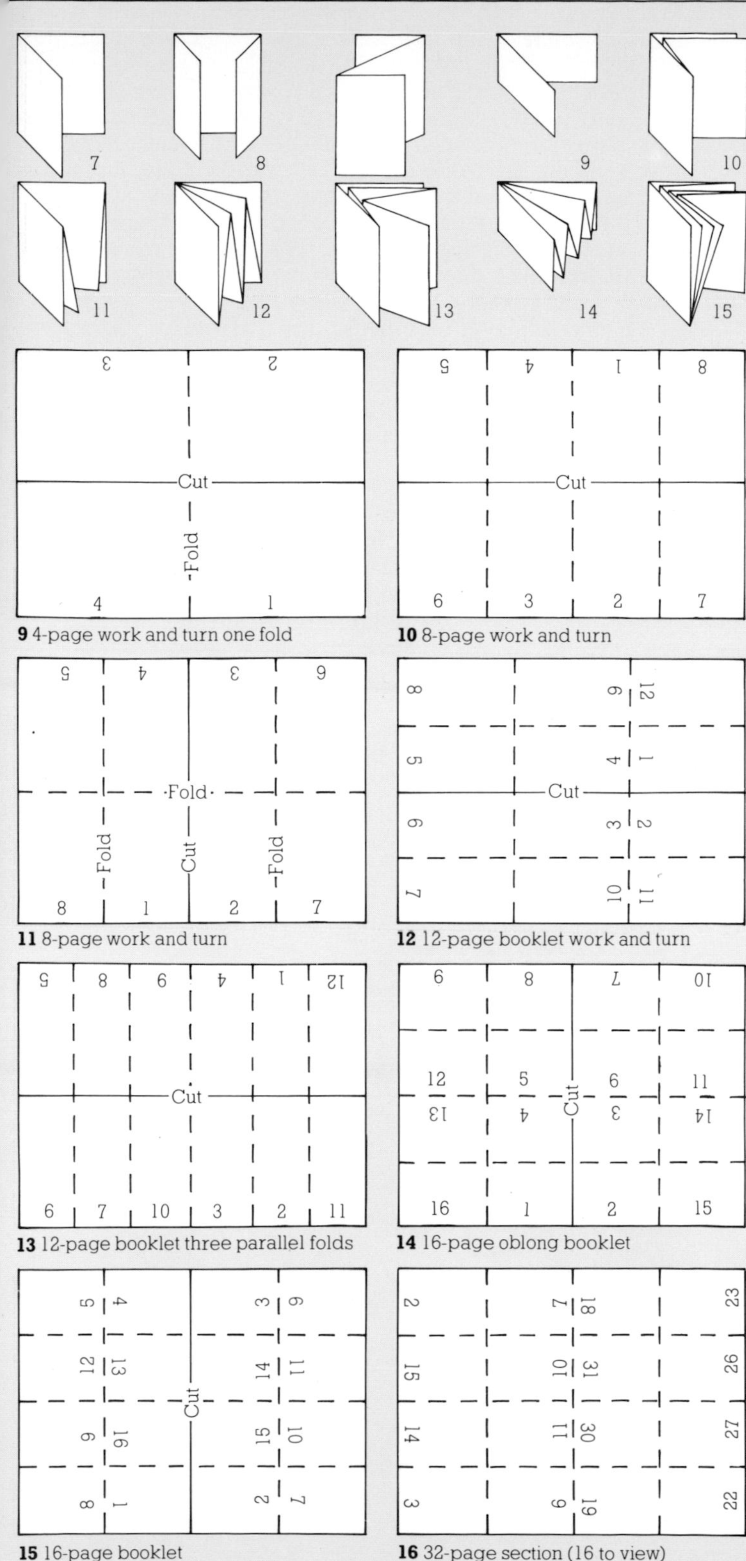

9 4-page work and turn one fold

10 8-page work and turn

11 8-page work and turn

12 12-page booklet work and turn

13 12-page booklet three parallel folds

14 16-page oblong booklet

15 16-page booklet

16 32-page section (16 to view)

The imposition itself, like film assembly, is normally done with adhesive tape on clear plastic film, which has previously been drawn up with the layout grid. This is a slow and expensive hand operation and some printers now use electronic imposition devices such as the Opticopy. These are like a camera with a large piece of film, the same size as the printing plate; the pages are photographed one at a time and the machine moves the film, so that each page is exposed in the correct position for printing. A microcomputer controls the operation, with different programs for the required imposition schemes. Even more advanced machines can expose direct to plate, without using film.

Once the imposition is complete, the printer produces the blueprints or 'blues' from the imposed films and these are sent to the publisher for checking. They can usually be produced two-sided and are folded, so the publisher can see how the book will be printed. (See Checking blueprints below.)

Platemaking When the blueprints has been approved by the publisher, the printer makes any corrections required and then makes plates from the imposed films (foils). The metal plate is usually 'presensitized' (that is, it has been coated with a chemical that reacts to light) and this is placed in an exposure frame. The imposed film is placed over the frame and a light source shines light through the clear parts of the film, which has the effect of sensitizing the image area. When it is developed and washed (normally on automatic machines), the image area will attract ink and repel water and the non-image (background area) will repel ink and attract water (see Offset Lithography, page 116), if it is a negative-reading plate.

Checking blueprints

Receiving a blueprint back from the printer is a bit like collecting your snapshots from the photographic shop — there are the text and illustrations in their correct positions in something that looks

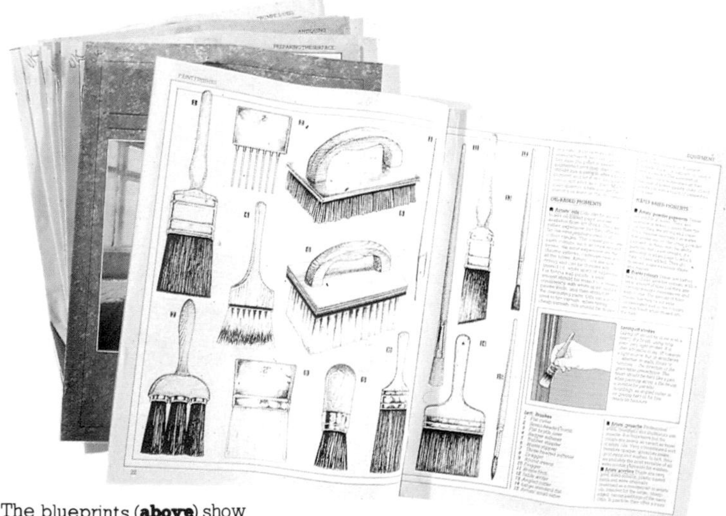

The blueprints (**above**) show exactly how the text and illustrations will appear in the final publication. They are prepared by the printer from the imposed films just before platemaking starts, allowing the editor and designer to make last minute positional changes or replacements.

like a book. A blueprint is a photographic proof of the black film plus one, or occasionally two, of the other colors to show up the illustrations. The whole thing is blue or murky gray in color and usually smells strongly of ammonia.

Checking blueprints requires concentration. It is not something you should dip into at odd intervals throughout the day but go through quietly page by page until you have finished. First flip through the pages checking that all the sections are present and in their proper sequence. Since a blueprint is not bound, the sections may easily be out of order. Do try to keep the pages within each section in place; if they get jumbled up it can take a fair time to put them back in the correct order. If you have two blueprints, and time permits, send one to the author with strict instructions for haste; you can share the remaining one with your designer.

The printer may return the master paste-up with the blueprints, so you may be able to turn over the spreads of the paste-up as you check each page of the blueprints. Your designer will usually check that the illustrations and text have been precisely positioned according to the grid, but you should also check this, at least in a general visual way. Also check the blueprints closely bearing the following points in mind:

1 That the text and illustrations have been correctly positioned according to the paste-up and the design grid. It is quite possible for illustrations to be transposed between sections, to be out of alignment, incorrectly cropped (masked) or simply upside down. Many photographs, particularly of plants and other natural history subjects taken from odd angles or from overhead, look surprisingly right when viewed in one color when they are, in fact, the wrong way round. Printed in full color, the angle of the light in the photograph usually shows the correct orientation much more clearly.

2 That nothing is missing. Frequently, tint backgrounds appear to have been left off because they do not show up on the color film used to make the blueprint. Always query these apparent omissions. Unless one-piece text film has been used, always check that all the text is present and correct, particularly headings, folios and rules.

3 That the film has not been damaged during transit or during the film assembly process at the printer. Blueprints usually have apparent 'scratches' from the edges of tape used to fix the films in position. Often there are odd marks and spots, which should be pointed out, but fortunately usually they do not appear in the final printing.

4 That everything is editorially correct. In many cases, there is not time to read a blueprint for sense and accuracy. However, there can be glaring errors that leap out of the page at you. This should not be cause for undue alarm – in most cases you can effect some 'repair', for instance, stripping in corrections to captions or text and repositioning annotation.

If these are the major points to be checked, what changes can be made at this stage? Any of the following, if you can afford it:

1 Change the position of any piece of text or illustration. Usually only minor adjustments are needed, but if necessary you can redesign at this stage. The printer will either cut and reposition the pieces of film to comply with your wishes or reshoot it, but time and money usually overrule all but the most essential changes.

2 Insert new or replacement pieces of text or illustration film. Often the master paste-up goes off to the printer with a few pieces of film or artwork missing. In the time the printer takes to assemble the film you can make amends for such oversights and insert these pieces at this stage. The same applies to text corrections you may have requested after the master paste-up left the publishing house. Simply insert a proof or photocopy of the replacement pieces in the appropriate places on the blueprint and draw attention to them, using a bright pen, with notes such as 'Please insert new film supplied'.

Whatever changes or insertions you wish to make, always mark the blueprint clearly and type out a checklist for the printer. List the page numbers and describe the action required. You can supply any new pieces of text on one piece of film as long as the relevant page numbers have been typeset to identify each piece, or you have marked the numbers on the film. Since this is your last opportunity to make any changes, always make your instructions crystal clear.

Unless you visit the printing house you may not see a corrected blueprint to confirm that your changes have been made. The next time you see those by now familiar pages again will probably be as unbound printed sections or the final bound book – the editor's work is done.

Print processes

Once you have checked and corrected the blueprint and returned it to the printer, what happens next? What printing process will be used? Almost invariably, your book, or magazine will be printed by offset lithography, the most popular, adaptable and economic printing process currently available for a wide range of published material. If your publication is a relatively short-run 'special' edition or issue demanding crisp black text and dense colors on art paper, then it may be printed by the letterpress process, although this process is now quite rare. On the other hand, if you work on a national magazine of over 300,000 copies, then gravure printing might prove the most cost-effective strategy. The choice depends on the nature and size of the publication and on the time and money available to print it. Here we review the basic printing processes in common use today.

From the 'instant print' shop at the corner of the street to the massive printing plants that are active 24 hours a day, there are countless types of printing presses working at various speeds, using various sizes of paper in sheets or in roll (web) form, printing in one, two, three, four or more colors, with or without sophisticated folding equipment and other features. Underlying this multiplicity of machinery are three basic printing processes categorized by the way in which the ink is transferred from the plate to the paper. These are letterpress, offset lithography and gravure.

Letterpress The name 'letterpress' is an apt description of its working principle, for the inked letters of type (and illustrations) are pressed against the paper by force to make an impression. The printing areas of the plate are raised above the surface of the non-printing areas, just as handset or hot metal type stands above the surface. Thus, letterpress is the traditional method of printing from metal type and etched metal blocks of line illustrations or photographs, assembled in a rigid frame (chase) to create a 'form' (printing plate).

In a platen press – the simplest arrangement for letterpress printing – the flat surfaces of the assembled form and a sheet of

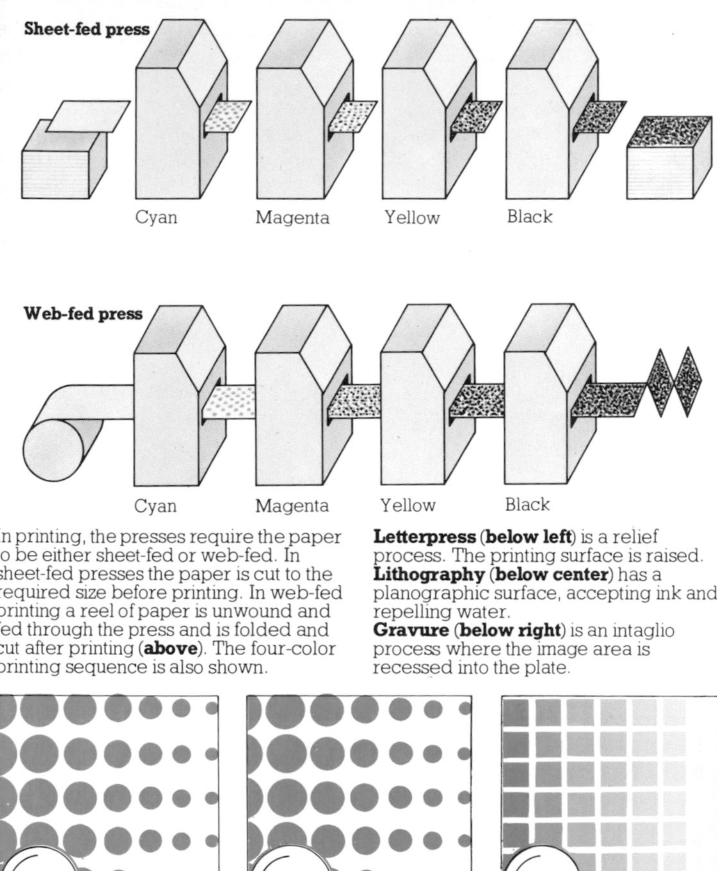

In printing, the presses require the paper to be either sheet-fed or web-fed. In sheet-fed presses the paper is cut to the required size before printing. In web-fed printing a reel of paper is unwound and fed through the press and is folded and cut after printing (**above**). The four-color printing sequence is also shown.

Letterpress (**below left**) is a relief process. The printing surface is raised. **Lithography** (**below center**) has a planographic surface, accepting ink and repelling water. **Gravure** (**below right**) is an intaglio process where the image area is recessed into the plate.

paper are brought together vertically under pressure to create the printed page (an impression). Mechanical variations of this basic principle include the flat-bed cylinder press, in which the form is horizontal and the paper is rolled over it on an impression cylinder; the rotary press, in which both plate and paper are carried on cylinders; and the belt press (Cameron is a commonly used belt press), in which a number of flexible plates mounted on two continuous belts come into contact with a web of paper. The curved or flexible plates are made of metal or plastic and are produced either from a mold made from the form or photographically.

The letterpress process is used for commercial work and stationery, for fine book work and where hot metal setting is the norm, such as on newspapers. Its advantages are that it produces a dense, crisp image (particularly of type on good-quality paper), it is suitable for short runs, and it wastes less paper in the setting up, or 'make-ready' period. The disadvantages of the process are the relatively high cost of producing the plates, the slowness of the sheet-fed presses using the letterpress process and the need for higher quality paper to emulate the results produced by other processes.

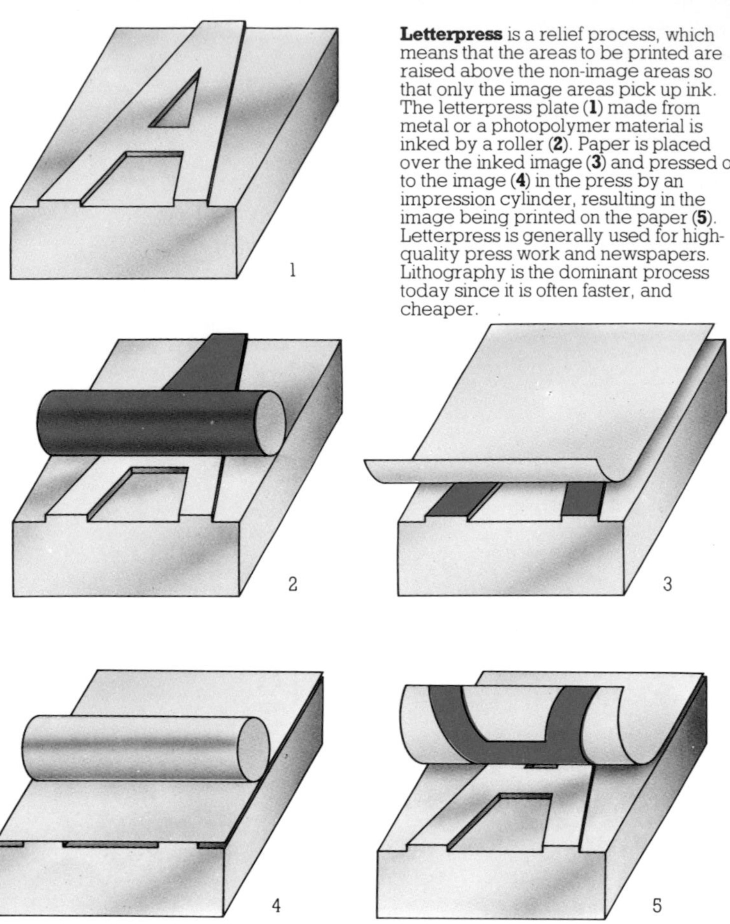

Letterpress is a relief process, which means that the areas to be printed are raised above the non-image areas so that only the image areas pick up ink. The letterpress plate (**1**) made from metal or a photopolymer material is inked by a roller (**2**). Paper is placed over the inked image (**3**) and pressed on to the image (**4**) in the press by an impression cylinder, resulting in the image being printed on the paper (**5**). Letterpress is generally used for high-quality press work and newspapers. Lithography is the dominant process today since it is often faster, and cheaper.

Offset lithography Offset lithography is by far the most widespread printing process in use today. The essential difference between a lithographic and a letterpress plate is that the printing area is flat rather than raised above the surface of the non-printing area as in letterpress. The basic principle of lithography — literally 'stone printing' — was developed in 1798 for the production of art prints from stone surfaces. Today, the printing images are created photographically on metal, plastic or paper plates, but the chemical and physical forces at play remain essentially the same.

The image area on the plate accepts greasy printing ink and repels water, and the non-printing area retains water and repels ink. These properties are achieved in a complex series of chemical treatments following the exposure of the presensitized plate to a negative image ('negative-working' plates) or a positive image ('positive-working' plates). Once fitted on the printing machine, the plates are first dampened and then inked; the ink is retained only by the greasy image areas.

The term 'offset' arises from the way in which the image is transferred from the plate onto the paper. The plate and paper do not come into direct contact; the inked image is transferred (thus offset) first onto an intermediary cylinder with a rubber surface (a 'rubber blanket') and from this onto the paper. The main purpose of this is to avoid contact between the relatively abrasive texture of the paper and the delicate surface of the plate. The resilience of the rubber blanket also allows for any slight irregularity in the surface, making offset lithography ideal for printing on a wide range of papers and other materials. A further advantage of the offset principle is that less water reaches the final printing surface, reducing the tendency for the paper to become damp and stretch.

Most color-illustrated publications are printed by offset lithography on sheet-fed or web-fed presses, depending on the size of paper and on the print run. Both types of press use the rotary principle, making reliable, high-speed printing possible.

Sheet-fed presses can handle paper in a vast range of sizes and offer the most flexible printing method for everything from one-color, single-page leaflets to complete four-color illustrated books. The largest sheet-fed presses may be used for print runs of up to 100,000 copies, but if the format is suitable a web-offset press usually makes better economic sense for four-color work on print runs of 50,000 copies or more.

A web-fed offset press prints on a continuous roll of paper and operates at higher speeds than sheet-fed presses — up to 50,000 impressions per hour compared with a maximum of 12,000 per hour for sheet-fed presses. As the web of paper flies through the maze of cylinders on a large multicolor web-offset machine, both sides are printed at the same time with each of the four process colors to build up full-color images — the inks are dried by hot air, ultraviolet or infra-red light, and the printed paper is cut, folded and collated into sections ready for binding. Such high-speed operation is controlled by sophisticated sensors and feedback devices such as those that constantly adjust the ink flow according to the depth of color required in various parts of the plate.

Offset lithography, whether on sheet-fed or web-fed presses, is a fast and flexible method of printing, capable of producing high quality work. The plates are cheaper to prepare than letterpress

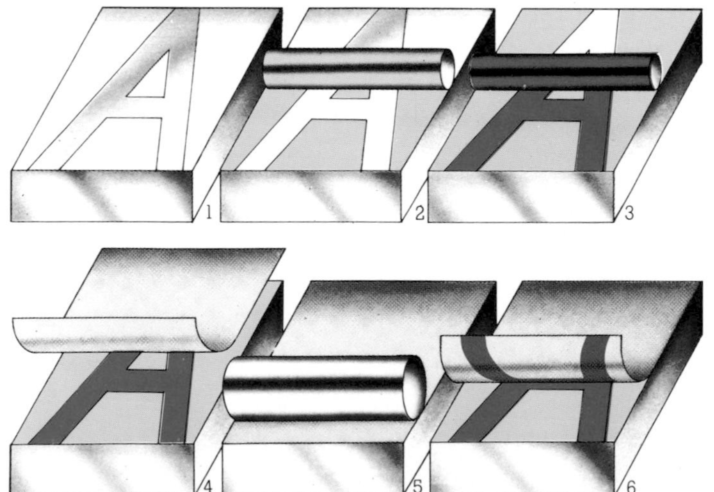

Lithography is a planographic printing method. The image area of the plate is treated with a greasy medium (**1**) and then dampened by rollers (**2**). The plate is inked (**3**), the ink adhering to the greasy image but not to the dampened areas. The paper is placed over the plate (**4**) and then plate and paper are run through the press (**5**), producing the printed page (**6**).

A platen press (**right**) is the simplest letterpress press: paper and plate are brought together vertically under pressure to produce the 'impression' (the printed sheet).

A web-offset printing press (**below**) prints on both sides of a continuous reel (web) of paper at high speed.

Gravure uses the process of etching (**center**)

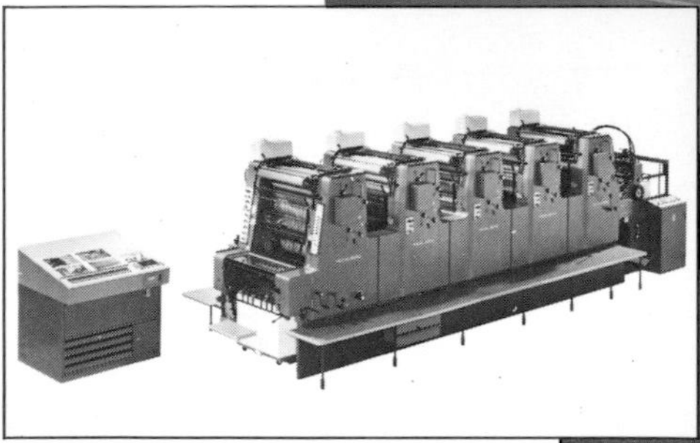

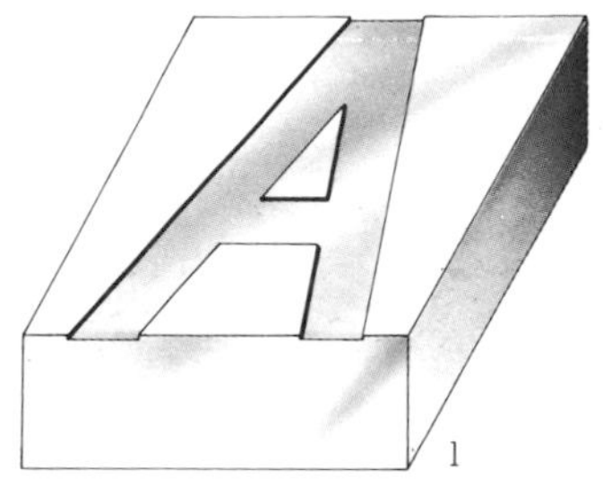

1

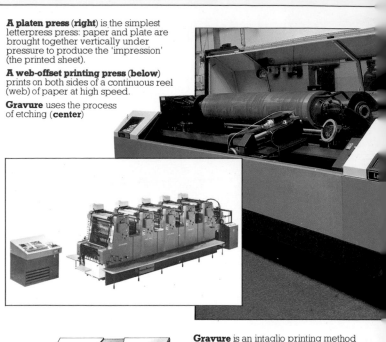

Gravure is an intaglio printing method and, as such, uses the process of etching to incise the image area into the plate (**1**). Ink is applied by a roller and a thin, flexible steel blade (a doctor blade) is drawn across the plate, removing the excess ink from the non-printing areas (**2**). The paper is then positioned over the plate (**3**) and pressed against it by a rubber-coated roller (**4**). The pressure forces the paper into the recesses of the plate so that it picks up the ink, thus forming the image. The finished print is then removed (**5**).

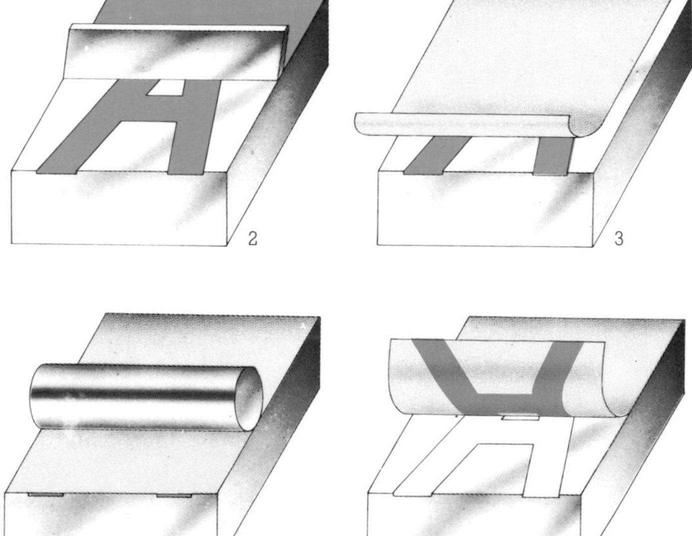

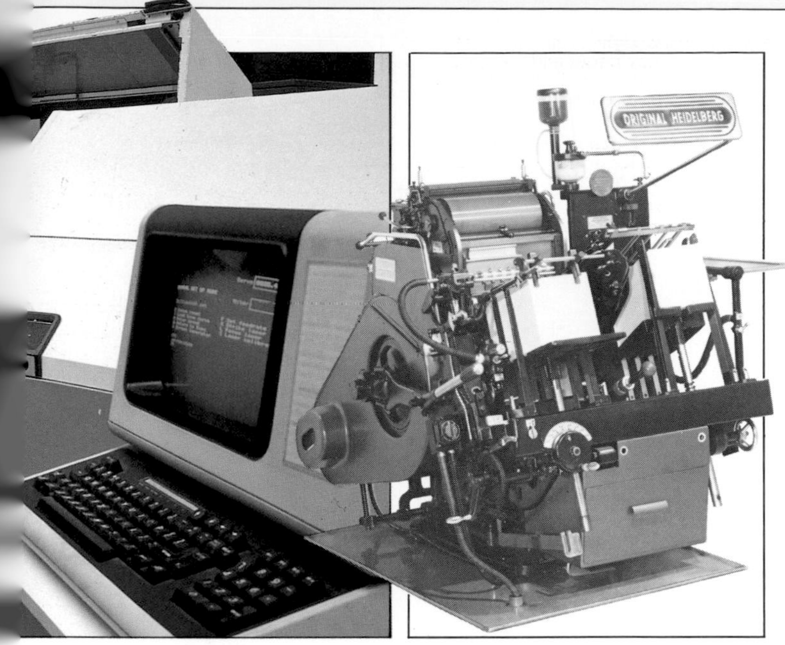

ones and are ideally suited to photographic typesetting and color separation techniques. Maintaining the correct ink/water balance has caused color variation difficulties in the past, but modern inks and electronic controls have largely overcome this problem.

Gravure The word 'gravure' refers to carving or cutting a surface. Thus, a gravure printing plate has the image cut or recessed into its surface rather than standing above it, as in a letterpress plate, or defined by physical and chemical interactions, as with a lithographic plate. The word 'intaglio', derived from the Italian word meaning 'to cut in', is also used to describe the principle of the gravure plate. The modern printing process using the gravure principle is really photogravure because the image is produced photographically rather than by hand.

The detailed image on a gravure plate is formed by a latticework of recesses, or 'cells', that hold droplets of thin, spirit-based ink. In conventional photogravure plates all the cells occupy the same surface area but vary in depth; the greater amount of ink in deeper cells produces a darker image on the paper. Variations on this basic approach include plates with cells of the same depth but variable surface area, and plates with cells that vary both in depth and surface area.

On a gravure press the plate (usually a cylinder) is inked and the excess ink scraped off by a flexible 'doctor blade' before the paper is pressed against it by a rubber-covered cylinder. The paper 'blots' the ink from the recesses to form the image. As you would expect, the printed result has a different texture from that produced by lithography or letterpress. Each individual 'dot' of ink spreads slightly, to produce smooth gradations of tone from light to dark areas. This is particularly effective for photographs, and many fine art books benefit from the finer screens and wide tonal values possible with gravure printing.

Gravure does, however, have its drawbacks. The major ones are the high cost of producing the plates or cylinders and the difficulty of making changes once the plates have been made. The printing surface usually consists of a layer of copper, electroplated onto a solid steel cylinder. The image can be transferred onto this either by a complex series of processes using a sensitized transfer medium, called a carbon tissue, followed by etching and washing or by means of electromechanical or laser engraving heads linked to a scanner that 'reads' the original image. Once formed, the printing surface may be chromium plated to improve its wearing qualities for long runs.

The advantage of the gravure process is its relative simplicity: the thin ink used dries almost instantly, there is no ink/water balance to adjust and a good result can be produced on even quite low-quality, absorbent papers. But in view of the high initial costs involved, gravure is really only suitable for high volume, standard format publications, such as national magazines and color supplements, with print runs in excess of 300,000 copies, although short runs of high-quality photographic books are often printed by sheet-fed gravure.

Finishing and binding

Folding Where an item has been produced on a web-fed press, the press will usually produce folded sections, of 16 or 32 pages, ready for binding, as web presses mostly include a folder. However, with sheet-fed presses, the sheet has to be folded after printing, on a separate folding machine. The flat sheets are fed in at one end and the machine folds and delivers the sections as 8, 16, or 32 page sections, depending on the imposition scheme used (see Imposition page 109-111). Most folding machines process 10,000 sheets an hour or more.

Normally, the sheet is folded so that the grain of the paper runs parallel to the spine of the end product, as this means that the pages will open more easily. However, sometimes the printer will want the grain running in the other direction to avoid paper stretch when printing.

Hardback (cased) bookbinding The process starts with folding and the sections are then gathered in the correct order. Before this, the endpapers (leaves of paper at the front and back of a book, half of which covers the inner sides of the board, securing the book to its cover (case), half forming the fly leaf) are glued onto the first and last sections. Where the paper is strong enough, 'self endpapers' are used. That is, the first page of the first section and last page of the last section act as endpapers and are glued down to the case.

If the book has plates in color or black-and-white, on a different paper to the text, these can either be incorporated as sections of 2, 4, 8, 16, 32 or 64 pages, or as 'wraps and inserts', which are four or more pages wrapped around or 2 or more pages inserted into a section. This is more expensive, but spreads the plates more evenly through the book.

The books are then sewn after gathering. The sewing machine inserts threads through the spine of each section, the thread joining the sections to each other to form the book block. The next operation is lining, where a strip of paper or linen is glued to the spine to help reinforce the joint when the case is attached. At this stage, head and tailbands (strips of plain or striped cloth glued to the top and bottom of the spine) can be applied. These do not really add any strength to the book, but look attractive and cover up the tops and bottoms of the sections. The book block can then be left with a flat spine (flat back or square back) or rounded and

Bookbinding methods will vary depending on the materials used and the nature of the job. The elements involved in the binding of a conventional jacketed hardback (**right**) are endpapers (**1**), headbands (**2**), dustjacket (**3**), spine (**4**), case (**5**), metallic foil stamping (**6**) and tailbands (**7**). This form of binding is known as cased binding: paperbacks are perfect bound, a preprinted cover being glued to the spine.

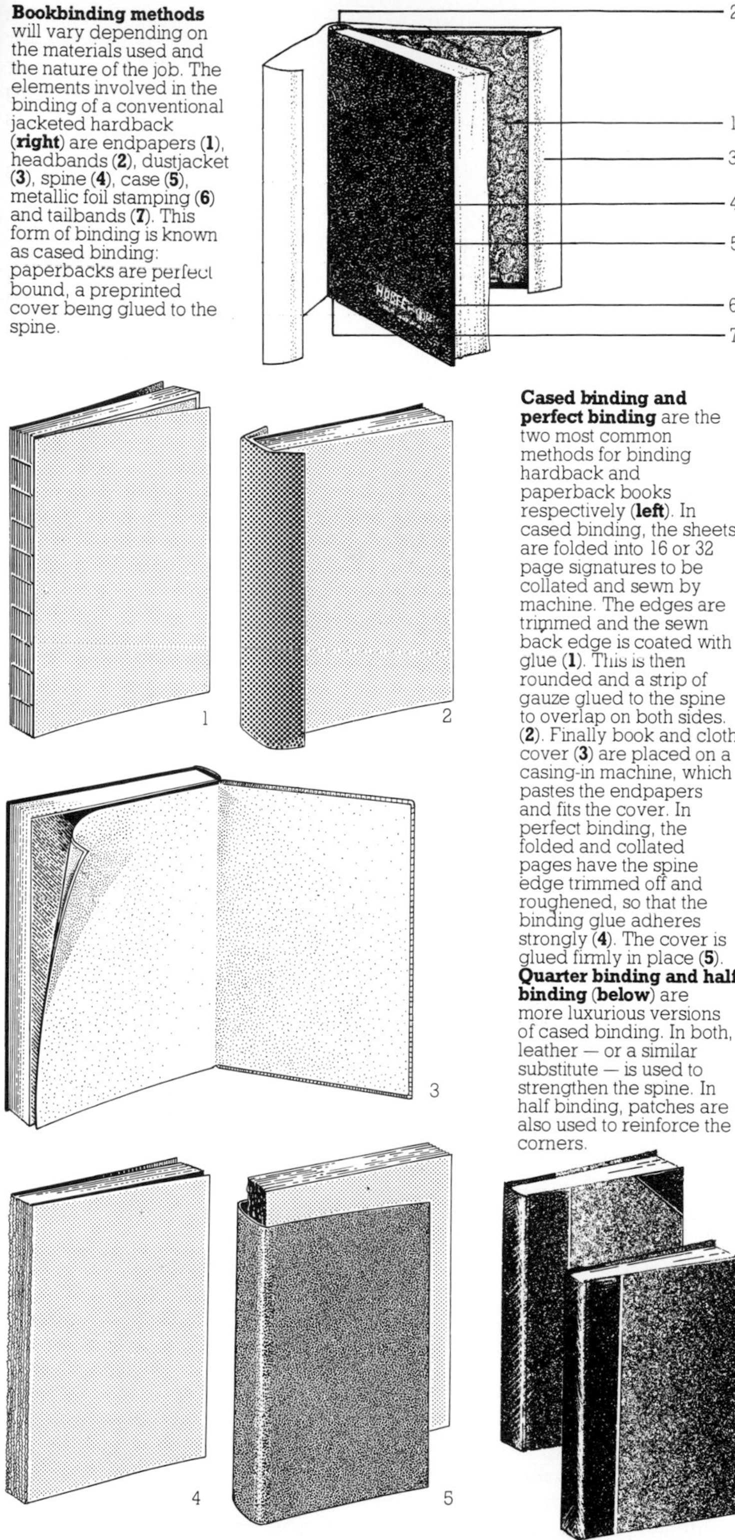

Cased binding and perfect binding are the two most common methods for binding hardback and paperback books respectively (**left**). In cased binding, the sheets are folded into 16 or 32 page signatures to be collated and sewn by machine. The edges are trimmed and the sewn back edge is coated with glue (**1**). This is then rounded and a strip of gauze glued to the spine to overlap on both sides. (**2**). Finally book and cloth cover (**3**) are placed on a casing-in machine, which pastes the endpapers and fits the cover. In perfect binding, the folded and collated pages have the spine edge trimmed off and roughened, so that the binding glue adheres strongly (**4**). The cover is glued firmly in place (**5**). **Quarter binding and half binding** (**below**) are more luxurious versions of cased binding. In both, leather — or a similar substitute — is used to strengthen the spine. In half binding, patches are also used to reinforce the corners.

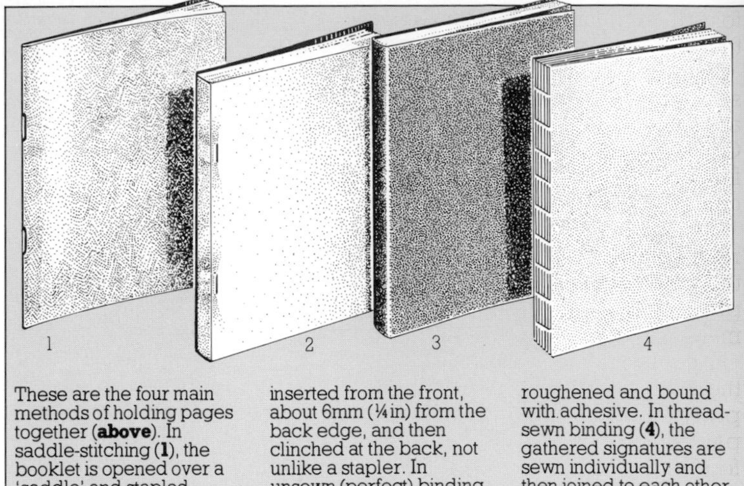

These are the four main methods of holding pages together (**above**). In saddle-stitching (**1**), the booklet is opened over a 'saddle' and stapled along the back fold. In side-stitching with wire (**2**), wire staples are inserted from the front, about 6mm (¼in) from the back edge, and then clinched at the back, not unlike a stapler. In unsewn (perfect) binding (**3**), the gathered signatures are trimmed along the back edge, roughened and bound with adhesive. In thread-sewn binding (**4**), the gathered signatures are sewn individually and then joined to each other by thread.

backed. The rounding and backing operation gives a firm grip to the sections and helps to prevent the middles of the sections dropping forward.

The book block is then cased-in, that is glued into the case and pressed to make it firm and flat. Jackets, if required, are then wrapped round the book and this can be done by hand or machine.

Although most hardback books are still sewn, an increasing number are unsewn or burst bound (see below), as the strength of these techniques improves. Another technique used is thread-sealing, where, instead of sewing, plastic threads are inserted through the spines of the sections to hold the pages together and then the book block is glued at the spine to hold the sections together.

Paperback book binding Most paperback books (and many magazines) are 'perfect' bound and this method is also described as unsewn binding. After folding, the folded sections are loaded onto a perfect binding line, which first collates and gathers the sections in the right order and then the machine slices off the back fold, removing about 3mm (0·118in), and grinds the spine to roughen it. The book block (which now consists of individual leaves) is then glued at the spine, both to hold the leaves together and attach the book block to the cover. The books are then trimmed to give a smooth edge all around and are ready for packing.

A variation of this technique is known as 'burst', or 'notch', binding. The spine of the section is perforated on the folding machine and the sections then go through a perfect binding machine but the spines are not removed. Instead, glue is forced into the perforations to hold the sections together. This is stronger than unsewn binding and cheaper than sewn.

Some paperbacks are sewn, and in a separate operation, the cover is glued to the spine and the books are trimmed.

Binding brochures and magazines A common method of binding brochures and magazines is wire-stitching, by saddle-stitching or side-stitching (also called stab-stitching). In saddle-stitching, the folded sections are positioned on a metal 'saddle' under a head that inserts wire staples through the spine.

Side-stitching is used for thicker publications and here the folded sections are gathered (collated together in order) and the staples are forced through the side about 3mm (0·118in) in from the spine. Obviously, this means that a side-stitched publication will not open flat easily and, therefore, the designer should allow a wider center margin to compensate for this.

Other magazines are bound by the perfect binding process. The result looks somewhat like side-stitching and the cover is glued to the body of the paper. A very attractive and neatly cut package is produced. This method is gaining popularity among quality magazines that used to use a side-stitching method.

For small-circulation magazines that do not contain many pages, the paper is initially delivered flat and unfolded from sheet-fed presses of the printer. The sheets are folded into eight- or sixteen-page signatures that are stitched and then trimmed. But many roll-fed web presses now have bindery folding equipment attached directly to them. They have the capabilities to use folders that fold the sheets after they have been slit by a rotary chopping blade. Using the roll method, it is possible to print on both sides of the roll at the same time, greatly speeding up the printing process.

All sheets, including the body, the cover, and inserts, are all gathered and collated together stitched, trimmed, and separated into piles of fixed amounts. For subscription mailing, the magazine circulation department can give the printer a roll of names that are alphabetized and arranged in regions so that these mailing stickers can be applied to the magazines on the binding line.

Spiral, wire-O and plastic comb binding These methods are used for manuals and short runs of publications, or where the ability of the item to lie flat is important, such as computer manuals.

In spiral binding, holes are cut through the cover and pages, which are then joined together with a wire or plastic coil. Wire-O binding is similar, but the 'fingers' of wire go through slots, as with plastic comb binding.

Casemaking and stamping

For hardback books, the cases are made separately on a casemaking machine. This machine wraps cloth or imitation cloth around the three pieces of board (front, spine and back) and glues it to make the case. Often the case is a plain color, but it can also be a design printed on white imitation cloth.

Stamping is the term used to describe the method of impressing the title and publisher's imprint on the spine and front of the case. A 'die' is made (very often from the jacket artwork) and it has the image area raised above the background, rather like a letterpress block. On the stamping machine, the die is heated and pressed through metallic or colored foil onto the case.

The publisher normally requests a specimen case and the editor and designer check it before all the cases are made.

5
PROMOTION, PUBLICITY AND PRESENTATION

Book jackets/Synopses and catalog copy/ Sales conferences and book fairs

Successfully completing one book or one issue of a magazine is not an end in itself. As an editor, you will be involved throughout the year in helping to prepare publicity and promotional material of all kinds. Here we look briefly at the range of tasks and experiences that may present themselves.

Book jackets

Your participation in preparing book jackets is usually restricted to writing the copy. Generally, this task applies to the following areas on the jacket:

1 Front If you have been using a working title up to the jacket design stage, now is the time to decide on the actual title. It can be very difficult to think of an original title for a book, say, on houseplants or any other well-covered subject. Most general, color-illustrated books display a subtitle, on the front cover to qualify or expand on the title. This gives more scope as the title can clarified with its meaning extended in the subtitle. It is always a good idea to prepare several combinations of main title and subtitle to show to your superiors or the sales department. If the book is one of a series, then the front cover will carry a

A book jacket can be broken down into clearly defined areas, each performing a different 'promotional' role (**right**). Writing copy ('blurbs') to fit these areas can be quite a taxing task, especially when the jacket is required well before the finished book.

Author blurb
Back
Back flap
ISBN number
Geoffrey Rogers began his editorial career in 1967 as an assistant editor, working on scientific and technical books. For the following 16 years he worked on a wide range of illustrated books for the international market. During that time he represented publishers at Frankfurt Book Fairs and became involved in all aspects of book publishing, from caption writing to commissioning authors.
print production
budgeting
scheduling
contracts
copy-editing
typesetting processes
proof-reading
computers and the editor
working with the designer
commissioning artwork
picture research
working on a layout
origination
checking proofs
publicity and presentation
glossary

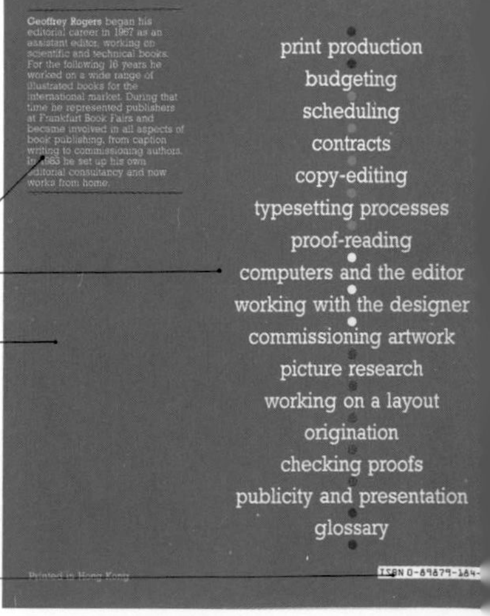

series title, a book title and an explanatory subtitle. Since the shortest descriptions are often the hardest to formulate, try writing the main blurb for the book first and distilling the essence of that for the subtitle. Do not forget the author's name on the front cover and optional things like the name of the publisher, 'As seen on TV' or the writer of the foreword if he or she is well-known.

2 Front flap This usually carries the main blurb describing the content of the book, which may continue onto the back flap. You may have phrased this information several different ways for synopses and catalog copy. The ideal approach is to encapsulate the subject and value of the book in the first paragraph and then describe exactly what the book contains in the following two or three paragraphs. Avoid exaggerated claims but certainly point out what sets this book apart from its various other competitors in the same subject area. Sound confident. The price of the book also often appears in the lower right-hand corner of the front flap along with the name of the photographer or artist who provided the cover illustration.

3 Spine The title of the book, sometimes the subtitle, the name of the author and the publisher's logo, or colophon, appear here.

4 Back Designs vary, but the back of the jacket usually carries some illustrations and/or photographs plus a 'mini' version of the blurb and an abbreviated specification with, for instance, the number of pages, wordage, number of illustrations in color. The back cover corroborates the message of the front flap more briefly. The mini-blurb can be the essence of the main one, perhaps using phrases you considered for the main blurb but put aside at the last moment. It is important that all the 'selling messages' carry the same angle and tone. An ISBN (International Standard Book Number) and sometimes a bar code also appear on the back.

5 Back flap Traditionally, the author blurb appears here. Rewrite this from the original the author sends at your request. Most authors are shy about describing themselves in the third person, so you will probably need to polish this a little. The back flap may also mention other books in the same series or closely related ones from the same publisher.

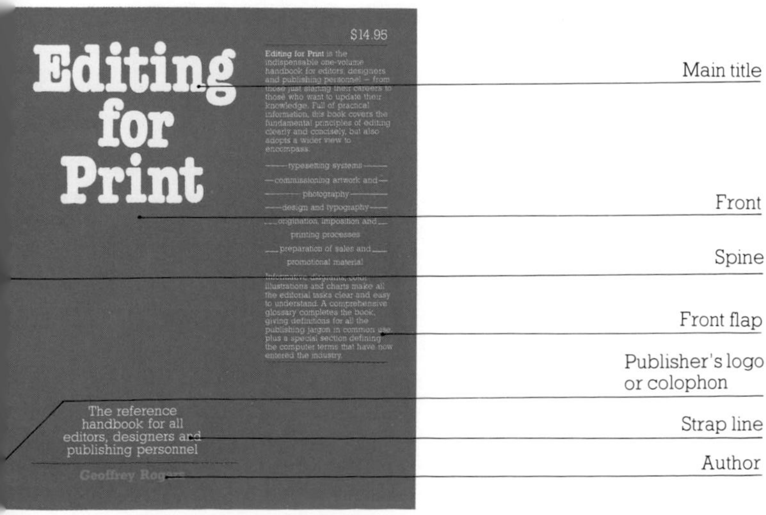

Magazine covers It is the front page of the magazine that entices people to buy even the most popular and well-known titles at news-stands. Even if yours is a direct-mail, controlled circulation title it is equally important as a means of encouraging your readers to pick up and read each issue. Consequently it is worth spending some time and effort (and often money) on its design and content.

On a trade publication with a very small budget for photographs or artwork a good choice will be the best quality press shot relevant to that issue or a company-sponsored photograph. For others there will be good commissioned or bought-in material already within the content of the magazine that can be used for the front cover. A single full page with perhaps a few insert shots is more effective than a hogepodge of images, but the exact layout will depend on the style of your magazine.

Naturally, specially commissioned shots are the ideal as clear or unpatterned areas can be left to accommodate the title, coverlines (a list of the main features) and flashes (a colored star, circle or other shape drawing attention to a special offer) without it looking confusing. Even more important perhaps than the cover pictures is the choice of words. They should provide a quickly assimilable summary of the magazine's contents, which should be clear to read and easy to understand. Bands of color containing each coverline may be needed to help them stand out, but aim for a contrast — black on white, yellow on black, for example, or red, always a highly efficient attention-grabber. Coverlines should be short and to the point, never too clever or obscure, picking out the most important features, such as competitions, interviews and so on. And always double-check that the date, price and issue number are correct as it is very easy to overlook seemingly obvious details.

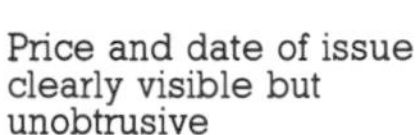

Price and date of issue clearly visible but unobtrusive

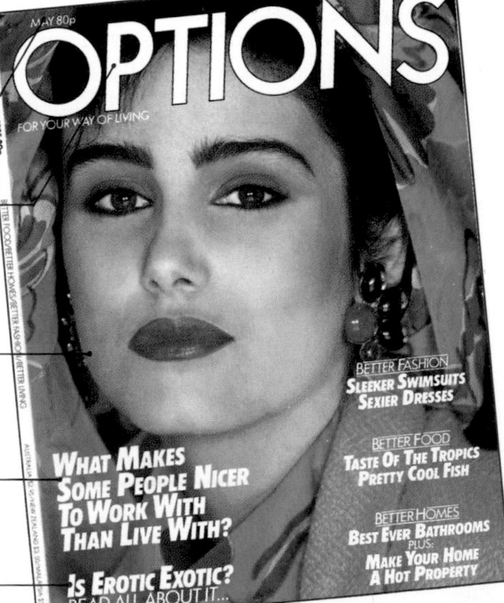

Regardless of the magazine's content, it is usually the strength of the front cover which will attact people initially. The choice of words should give readers a clear guide to the subjects covered, and perhaps some unanswered questions, and offers to encourage them to buy the magazine.

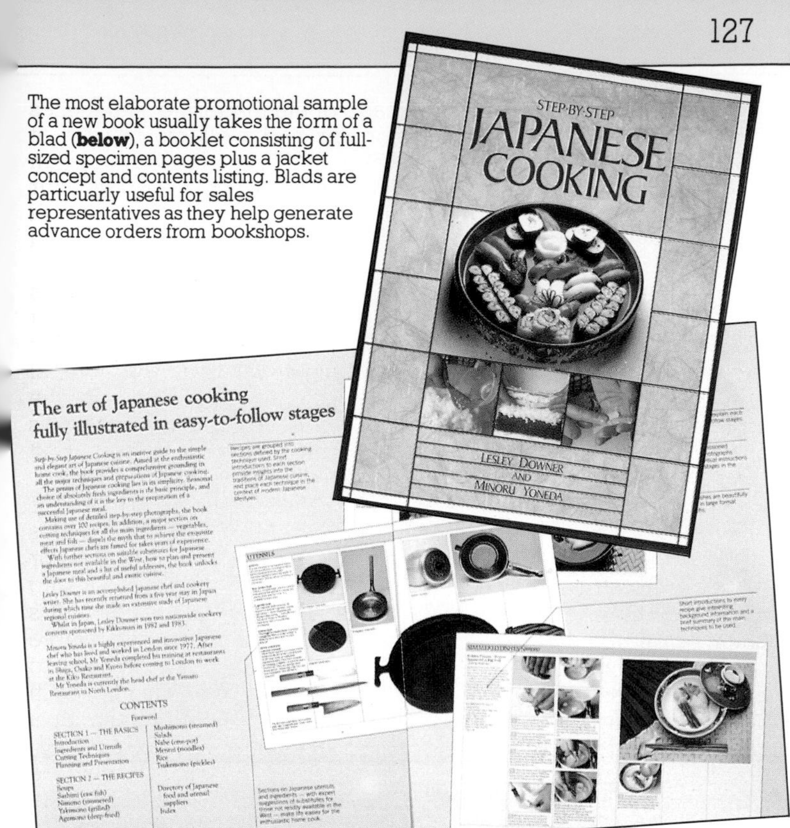

The most elaborate promotional sample of a new book usually takes the form of a blad (**below**), a booklet consisting of full-sized specimen pages plus a jacket concept and contents listing. Blads are particuarly useful for sales representatives as they help generate advance orders from bookshops.

Blads and sales presentation material

As you try hard to encapsulate the excellent qualities and special features of books in progress, you may also be asked to write similar descriptions of books that are still only ideas. Preparing blads (usually three- to eight-page booklets with sample pages from the planned book, complete with cover and contents) and other sales material can stretch your powers of imagination.

To make a blad or any effective sales presentation, real text is required. This means that you must either ask the author to prepare sample pages out of context or, if there is no author at this stage you may have to write the text yourself.

Real artwork illustrations and photographs are also necessary. The designer will commission the illustrations specifically for the presentation and hope to use them in the real book to recoup the money spent on them. It is usually possible to obtain suitable photographs from photo agencies and, if you do, ensure that a compromise fee is arranged if they will be used for sales purposes only. In a blad the illustrations and photographs are printed (usually on a proofing press). Other forms of presentation may use color prints to save the cost of separation and proofing. If time and money are short, it is possible to prepare presentation material using 'bodytype' or 'bodycopy' (dummy text, usually in Latin) and illustrations and photographs assembled to approximate the intended layout style.

Once prepared, such presentation material is used for a variety of promotional purposes, some of which are listed below.

- Sales people from the publishers show it at conferences to inform the sales representatives (not necessarily employed directly by the publishers) about forthcoming books.

- Sales representatives take it to bookstores to illustrate in a concrete way what is coming from the publisher and, hopefully, to gain advance orders.
- Foreign rights people take it to show prospective publishers in other countries.
- The foreign rights people plus some members of the management and editorial staff bring it to the international book fairs to gain orders and illustrate the kind of work the publishing company produces.

Synopses and catalog copy

To accompany the full color presentation material, you will need to prepare synopses and copy for the catalog. The synopses used for promoting future projects are very similar to those you request from authors, only with a little more sparkle about them. A typical 'selling' synopsis might have the following pages:

Title page: complete with blurb line.

Specification: proposed publication date, author's name, page size and extent, number of words and illustrations, plus printing and binding specifications.

Contents: a breakdown of what is in the book, usually headed by a paragraph to summarize its value and relevance.

Author and consultant biographies — with particular reference to their qualifications and experience.

Readership and sales points: who the book is aimed at and how it scores over the opposition.

To write catalog copy you can usually draw on the corpus of information you have built up for the synopses and jacket blurbs.

Sales copy for magazines With the editor as spokesman for the magazine and vital link between it and the rest of the industry, it is often necessary for him or her to provide advance information of the issue's contents for advertising and promotional purposes. This is one of the reasons why it is essential to finalize feature details as early as possible, saving you the work of circulating amendments and revisions.

Your advertising department will need a detailed breakdown of features, sometimes with a rough idea of any companies likely to be mentioned, so that they can sell the issue to potential advertisers as convincingly as possible. Companies themselves will often approach you at the beginning of the year for a features schedule so that they know in advance when to send the relevant press information, and there will be several press directories requesting the same kind of information. A more general breakdown, a sort of promotional summary of the issue, may be required well in advance by your distributors to persuade retailers to stock it in greater numbers; a similarly styled piece makes a good advertisement for the issue if it is placed in the previous magazine with a few carefully chosen photographs. If a particular issue is to be given television, radio or other media promotion, the advertising agency handling the campaign will also need a detailed and accurate breakdown of its best features as well as an advance copy of the front cover.

When writing any summary for promotional purposes, whether for the trade or to attract new readers, aim at a confident, enthusiastic style without being excessive, capturing the essence of the magazine as clearly and succinctly as possible.

There are many ways to circulate sales copy for the magazine in an attempt to promote subscriptions and boost single-copy sales. One popular method is to insert a brochure or reply card in a newspaper and pay the paper for use of the exposure. Cooperative mails involve many products other than the magazine alone combined in one advertising pull-out brochure.

At many college bookstores, the same brochures are distributed offering special discounts to students. Department stores often participate in solicitations for subscriptions through their charge account plans. The subscriber is billed directly on the charge account and the store receives a commission. Other times, an organization will lend its name to endorse a magazine and will receive a commission for each subscription. The endorsement is sent with other organization material through the mail. Telephone solicitation is also an expedient method and is used particularly for renewal of magazine subscriptions.

Another cooperative system used is for magazines to trade space to advertise each other. Additionally, many magazines advertise through wire photo services, gaining both extra revenue and exposure. Commonly the press wire services can even pick up a story for worldwide coverage, particluarly if it is a sensational feature story. There are also many industry newsletters and media magazines that promote each other in the trade.

Perhaps the three most effective ways of yielding subscriptions are through radio, television and the direct-mail campaigns. Radio advertising is extremely effective, especially if the magazine develops a jingle of some type that will create a memorable and pleasant impression in the listener's mind. Of late, there has been a great deal of television advertising for magazines, and some very convincing campaigns have been devised for promoting subscriptions. Being a visual and verbal medium, television can thoroughly arrest the potential subscriber's attention. An effective way of ensuring a high response is to use only a toll-free telephone number. People will not respond as quickly or as often if they have to take down an address. It is far more powerful to reach immediately into the home with a phone conversation. Also, the commercials for magazines are quite lengthy in comparison to others. The reason for this is that at least fifteen seconds must be spent on repeating the telephone number.

Once the television viewer calls in, he or she should not be discouraged by a lengthy billing and information-gathering service. The subscriber should be told that he or she will be billed later, and use of credit cards should be encouraged, perhaps coupled with the incentive of a free gift. For the bill-me-later format, it is best to send the issue fairly soon after the order has been placed so that reader curiosity is still high and the likelihood is greater that the subscriber will indeed pay for the subscription. Special issues, anniversary issues, and bonus issues should be mentioned in the commercial as additional enticement.

The direct-mail campaign is another viable way of raising circulation and subscriptions. Generally, the direct-mail package consists of five selling pieces. An external envelope will be attractively designed, usually with typography on the outside, inviting the reader to open it up and find the ultimate magazine description inside. The envelope will contain a letter from the publisher explaining the scope of the magazine and why it is right for upscale, discriminating people. A four-color brochure will show sample spreads, and a subscription form, and reply

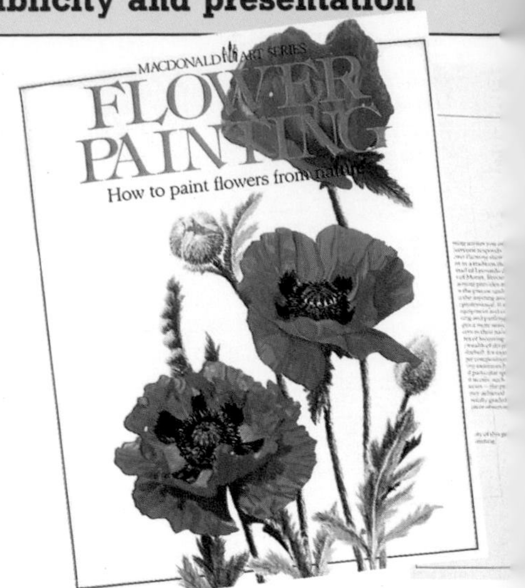

Book dummies are prepared to help sell the idea for a new book at book fairs, sales conferences or bookstores. Once the size, extent and bulk of the book have been chosen, a blank version can be used to make the dummy book. Designs for the jacket, title page and a few sample spreads are drawn up and then prepared in such a way that they look almost like the real thing. Headings and bodycopy (totally meaningless Latin text) are stuck down in the text or caption areas. If they are carefully made, book dummies will leave prospective clients eager to place their orders for the new title.

envelope will also be contained. Generally, a sample copy is promised for inspection as a charter subscriber. When starting a new magazine, it is best to send the direct-mail piece before the magazine is launched, because anticipation of the magazine will be at its peak. The mailing piece should reflect the quality and content of the magazine so as to avoid later cancellations. The brochure should have numerous photographs arranged in a memorable and appealing layout.

Another way to increase magazine awareness is for the advertising department to engineer a 'complimentary' copy campaign, whereby free copies are sent to prospects. The letter included will extol the magazine's effectiveness in selling their product. A magazine will often identify itself with a well-known product in its advertising campaign.

Still another method of attracting attention is to send useful items to potential advertisers bearing the name of the magazine. A magazine may sponsor a competition, associate itself with a cause, or offer its services by setting up a booth at a trade convention. Trade magazines should keep abreast of conventions of different manufacturers and industries since it is often possible to make many bids for advertising business at such events.

If a magazine wishes to redefine its image or assert a special quality, launching a campaign with a theme is an excellent approach. The campaign may be topical, using themes such as fitness and health, beauty, self-discovery, fashion awareness, or even politics. The campaign will often travel to department stores and public meeting halls, or hold open forums in association with youth, religious, and hobby groups.

Sales conferences and book fairs

Having helped to prepare promotional material, you may be asked to represent your company at a promotional event.

If you are to address a regional conference of sales representatives, bear in mind that over the two days such conferences usually run the representatives will be bombarded by an abundance of information that may begin to blur in their minds. Do whatever you can to make your remarks lively and memorable. Since each representative will have a copy of the

presentation material, your main purpose is to explain how the new book relates to existing ones on the market. You are providing them with their sales strategy for the bookstores.

The closest an editor usually gets to selling foreign rights is at the Frankfurt Book Fair — an annual fall gathering that attracts publishers from all over the world. Your role at Frankfurt, or any other international book fair, is to fill the gap between the presentation material and the real thing. Knowing something about the subject from your editorial research and/or previous work, you should be able to answer searching questions on the content and merit of the proposed book. A certain diplomatic skill and a little knowledge of Continental languages will help you.

Sales conferences for magazines As well as meeting press and company personnel on a regular basis, it is sometimes the editor's job to represent his or her magazine at distributor's sales conferences, publishing industry gatherings and even, if you work in a specialist field, phone-in and interview programs on radio and television. The exact nature of the occasion will determine your role and the level of expertise you will need to display. At a trade conference, for instance, you may be required to give a short speech or presentation on who you feel your magazine is aimed at and its future plans in relation to the rest of the industry. Such material can be prepared well in advance and even rehearsed if necessary. Think about who you will be addressing and gear your information accordingly.

Do not be too nervous about the prospect of a radio or television assignment. Program presenters and interviewers are experienced at making their guests feel at ease and covering up embarrassing pauses or mistakes — confidence only comes with practice. An interview may only take the form of a quick telephone call from a news program to ask your opinion on a current topic, but interviews can be prepared in many ways: live from the studio in between snatches of news or music, or pre-recorded for syndication to radio stations across the country. Live phone-ins can be a little more difficult, but if you know your subject there should be no problem as awkward callers are usually kept at bay and there are usually other experts on the program to help spread the load.

6
REPACKAGING PRINT

Repackaging books and magazines/Repackaging with computers

Repackaging the material in books ranges from using one or two photographs from one book in another to reshaping the entire structure of a book or books into a completely new format. Although reusing the odd photograph or illustration from an existing book hardly merits the title 'repackaging', it can be an effective way of saving time as well as money for new projects. Repackaging in a comprehensive way to create 'spin-offs' (see below) makes excellent economic sense and there is no reason why the derived publications should be any less worthy than the original ones.

Repackaging

Apart from the money-saving aspects of repackaging, the most important implications are creative and legal. From the purely creative angle, repackaging challenges you to be as innovative as possible within a restricted set of options. In some cases this can be more enjoyable than having no such restrictions. At least some decisions are made for you before you start. Common reasons for repackaging are:

- Deriving several small format guide-type books from one large format volume.
- Compiling one large format volume from several small format guide-type books.
- Distilling the essence of several books into a new one of similar proportions.
- Taking just one part of a book, say the purely practical section of a 'how-to' book, and making this into a book in its own right.
- Creating a slimmed-down version of a book to fit a lower price bracket and/or a different readership.

Many of these options involve a simple 'cut-and-paste' level of effort whereby you and your designers cut out the text and illustrations and rearrange them on a different layout grid. Naturally, to do this the text must be set to a width that will look at home in a variety of designs. You can crop photographs when moving from a large to a smaller format and either allow more white space or fit in more photographs per page when moving from a smaller to a larger format book. Since you will need to duplicate the color separations at some stage you can ask the separation house or printer to increase or decrease the size of the image within certain limits. This is especially useful when a photograph does not quite fit the new grid.

Preparing this creative 'jigsaw' may involve cutting and re-editing of the text, as well as writing additional text and captions to fit the new layout. Your typesetter should have films or bromides of the original text and should therefore be able to create a new text film from your rearranged layouts, adding in the new setting where necessary.

The legal aspects of repackaging involve the photographs. Unless your company owns the copyright of the photographs, you will need to pay an additional copyright fee for reusing them in a new book. Agreements vary, but you may pay from 50 to 100 per cent of the original fee again. If you pay exactly the same fee again, then you are saving money only on the cost of color separations, although duplication costs will be involved. Naturally, because of these charges, fully commissioned photographs that belong to your company are the first source for reuse, but be careful not to do this too often.

If your author's contract assigns the copyright of the text to your company, then you can recycle the words as you wish. Authors with different contracts must reach suitable agreements over repackaging. In most cases the copyright of the artwork illustrations belongs to the company that commissioned them.

Repackaging magazines Because a magazine's main strength lies in the fact that it provides current, up-to-date information, it is not easy to reuse material from back issues directly. Readers expect to see something fresh and new in both words and pictures and many will be regular subscribers with a large collection of back issues themselves. Yet certain subjects do come up with seasonal regularity and, while you may be using a new angle, the original information makes a useful reference and may simply need updating and rewriting. Standard 'how-to' and 'step-by-step' features can be repeated as they are with discretion, maybe using new artwork or a different format, but the words themselves can remain virtually unchanged.

Product features are obviously unusable since very soon after publication, models and prices are out of date. But one way magazine material can be reused to attract new readers is to alter it and make it into a 'special publication', an issue concentrating on one particular subject but drawing on several issues for relevant features that will not date. Often, general information features can be lifted complete with illustration, then supplemented with one or two items of new, currently relevant material. With high quality production, a new cover and a slightly higher cover price, old magazine material can be reused in this way for minimum cost and effort.

Another practical way to use recycled material is to bind it in a separate booklet and give it away with the magazine as a free gift: a beauty guide, a tips and hints booklet or decorating manual all can be gleaned from past features, amended and rewritten for a smaller format, using the same diagrams and illustrations.

In the same way, you may be approached by a book publisher interested in utilizing such material in a book concentrating on beauty, health, do-it-yourself or even fiction, and using the name of the magazine to promote it. Once you have compiled the relevant features from back issues, editing and cutting is generally handled by the publishing house's own editors. However, you may be called upon to go through it using your experience to pick up any discrepancies or repetition.

As with the recycling of magazine material into any new format, it is very important that you check who owns the copyright of both words and pictures. You may need permission and even have to pay a fee to reprint if you only hold first national publication rights — as is likely in the case of photographers for whom syndication of their photographs is an important aspect of their business.

Using the resources you have built up over a year or so of researching and studying topics for articles, it will not take too much time to compile alphabetical and subject-oriented lists of suppliers and manufacturers of goods and services. Again, consult your editorial research department for additional information and also consult the promotional research department to find out the things your readership would like to see in special issues.

The year-end wrap-up is a popular way of putting together existing material in an interesting and enlivened format. For retrospective and anthology issues, several articles written by a well-known writer can provide the proper cohesion.

You might also want to consider moving into a different medium with your magazine product. Some companies have put their magazines on cassettes or disks, sometimes combining the printed magazine in the package. The two formats of the magazine will serve to complement one another and will usually examine a particular topic. This method of packaging is predicted to be a popular and growing trend for the future. For those magazines devoted to education or carrying regular columns on education, the cassette/disk/magazine format can be used in the classroom. For magazines that cover hobbies, special techniques can be dictated on tape while the magazine acts as a visual guide. Further, a videocassette can replace both elements and act as a spin-off to the magazine.

Repackaging with computers If a book or magazine is successful, the publisher will often want to use the same material again — in new editions, new formats (for instance, paperback versions), or 'spin-offs'. Using material twice is clearly advantageous to the publisher: the cost is a fraction of that paid for the original material, and if he or she has been clever with the copyright agreements made with the authors, repackaging may cost almost nothing at all.

One of the most convenient things about word processing and computer typesetting is that the publisher is left not only with a printed record of the book or magazine in question, but a disk containing exactly the same information.

Until now, the practical organization required when reusing material in a printed work — 'rehashing' it — has been expensive and time-consuming. Printed works have been recorded on sheets of clear film, so any alterations mean cutting up the film and repositioning it, or typesetting passages and working them into the text (stripping them in). Clearly, no drastic revisions are possible without considerable expense. The typeface, size and measure must stay the same. And alterations are restricted to moving or adding manageable chunks of text.

If the work is recorded on disk, however, it is much easier. It is both cheap and easy to change the format — the typeface and size. All that needs to be done is for the original typesetting instructions to be deleted and for the new ones to be inserted and the computer can be used to reset the type. It is then cheap to produce new galleys, paste them up and photograph them to make new film. If there is a demand for a new edition of a book and it needs to be corrected and updated, it is equally simple to

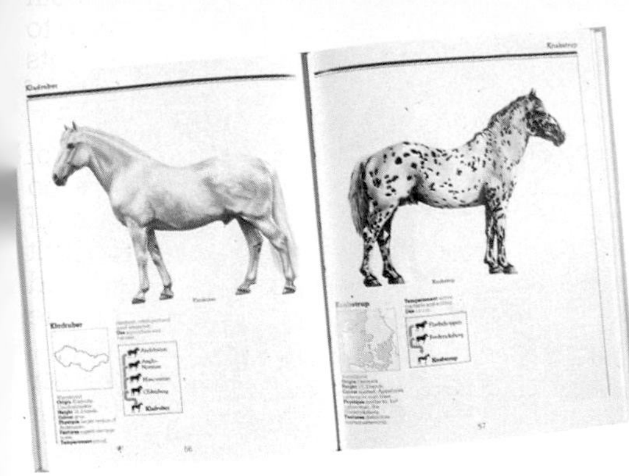

The repackaging of the book (**below**) to produce the smaller format book (**left**) illustrates one method of utilizing existing material in a creative way. The spin-off book uses a different typeface and grid, new illustrations have been commissioned and the contents have been arranged to provide a different angle on the subject.

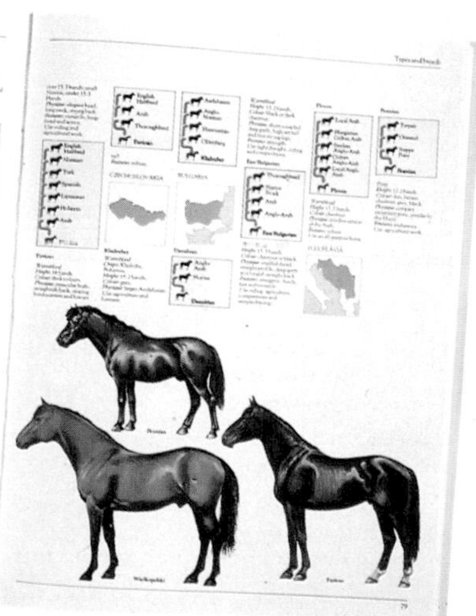

insert the alterations on the disk, and typeset them. Changes can then be dealt with, cheaply, page by page — so that, instead of the difficult business of stripping in, all that needs to be done is an ordinary paste-up of ordinary galleys.

This gives the editorial department a great deal more freedom. Instead of having to make piecemeal corrections, which often means having to perpetuate past mistakes or settle for a halfway solution, it can produce a really good — and effectively almost 'new' — work. And even routine matters, such as producing foreign editions become easier — there is even a program available to anglicize American words.

It is becoming increasingly possible for publishers to see their own existing published works as a store of information that can be transferred to other books quickly and easily. The implications are the most far-reaching in the field of reference books such as dictionaries. With a little forethought, the editor of a general dictionary, for instance, can code entries on different subjects. When the time comes for, say, a botanical dictionary, it can be produced in no time at all by asking the computer to select all the coded botanical entries from the general dictionary.

7 GLOSSARY

This glossary contains the terms most frequently encountered in day-to-day editorial work — but note that different houses and types of publishing tend to generate their own standard usages. Cross-references to other entries in the glossary are indicated by the use of SMALL CAPITALS.

A

Acknowledgment A statement expressing gratitude for contributions to a work by an organization or individual. Generally, but not always, distinguished from a CREDIT.

Addendum (**1**) Material supplementary to the main content of a book, printed separately at the beginning or end of the text. (**2**) An additional piece of copy, attached to a MANUSCRIPT page, and to be taken in where indicated on that page.

Advance An agreed prepayment to the author or other contributor, paid either before or at the time of publication, to be offset against future ROYALTY payments. Frequently, advances are paid in three stages: on signature of contract, on delivery of acceptable manuscript, and on publication.

Advance copies/advances Copies of a new publication made up in limited quantity for promotional purposes before delivery of the main PRINT RUN.

Afterword (**1**) Information on a work or its author added at the end of the main text. (**2**) A final concluding section by the author; an envoi.

Agent see LITERARY AGENT.

Alignment The arrangement of type or graphic material to level up at one horizontal or vertical line; in particular, the correct leveling of all the characters in a line of printed type.

Alphabet/alphabet length A measure derived from the length in POINTS of the 26 alphabet letters set in LOWER CASE; thus 39 characters have a measure of 1½ alphabets.

Alphanumeric set A full set of letters and figures, possibly including also punctuation marks and certain commonly used symbols.

Annotation (**1**) Explanatory notes printed in the MARGIN of a text. (**2**) A type-label added to an illustration. (**3**) Explanatory matter incorporated in an edition of an established work (eg, a Shakespeare play).

Anthology A collection of essays, stories and so on, which may or may not have appeared in print before, by a number of different authors or by the same author. (In the latter case, the term 'collection' is sometimes preferred.)

Appendix MATTER subordinate to the main text of a work and printed after it.

Artwork MATTER other than text prepared for reproduction, such as illustrations, diagrams, photographs and specially produced lettering for chapter headings, jackets, and so on.

As to press In the production of gravure-printed magazines, proofs showing final position of color material.

Ascender The section of a LOWER CASE letter rising above the X-HEIGHT, such as the upper part of a d or h.

Assembled negative Negative of line and HALFTONE copy used in preparing a printing plate for PHOTOLITHOGRAPHY.

Author's alterations (AAs'/author's corrections (ACs) Changes made by the author at PROOF stage other than those made necessary by typesetting or editorial errors.

B

Back The part of a book nearest the fold or edge at which the pages are bound.

Back jacket flap see FLAP.

Back lining A paper or fabric strip fixed to the back of a book before CASING IN.

Backlist The books, or a catalog thereof, which a publisher has produced in previous years and intends to keep in print for the foreseeable future, reprinting if and when necessary.

Back margin The MARGIN of a page nearest to the book's SPINE.

Back matter see END MATTER.

Back to back Printing on both sides of a SHEET. See BACK UP.

Back up To print the second side of a SHEET. 'Backed' refers to the sheet when it has been backed up.

Base artwork ARTWORK requiring the addition of other elements, such as HALFTONE positives, before reproduction.

Base film The basic material for contact film in platemaking for PHOTOMECHANICAL reproduction, onto which film positives are stripped.

Base line (**1**) An imaginary line on which

the bases of CAPITALS and LOWER CASE characters lacking DESCENDERS rest. (**2**) *(US)* The last line of space on a page containing type MATTER.
Bed The steel table of a printing press on which the FORM is placed for LETTERPRESS printing.
Biblio A page in the PRELIMS of a book (usually the TITLE VERSO) giving details of the publisher and publishing history of the book.
Bibliography List of publications providing reference material on a particular subject, usually that of the book, and often including the sources used by the author as well as suggested further reading. Generally included in the END MATTER of the book.
Binder A device designed to hold the collected issues of a magazine such that they may be read as if bound as a book.
Binding methods Methods of securing the leaves of a book, manuscript or brochure. See PERFECT BINDING, SADDLE-STITCH, SECTION-SEWN BOOK and SIDE-STITCHING.
Black printer The film that prints black in the COLOR SEPARATION process.
Blad Sample pages of a book produced in booklet form for promotional purposes. See also DUMMY
Blanket cylinder The cylinder of an OFFSET press that transfers the ink image to the paper.
Bleed The part of an image that extends beyond the TRIM MARKS on a page. Illustrations that spread to the edges of the paper allowing no MARGIN or margins, and one or more edges of which are therefore trimmed off after printing but before casing, are described as 'bled off'.
Block (**1**) HALFTONE or line illustrations engraved or etched into a zinc or copper plate for use in LETTERPRESS printing; also a proof thereof. (**2**) A metal stamp used to impress a design on a book COVER. (**3**) As a verb, to emboss a book cover.
Block in To sketch in the main areas and reference points of an image in preparation for a drawing or a design layout.
Blues/blueprints Low-quality PROOFS for initial or occasionally last-minute checking, appearing as if printed white REVERSED OUT of dark blue. See also OZALID.
Blurb The description of a book or author printed on the JACKET, in promotional material, in the PRELIMS or as an AFTERWORD (**1**).
Boards The stiff card in the CASE of a hardback book.
Body (**1**) The surface area and/or shank of a piece of TYPE. (**2**) The main portion of a book, excluding PRELIMS, APPENDICES, END MATTER, etc.
Body copy/matter/type (**1**) Printed MATTER forming the main part of a work, but not including HEADINGS, etc. (**2**) The actual type used in setting a text. (**3**) In the preparation of a DUMMY, the sections of PRINTER'S LATIN that are STRIPPED IN to give an impression of the final page appearance.
Body size POINT measurement of a body of type as cast.
Bold/bold face Type with a conspicuously heavy, black appearance; the keywords of this glossary are set in **bold**. It is based on the same design as MEDIUM-WEIGHT type in the same FONT.
Book block A book that has been FOLDED AND GATHERED and stitched, but not CASED IN.
Book club An organization that offers its members, either by mail-order or (in some countries) by door-to-door selling, books at reduced prices. The books concerned may be REPRINT editions or RUN-ON EDITIONS. Members must usually make a commitment such as to buy a certain number of books in the first year of membership.
Book proof IMPOSED PROOFS or PAGE PROOFS put together in book form.
Booklet A publication with more pages than a PAMPHLET but less than a book (usually no more than 24 pages long).
Box/box rule An item of type or other graphic MATTER ruled off on all four sides by a RULE or border, or otherwise segregated from the BODY-COPY — for example, by being overprinted with a pale TINT.
Box feature/story Information in a book presented separately from the RUNNING TEXT and illustrations and generally marked off in a BOX rule.
Brass A bookbinder's engraved plate used to BLOCK a book COVER.
Brief To instruct artists or authors, in general or in detail, as to what one wishes them to produce.
Brochure A PAMPHLET or other short publication with stitched page.
Bromide (**1**) A photographic print on bromide paper. (**2**) A PROOF from PHOTOCOMPOSITIOH made on paper rther than on film.
Budgeting ESTIMATING in advance the cost of a particular project, in terms of production costs illustration fees, author's payments, FREELANCE payments, etc. A budget can be in terms of the project as a whole or the UNIT COST.
Bulk (**1**) The thickness of the assembled pages of a book, generally excluding the COVERS; jacket designers and marketing people often use the term to include the covers. (**2**) The thickness of a SHEET of paper related to its area weight.
Bullet A large dot used to precede listed items or to add emphasis to particular parts of a text: ●. Compare with OPEN CIRCLE.
By-line The author's name appearing above or below an article.

C

© Copyright mark. See UNIVERSAL COPYRIGHT CONVENTION.
C type A photographic color print produced directly from a negative. The method of processing was developed by Kodak.
Camera-ready Adjective applied to ARTWORK, COPY or PASTE-UP that is ready to be photographed without alteration for reproduction.
Capital/cap The term for UPPER CASE letters, derived from the style of inscription at the head, or capital, of a Roman column.
Cap height/CH The POINT SIZE of the capital letters in a particular

FONT. Commonly quoted in millimeters for modern typesetting systems.
Caps and smalls Type set with most or all INITIALS in CAPITALS and other letters in SMALL CAPITALS rather than lower case.
Caption The descriptive MATTER printed above, beside or beneath an illustration, diagram, table, etc.
Carry forward/over See TAKE OVER.
Case (**1**) The stiff COVER of a book, comprising two BOARDS, a HOLLOW and a binding material. (**2**) In LETTERPRESS printing, a box with separate compartments in which pieces of type are kept (hence the expessions LOWER CASE and UPPER CASE).
Cased/case-bound Adjective describing a HARDCOVER BOOK.
Cash-flow The turnover of money in a business.
Casing in (**1**) The process of inserting a book in its CASE (**2**) and pasting it down.
Casting off (**1**) Calculating the space a MANUSCRIPT will occupy when typeset in a particular TYPEFACE. (**2**) Calculating within reasonable limits the number of words (or occasionally characters) in a given manuscript.
Catchline The temporary, identificatory heading at the top of a GALLEY PROOF.
Center fold/center spread The central SPREAD of a SECTION. Because the two facing pages are printed on the same side of a single sheet of paper, a single PLATE may be used to print both pages. Alternative terms are 'natural' and 'true double'.
Centered TYPE placed in the center of a sheet or TYPE MEASURE; MATTER with uneven lines (for example, poetry) may be 'visually centered', so that it looks as if it is centered when in fact most lines of it are not.
Centered dot A dot (for example, the decimal point) raised above rather than on the line, as in 3·6.
Chapter drop The level at which text begins underneath a chapter HEADING, or the number of lines allowed for both chapter heading and the space above and beneath it within the TYPE AREA.
Chapter opener see SECTION OPENER.
Character (**1**) An individual item cast in type, such as a letter, numeral, punctuation mark or, in typesetting, space between other characters. (**2**) A set of symbols in data processing that represents a figure, letter, etc.
Character count The number of CHARACTERS (**1**) in a piece of COPY.
Cromalin A fast proofing system in which powder is used instead of ink.
Cicero European unit used to measure the width, or TYPE MEASURE, of a line of type and the depth of a page. One Cicero = 4·511mm = 12 DIDOT POINTS = 12·835 POINTS.
CIF Commercial term denoting that a price-quote includes delivery (Carriage, Insurance and Freight).
Classified ad Unillustrated newspaper or magazine advertisement, sold by the line. Compare DISPLAY ADVERTISEMENT.
Clean proof A printer's or typesetter's PROOF relatively free from errors.
Close up Instruction to DELETE a space between characters or lines.
Cloth The binding material used in the CASE (**1**) of a HARDCOVER BOOK, traditionally cloth but nowadays almost always a synthetic textured paper.
Coated paper/surface paper A paper to whose surface a mineral coating has been applied after the body paper was made.
Co-edition A (usually) highly illustrated book assembled by one or more PUBLISHERS, or often by a PACKAGER, in such a way that parts or all of it may be produced in a single production run with only minor alterations (such as change of IMPRINT (**2**)) for the various different intended markets. Most often co-editions are produced in the form of finished books, but sometimes each participant publisher merely makes use of duplicate FILM produced by the project's initiator.
Cold composition/type Typewriting or any TYPESETTING technique in which molten metal is not used, such as PHOTOCOMPOSITION. Compare HOT METAL SETTING.
Collection see ANTHOLOGY.
Collotype A PHOTOMECHANICAL printing process suitable for fine-detail reproductions. Printing is from a raised gelatin film on a glass support, and gives CONTINUOUS TONE.
Colophon (**1**) Emblem identifying a printer or publisher appearing usually on the SPINE, TITLE PAGE and JACKET spine of a book; often called a 'logo'.
(**2**) Inscription at the beginning and/or end of a book giving title, printer's name and location, and printing date.
Color In typography, the light or heavy appearance of a particular TYPEFACE.
Color bar/code Standard set of bars on PROOFS in FOUR-COLOR PROCESSING, showing the strength and evenness of ink and the registration of the colors.
Color cast An excess of one color in a printed or PROOFED color subject; a picture that looks too red is said to have a 'red cast', etc.
Color correction Adjustment of color values during reproduction or on color PROOFS to obtain a correct image.
Color fall (**1**) The pattern of appearance of the color subjects in a book. (**2**) In books which are not printed in color throughout (FOUR BACKED ONE, for instance) the pattern of appearance of pages on which color illustrations may appear.
Color positives A set of SCREENED positive COLOR SEPARATIONS.
Color separation Division of colors of a CONTINUOUS TONE multicolored original into basic portions (usually CYAN, MAGENTA, yellow and black) by a process of photographic filtration. The portions are reproduced by separate PRINTERS.
Color transparency Positive photographic image reproduced in color on transparent film.
Column (**1**) The body of text on a single page of a book. (**2**) A section of a page divided vertically,

containing text or other MATTER (this page has three columns). (**3**) In tabulated work, a vertical section.

Column centimeter/ column inch Measure of space used to calculate the cost of DISPLAY ADVERTISEMENTS in a newspaper or periodical, equal to one COLUMN WIDTH by 1cm (or 1in) depth.

Column width The width in EMS, millimeters or other measure of a COLUMN (**1**) or (**2**).

Commercial art ARTWORK produced for commercial use, as distinct from fine art.

Commission To request an artist, author or FREELANCE to produce a particular piece of material, usually according to a BRIEF, for an agreed fee, hourly payment or ROYALTIES.

Compose To typeset copy.

Composition Type which has been set in a form ready for reproduction by LETTERPRESS printing or PHOTOLITHOGRAPHY.

Compositor/comp The person who sets type, whether by hand or by any other process. Also called a typesetter.

Condensed face TYPEFACE with an elongated, narrow appearance.

Contact print/contact Photographic print made by direct contact with an original POSITIVE (**1**) or NEGATIVE at same size.

Contact screen HALFTONE SCREEN made on a film base which has a graded DOT pattern. It is used in direct contact with a film or plate to obtain a halftone NEGATIVE from a CONTINUOUS TONE original. This provides better definition than a conventional glass screen.

Contents A page of a book, usually in the PRELIMS, listing the chapters or articles in it.

Continuous tone Photographs or colored originals in which there are continuous shades between the lightest and the darkest tones, without being broken up by DOTS

Contract A signed document between two parties specifying the precise terms and conditions under which they will trade in a particular case or in a general sense; especially the agreement between an author and a publisher specifying, on the author's part, proposed length of typescript, delivery date, etc, and, on the publisher's, details of ADVANCE, ROYALTIES, etc.

Contributor Someone who has contributed copy or illustrations (usually original rather than previously printed work) to an ANTHOLOGY, periodical or multi-author work.

Copy MATTER to be typeset.

Copy/content editing Preparing material for press in terms of consistency, HOUSE STYLE, but also including such functions as grammatical correction, altering the text to enhance readability, inserting subheadings and, in periodical publications, adjusting type sizes and style and amending COPY to fit specific spaces. Both copy-editing and EDITING however, are variously defined in the workplace.

Copy-fitting (**1**) See CASTING OFF (**1**). (**2**) Making a piece of COPY fit into an allocated space, either by editing or by typographical means.

Copy preparation (**1**) The processes of COPY-EDITING and EDITING. (**2**) Marking up COPY with instructions for the typesetter.

Copyright see UNIVERSAL COPYRIGHT CONVENTION.

Copywriting Writing COPY for use in advertisements or BLURBS.

Corrigendum/ corrigenda A note (or notes) inserted in a publication after printing, or sometimes printed in the PRELIMS or ENDMATTER of a subsequent printing, to correct an item or items in the text.

Cover (**1**) The paper, board, cloth or leather to which the body of a book is secured by glue and thread. (**2**) The JACKET.

Credit/courtesy line A line of text accompanying an illustration, table or other quoted material giving the name of the organization or individual that supplied the artwork or granted the permission to quote.

Crop (**1**) To specify that part or parts of an illustration not to be reproduced. (**2**) The part of an illustration that is discarded after it has been trimmed.

Crosshead Subsection, paragraph HEADING or numeral printed in the BODY (**2**) of the text, usually marking a subdivision of a chapter. Compare SUBHEAD.

Cross-reference Instruction to the reader to refer to another part of the text for related information.

Cutting Reducing text by excision or condensation in order that it will fit a given space.

Cut-out (**1**) A HALFTONE that has been CROPPED (**1**) such that the background has been removed, leaving only the main subject. (**2**) A shape cut out of paper stock with a steel DIE, for example in the cover of a PAPERBACK book to expose copy on the TITLE PAGE beneath.

Cuts and fills/makes and saves Bits of copy removed or inserted after page design stage in order that the MATTER will fit the design precisely (eg, without short COLUMNS).

Cyan Shade of blue used in FOUR-COLOR PROCESSING. See PRIMARY COLORS.

Cylinder press Printing press in which the FORM is carried on a flat BED under a paper-bearing cylinder for an IMPRESSION (**2**) to be made at the point of contact.

D

Deluxe edition (**1**) An edition produced of an existing work with additional illustrations, more luxurious binding, etc. (**2**) An additional run of copies produced at the same time as the original edition but on better paper, with more luxurious binding, etc, and often given the status of a LIMITED EDITION.

Dead matter (**1**) Leftover MATTER that is not used.

Deadline The date by which a particular job must be finished. (**2**) Manuscript that has been typeset and from which proof-reading corrections have been made.

Deep-etch halftone A HALFTONE plate with unwanted screen dots removed, leaving areas of plain paper on the printed sheet, in order to

produce, for example, a CUT-OUT (**1**).
Delete Take out.
Descender The part of a LOWER CASE letter such as a 'y' that falls below the X-HEIGHT.
Detail paper/layout paper Thin, translucent paper with a hard surface used for LAYOUTS and sketches.
Dewey decimal classification Classification system used in libraries, devised by Melvil Dewey (1851-1931). Knowledge is divided into 10 main numbered areas, each of these is subdivided 10 times, and so on, so that the exact subject of a non-fiction book can be specified numerically very precisely, while the book is located on the shelves near to books on related subjects.
Didot point Continental unit for type, measuring 0·0148in (0·37592mm) and thus slightly larger than the UK/US POINT.
Die An INTAGLIO engraved stamp used for impressing a design.
Die cutting Cutting paper, card or board to a particular design using a metal DIE.
Digital typesetting Typesetting in which the characters are broken down into dots which are set so close together that the 'dottiness' is invisible to the reader, and so that FILLING IN reduces yet further any possible particulate appearance.
Diphthong (**1**) A pair of vowels pronounced as one vowel sound, as in 'Caesar'. (**2**) A LIGATURE.
Direct cost The cost incurred directly from a project, excluding normal business overheads.
Direct/directional Term such as 'far left' or 'above' in a compound CAPTION to direct the reader to the relevant picture.
Dirty proof A PROOF requiring heavy correction, or one that has received heavy correction and amendment.
Display advertisement Advertising material designed to a size or quality to attract immediate attention.
Display matter/type Larger TYPEFACES designed for HEADINGS, etc.
Dot Smallest basic element of a HALFTONE.
Dot area The pattern of a HALFTONE; ie, both the DOTS and the spaces in between.
Dot etching A way of reducing the size of the DOTS in a HALFTONE by chemical action in processing to alter the tonal values of an image.
Dot-for-dot reproduction A way of reproducing a previously screened image, in which the collection of DOTS, rather than the overall image, is reproduced. A maximum enlargement or reduction of about 10 percent can be achieved.
Dot gain An aberration in the making of HALFTONE film or plates whereby the DOTS become slightly, and undesirably, enlarged. A dot gain scale is often included in PROOFS to check for this.
Dot loss The devaluation or disappearance of a DOT on a HALFTONE printing plate.
Double page spread see SPREAD.
Draft A preliminary version of COPY or an illustration, later to be refined to produce the 'final draft'.
Drop The number of lines of text in a COLUMN as allowed on the GRID.
Drop cap/dropped cap A large initial at the beginning of a section of text that drops into the lines of type below.
Dummy The prototype of a proposed book, produced in the correct format and with the correct paper, but with blank pages, or with some pages to which illustrations and BODY TYPE (**3**) have been affixed, or containing only a repeated SIGNATURE of printed material (this is a repeated BLAD).
Duotone/duplex halftone Illustration process using two colors to produce the effect of one. Two NEGATIVES are made from a MONOCHROME original, one for the darker shade with the greater detail, the other for the lighter flat tint. The resulting image has a greater depth and weight than a standard HALFTONE reproduction.
Dust jacket see JACKET.
Dyeline/diazo/diazonium A method of reproduction in limited quantities from a transparent or translucent original on paper, cloth or film. The image is exposed to a light-sensitive coating of diazo salts and dyestuffs and the print may be blue, black or another color.

E

Editing (**1**) Overseeing and controlling the contents of a periodical.
(**2**) Overseeing, controlling and commissioning the contents of a book publisher's list.
(**3**) Working in conjunction with an author or authors to produce the desired final manuscript.
(**4**) Preparing copy for press — see COPY-EDITING.
(**5**) Overseeing, controlling and commissioning the illustrative contents of a book, periodical, etc, (picture or art editing).
(**6**) Compiling an ANTHOLOGY, the papers from a symposium, etc.
Edition (**1**) The copies of a work printed and issued at one time. (**2**) A term used to differentiate two forms of a book which may or may not have been issued at the same time, as in 'paperback edition', 'UK edition', DELUXE EDITION and LIMITED EDITION. (**3**) A term used as in 'second edition' to indicate that the work is a revision rather than a straight REPRINT. (**4**) A version of a standard work (eg, a Shakespeare play) which has involved the matching and reconciliation of different versions, ANNOTATION (**3**), etc. (**5**) A reprinted set of books in a uniform format.
Editorial work That work involved in the production of published material that is concerned primarily with the words (although the term is occasionally extended to include PICTURE RESEARCH, EDITING (**5**), and other matters to do with illustrations such as CAPTION-writing). Functions can include COMMISSIONING, COPY-EDITING, EDITING, compilation of INDEXES, PROOF-READING, writing of BLURBS, etc.
Ellipsis A sequence of dots, usually three (. . .), indicating that part of a piece of quoted matter has been omitted.

Elliptical dot screen A HALFTONE SCREEN with a gradated DOT pattern that includes elliptical dots forming middle tones.
Em Unit of typographical and linear measurement: a pica em is 12 POINTS, 4·215mm or 0·166in (approximately.)
Em quad A space in the type equivalent to the square of the type size.
Em rule/dash A dash, one EM in length, used in punctuating text.
Embossing RELIEF PRINTING or stamping in which DIES are used to raise letters above the surface of paper, cloth, leather or board.
Emulsion The light-sensitive coating of a photographic material.
Emulsion-down In making a printing plate, the direct contact of film with EMULSION side down on the plate. If the emulsion is uppermost the image formed is slightly haloed due to the thickness of the film.
En A measurement used in CASTING OFF (**1**) equivalent to half an EM.
En quad A space in type the square of half the width of an EM QUAD.
En rule/dash A dash about half as long as an EM RULE/DASH.
End even Instruction to a typesetter to end a section of COPY with a full line.
End matter Parts of a book following the main BODY (**2**) of the text; see APPENDIX, BIBLIOGRAPHY, INDEX, GLOSSARY.
End-of-line decisions Decisions made by a COMPOSITOR or typesetter as to JUSTIFICATION of type and WORD BREAKS at the end of a line. In computer TYPESETTING this function may be included in the program.
Endpapers The leaves of paper at the front and end of a book which cover the inner sides of the boards, securing the book to its CASE.
Engraving (**1**) The design or lettering etched on a plate or block. (**2**) The print taken from such a plate.
Erratum An author's or typesetter's error discovered after the book has been printed, often acknowledged in an erratum slip TIPPED IN to copies of the book.
Estimate Precise or rough ('guesstimate') calculation of the cost of work on a production order, based on current prices and allowing for inflation.
Etching (**1**) Metal plate treated with acid and with certain parts protected by the application of a 'ground' (a thin coating made from pitch, gum-mastic, asphaltum and beeswax, or synthetic substitutes). (**2**) A print taken from such a plate.
Even smalls SMALL CAPITALS used with an initial CAPITAL. Compare CAPS AND SMALLS.
Exception dictionary A list of WORD BREAKS that are exceptions to the standard guidelines, stored in a computer used in PHOTO-COMPOSITION.
Expanded/extended type Type with a flattened, rectangular appearance.

F

Face (**1**) The printing surface of a CHARACTER (**1**). (**2**) An overall expression for a family of TYPEFACES that share distinctive characteristics but which may be BOLD, CONDENSED, EXPANDED, ITALIC, etc. (**3**) Short for TYPEFACE.
Fat face A TYPEFACE with extreme contrasts in the widths of thin and thick strokes.
Feature Usually a non fictional piece in a magazine which is not part of a series.
Figure number The reference number given to an illustration or, in academic books, occasionally to a table.
Figure title The title given to an illustration, as distinct from a descriptive CAPTION.
Filler An extra illustration or piece of COPY put into the text to fill space in a page or COLUMN.
Filling in/up The filling by ink of the spaces between halftone DOTS or the counters (interiors, such as the central space of an 'o') of type to produce small areas of solid tone. Usually undesirable, filling in is on occasion put to use, as in DIGITAL TYPESETTING.
Film (**1**) Transparent plastic material, usually cellulose acetate. (**2**) Such material coated with light-sensitive EMULSION for photographic recording of an image.
Film assembly FILM NEGATIVES or FILM POSITIVES (**1**) assembled in correct positions to make plates for PHOTOLITHOGRAPHY.
Film negative A photographic image on film in which the highlights and shadows are reversed; also used extensively in reprographic printing (techniques of copying printed material).
Film positive (**1**) A black image on a background of transparent or translucent FILM. (**2**) A POSITIVE image on a film base made as a contact print from stripped NEGATIVES. It is used as a MASK in INTAGLIO platemaking.
Filmsetting see PHOTO-COMPOSITION.
Final draft see DRAFT.
Fine rule A RULE of virtually hairline thickness. Compare HAIRLINE RULE.
Finished artwork ARTWORK that is ready for press.
Finished rough see PRESENTATION VISUAL.
Finishing (**1**) Putting a surface on paper during manufacture. (**2**) Inking over or otherwise 'finishing' ARTWORK prepared by another artist.
Fit The ALIGNMENT and registration of individual images within a page.
Fixed costs Those costs of a project (such as typesetting) which remain the same no matter how many copies are printed; compare RUNNING COSTS.
Fixed word spacing A method of typesetting employing a standard size for spaces between words, leaving lines UNJUSTIFIED.
Flap That part of the JACKET of a HARDCOVER book that is folded so as to lie between the ENDPAPERS at front and back. Usually the front flap carries the BLURB and the back flap an author blurb and/or advertisements for other related books from the same publisher.
Flat artwork CAMERA-READY artwork.
Flat plan (**1**) A diagrammatic plan of the pages of a book used to establish the distribution of color, chapter lengths, etc (also known as a story-board or flow chart.) (**2**) A diagram or chart showing the

sequence of events involved in a process or activity. (Also known as a flow chart).
Flat fee A negotiated fee whereby an author, illustrator or FREELANCE receives a set fee for a job of work, rather than ROYALTIES or any other form of graduated payment.
Flat sheets SHEETS printed but as yet unfolded.
Flat-tint halftone A HALFTONE printed over a background of flat color.
Flop A photomechanical image that has been deliberately or accidentally REVERSED LEFT TO RIGHT.
Flow chart see FLAT PLAN.
Flush COPY aligned at left (flush left) or right (flush right) MARGINS.
FOB Commercial term denoting that a quoted price does not include delivery costs (Free On Board).
Foil (**1**) Extremely thin flexible metal sheet, can be applied as decoration to a blocked or embossed design. (**2**) The large sheets of film on which the printer mounts the imposed film.
Folded and gathered sheets/F and Gs SHEETS that have been folded and collated but not finally trimmed or sewn, sent to the PUBLISHER for approval of printing before binding begins.
Foldout An extension to the LEAF of a book, making it wider than the standard page width so that it must be folded back onto the page.
Foliation The practice of numbering the leaves (ie, alternate pages) of a book, rather than each page.
Folio (**1**) The book size formed when a SHEET is folded making the pages half the size of the sheet. (**2**) A LEAF of paper numbered only on the front. (**3**) A page number and the RUNNING HEAD of a page. (**4**) A MANUSCRIPT page.
Follow copy Instruction to the COMPOSITOR/ typesetter to follow the spelling and punctuation of the COPY supplied, even if unorthodox or apparently inconsistent, rather than the HOUSE STYLE.
Follow on see RUN ON.
Fount/font (**1**) A complete supply of a typeface. (**2**) A TYPEFACE in one style only — for example, BOLD rather than ROMAN.
Foot (**1**) The MARGIN at the bottom of a page (FOOT MARGIN) or the bottom edge of a book. (**2**) The part of a letter that rests on the BASE LINE.
Foot margin The MARGIN at the bottom of the page in a publication.
Footnotes Short explanatory notes, ancillary to the main text, printed at the foot of a page or table, or gathered at the end of a chapter or the book. Compare SIDENOTES.
Foreedge The outer edge of a book parallel to the back.
Foreedge margin The outer-side MARGIN of a page in a publication.
Foreword Introductory remarks, usually by someone other than the author, concerning a book or its author. Compare PREFACE.
Format (**1**) The general appearance or style of a book. (**2**) The size of a page expressed in terms of its depth and height (in the UK height and depth), in inches or millimeters.
Form Type matter and blocks assembled into pages and locked up in a chase (metal frame) ready for LETTERPRESS printing.
Forwarding The binding of a book after sewing but before CASING IN.
Four backed one/color one side In illustrated books that are not printed in full-color throughout, a technique whereby some or all sections are printed in four-color on one side and only one (usually black) on the other, thereby creating the illusion in the final book that it has been printed in color throughout.
Four-color process A method of printing in full color by COLOR SEPARATION, producing four PRINTERS.
Freelance A general term for someone who is self-employed but who sells his or her editorial, design, etc, services on an hourly or other basis to a publisher; analogously, a journalist who is not employed by any one periodical but who sells articles to various periodicals.
Front jacket flap see FLAP.
Front matter The PRELIMS.
Frontispiece An illustration facing the TITLE PAGE.
Full binding A binding in which the outsides of the BOARDS are completely covered with cloth or leather. Compare HALF-BOUND.
Full measure Instruction to the typesetter to make the lines start at the MARGIN; ie, not to INDENT.

G

g/m²/gsm/grams per square meter A unit of weight measurement for paper used in printing.
Galley proof A PROOF taken from the 'galley' (the long shallow metal tray used by compositors to hold type after it has been set) before the COPY has been divided into pages; in modern terms, a proof taken before the division of the copy into pages.
Gathering Placing the SECTIONS of a book in the correct order for binding.
Ghosting/ghostwriting Writing a book in conjunction with someone else (usually a celebrity) as if it had been written entirely by that other person.
Gilt edges/top The edges or top of a book covered with gold leaf, which is rubbed down to prevent the absorption of dust.
Glossary List giving definitions of terms related to a particular subject.
Gold blocking The combination of blocking (see BLOCK (**2**)) and the application of gold leaf or FOIL.
Gravure see PHOTOGRAVURE.
Grid A measuring guide in the form of flat layout sheets used by designers to help ensure consistency. The grid shows type widths, column widths, picture areas, trim sizes, etc.
Gutter (**1**) The space made up of the FOREDGES of pages plus the trim.
(**2**) Commonly but incorrectly, the channel of space down the center of a SPREAD.
Gutter bleed An image allowed to extend unbroken across the central MARGINS of a SPREAD.

H

H&J/H/J Hyphenation

and Justification. See also END-OF-LINE DECISIONS.
Hairline rule The thinnest rule it is possible to print, rather thinner than a FINE RULE.
Half-bound Describes a book with its back and corners bound in one material, the sides in another.
Half-title (**1**) The title of a book as printed on the RECTO preceding the TITLE PAGE. (**2**) The page on which the half-title appears.
Half up ARTWORK completed to a size 50 percent greater than that at which it is to be reproduced.
Halftone Process by which CONTINUOUS TONE is simulated by a pattern of DOTS of varying sizes. A halftone BLOCK is a zinc or copper plate prepared by this process.
Halftone screen A sheet of glass or film bearing a network of lines ruled at right angles. The screen is used to translate the subject of a HALFTONE illustration into DOTS. See also SCREEN.
Hand press Printing press in which the plate is inked and the paper fed and removed by hand.
Handsetting TYPESETTING which is carried out manually by a COMPOSITOR rather than by any mechanical process; almost exclusively LETTERPRESS.
Hanging indent Form of typesetting in which the initial line of each paragraph is set FULL MEASURE and the remaining lines are INDENTED.
Hanging punctuation Punctuation marks allowed to fall outside the TYPE MEASURE of a piece of text.
Hard dot A halftone DOT in the second or third stage of processing, with good density and sharpness.
Hardcover book A CASED book with a stiff BOARD cover. Compare PAPERBACK.
Head The MARGIN at the top of a page.
Head- and tailbands Cotton or silk cords sewn to the back of a book at top (headbands) or bottom (tailbands) to cover up the ends of the sections.
Heading The title introducing a chapter or subdivision of the COPY. It is set in a style or size of type to distinguish it from the text and from other superior or inferior headings.
Headline (**1**) In newspapers and magazines, the main heading of a piece. (**2**) The title of a book as printed at the top of every page of text; compare RUNNING HEAD.
Head margin see HEAD.
Heavy Alternative term for BOLD.
Holding fees Fees charged by suppliers (especially picture libraries) for material borrowed by publishers or others and not returned within a set period.
Hot metal setting TYPESETTING that involves each character to be used being cast in molten metal.
House corrections (**HCs**) Alterations to PROOFS or manuscript made by the publisher or typesetter, as distinct from those made by the author. Compare AUTHORS' ALTERATIONS (AAs).
House style (**1**) The style of spelling, punctuation and spacing used in a printing or publishing house to ensure consistent treatment of COPY in preparation for or during typesetting. (**2**) Elements of design by which a company establishes a consistent and recognizable identity — for example, with a COLOPHON (**1**). (Also called 'corporate identity'.)

I

Illustration (**1**) A drawing, painting, diagram or photograph reproduced in a publication to explain or supplement the text. (**2**) A drawn image, as distinct from a photographic one.
Image area Amount of space given to a particular image in design and printing, assumed to be square or rectangular even if the image is not.
Impose To arrange pages of type so that when the SHEET is printed and folded the text will read continuously. The way in which the sheet is to be folded determines the exact arrangement of the pages, or imposition.
Imposed proof The PROOF from a FORM.
Impression (**1**) All copies of a book printed at the one time from the same type or plates. Compare EDITION, REPRINT. (**2**) The pressure applied to a frame of type by the cylinder or platen. (**3**) From (**2**), the printed image.
Imprimatur Latin for 'let it be printed'; a statement to show that permission to print a work has been given by the appropriate authority (eg, the Vatican).
Imprint (**1**) The name of the printer and the place of printing, required by law in many countries if the paper or book is meant to be published. (**2**) The name of the publisher with place and date of publication.
Imprint page The page, usually the TITLE VERSO, carrying the details of printing, copyright, etc. See also BIBLIO.
In-house Adjective applied to a process or service carried out within a company, not bought in from outside.
In print Adjective applied to books and other publications that are currently available from the publisher.
In pro A term used to direct the enlargement or reduction of an original image, that is, where originals are to be enlarged or reduced by the same amount as each other, so they are IN PROportion.
Indent Instruction given to compositor to set a line or lines short of the full COLUMN measure, most familiarly to indicate the first line of a paragraph (para indent).
Index (**1**) The section of a publication giving alphabetical listing of subjects, proper names, etc, mentioned in the book, with page references. (**2**) A SUPERSCRIPT. (**3**) The printer's mark used to draw attention to a section of MATTER (also known as a 'fist').
Indirect cost The cost of a project excluding the DIRECT COST.
Indicator see DIRECT/DIRECTIONAL.
Inferior figure/letter see SUBSCRIPT.
Initial A large CAPITAL, often found at the beginning of a chapter, and usually DROPPED to occupy a depth of two or three lines below the first line.
Initial caps Instruction to the typesetter to set the

first character of a word or phrase in CAPITALS.
Insert An instruction to the typesetter to TAKE IN extra copy.
Inset A SHEET or part of a sheet placed inside another which is not part of the book's normal PAGINATION.
Inspection copy (**1**) An ADVANCE COPY supplied to the publisher for final checking in case of absolute disaster. (**2**) A copy of a book in a bookstore put out for potential purchasers to examine, so that other copies of the book are protected from wear.
Intaglio A printing image below the surface of the plate.
Interleaved (**1**) Adjective describing a book that has blank pages between the printed pages, so as to allow for handwritten notes, etc. (**2**) Adjective describing a book that has thin tissue sheets inserted to protect the illustrations. (**3**) Adjective describing the situation where a plate page has a thin LEAF bearing a descriptive caption TIPPED IN to its inner MARGIN.
Internegative A photographic NEGATIVE forming the intermediate stage in making a print from a flat original.
Introduction The opening section of a book, written usually by the author as part of the text, or by another person commenting on the purpose and content of the author's work. Compare FOREWORD, PREFACE.
ISBN International Standard Book Number, a unique reference number given to every book, identifying area of origin, publisher, title and check control, all in the form of a ten-digit number. A new ISBN is given to each new EDITION (**3**) of a book.
ISO International Standards Organization. A Swiss-based organization which has been responsible for standardizing many elements common to design, photography and publishing.
ISSN International Standard Series Number, as used in a scheme analogous to the ISBN scheme, but for periodical publications.
Issue All the copies of a periodical produced on a particular publication day.
Italic Type with sloping letters: *italic*. Indicated in manuscript by an UNDERLINE.

J

Jacket The paper wrapper which goes around the COVER of a book (almost always a HARDCOVER) but which is not stuck to it.
Jobbing printer A printer who deals with small, everyday tasks, such as the production of printed invitations, as opposed to bookwork.
Joint The flexible part of a CASE between the boarded side and the SPINE.
Jump In a publication, printed MATTER carried over to continue on a succeeding but not the subsequent page.
Justification Spacing of words and characters such that each line of text starts and finishes at the same point. Compare UNJUSTIFIED.

K

Kern/kerning The part of a letter which overhangs the next.
Keyboarding The first procedure in PHOTOCOMPOSITION, typing in COPY to be recorded in the machine for setting.
Keyline An outline sketch on ARTWORK to show the size and position of an illustration or HALFTONE image which is to be incorporated.

L

Laminate To protect paper or card and give it a glossy surface by applying a transparent plastic coating through heat, pressure or a combination of the two.
Large face The larger version of type cast in two different sizes on one BODY (**1**). Compare SMALL FACE.
Lay edges The two edges of a SHEET which are placed flush with the side and front lay gauges or marks on a printing machine to ensure that the sheet will be removed properly by the grippers, and have uniform MARGINS when printed.
Layout (**1**) A PASTE-UP. (**2**) An outline or sketch which gives the general appearance of the printed page, indicating the relationship between text and illustration. (**3**) In a printed book or periodical, the overall appearance of the spreads.
Leading Space inserted between lines of text or between headings and text.
Leader A group of dots, usually three (. . .), at the beginning of a sentence, piece of quoted prose, etc. Compare ELLIPSIS.
Leader line/rule A line on an image keyed in to ANNOTATION (**2**).
Leaf (**1**) A very thin FOIL used in, for example, GOLD BLOCKING. (**2**) A newly formed sheet of paper before it has been dried and finished. (**3**) That element of a book carrying a RECTO followed by a VERSO; ie, two successive but non-facing pages.
Legend see CAPTION.
Letterpress (**1**) A printing process in which the image is raised and inked to produce an impression. (**2**) The text of a book, including line illustrations but excluding plates.
Letterspacing The insertion of space between the letters of a word or words to improve the appearance of a line of type.
Libel To publish a defamatory statement in permanent form.
Library binding A binding strong enough to survive frequent handling.
Library of Congress Catalog Card Number A reference number given to the US edition of a book and recorded at the Library of Congress. This is common practice but not required by US law.
Library shot/pic A picture or illustration taken from an existing source rather than specially commissioned.
Lifted matter Type MATTER already set which is taken out of one job to be used in another.
Ligature 'Tied' letter in type, such as fi. Compare DIPHTHONG.
Light face The opposite of BOLD.
Light table/box A table or box with a translucent glass screen top illuminated from below, used for viewing or working with any illustrative material — for example, when RETOUCHING.
Limited edition (**1**) An

EDITION (**1**) of a book where it is guaranteed that only a fixed number of copies will be produced, those copies usually being numbered. (**2**) A DE LUXE EDITION where similar constraints apply.

Limp binding Any form of binding which has no BOARD stiffener, especially a PAPERBACK binding. See also SOFT COVER.

Line and halftone Illustration process in which line and halftone NEGATIVES are combined, printed onto a plate and etched as a unit.

Line artwork Any artwork that can be reproduced using a LINE BLOCK.

Line block Printing plate made of zinc or copper consisting of solid areas and lines. It is reproduced directly from LINE ARTWORK without tones. It is traditionally mounted on a wooden block to type height, although today the term is often applied to any medium whereby a line illustration is to be reproduced.

Line board A smoothly finished support suitable for line illustrations and other artwork.

Line feed The measure, expressed in POINTS or millimeters, of the movement of paper or film from one line to the next in PHOTO-COMPOSITION.

Line up The situation whereby two lines of type, or a line of type and a BLOCK (**1**), touch the same imaginary horizontal line.

Linen tester A magnifying glass designed for checking the detail of a halftone DOT pattern.

Lining figures/numerals Numerals which are aligned at top and bottom, rather than having ASCENDERS and DESCENDERS; for example 296 rather than 296.

Linotype The first keyboard-operated composing machine to employ the principle of the circulating MATRIX and cast type in solid lines or SLUGS (**1**). It was invented by the German/US engineer Ottmar Mergenthaler in 1876 and first used, by the *New York Times*, in 1886.

List (**1**) The titles which a publisher presents to the market, including both BACKLIST and new titles. (**2**) The books produced by a publisher in a particular season, as in 'spring list'. (**3**) A publisher's catalogue.

List price/cover price see PUBLISHED PRICE.

Literal A typesetter's error, or misprint.

Literary agent A person acting on behalf of an author, offering projects and negotiating the contracts should those offers be successful. Artists' agents acting analogously for artists.

Lith film A film used in preparing PLATES in PHOTOCHEMICAL reproduction. It omits middle tones and increases contrasts.

Lithography Printing from a dampened, flat surface using greasy ink, based on the principle of the mutual repulsion of oil and water.

Logo (**1**) COLOPHON (**1**). (**2**) LOGOTYPE.

Logotype Words or several letters cast as one unit.

Long page A page with type extended by one or two lines either deliberately (to avoid an inconvenient break) or inadvertently.

Look-through/see-through/show-through The visibility of an image through paper when seen against the light, or the unwanted visibility through a LEAF (**3**) of the page beneath the upper one.

Loose leaf A binding method that allows the easy removal of individual leaves.

Lower case/lc The small letters in a FONT of type. See also U&LC.

M

Machine proof A PROOF taken when corrections marked on the GALLEY PROOF and PAGE PROOF have been made and the FORM is on the printing machine. This is the last opportunity for correcting mistakes before the final printing.

Magazine (**1**) A storage device such as that which holds the FONT in a HOT METAL composing machine. (**2**) A periodical other than a newspaper, or journal.

Magenta The shade of red used in the FOUR-COLOR PROCESS. See PRIMARY COLORS.

Make up (**1**) The SHEET indicating the placing of the various items on the page. (**2**) The actual assembling of the page.

Makes and saves see CUTS AND FILLS.

Make/making ready The operations on a press before the first good copies are produced; eg, setting up for size and thickness of paper, putting on printing plates, ensuring correct ink supply, and adjusting color strength and image position.

Manuscript/ms Written or typed work submitted for publication or typesetting.

Margins The blank areas on a printed page surrounding the MATTER.

Marked proof (**1**) The PROOF, usually the GALLEY PROOF, supplied to the author for correction and containing the corrections and queries made by the typesetter's PROOF-READER. (**2**) A set of proofs onto which have been collated all typesetter's, author's and editorial corrections.

Mask (**1**) A material used to block out part of an image in a photograph, illustration or layout. (**2**) A photographic image modified in tone or color.

Masking (**1**) Blocking out part of an image with opaque material to prevent reproduction or to allow for alteration in COPY. (**2**) Applying a protective layer to an illustration to cover an area while other parts are painted or airbrushed. (**3**) A technical method of adjusting values of color and tone in PHOTO-MECHANICAL reproduction.

Master paste-up The final PASTE-UP, showing exactly how COPY, illustrations, etc, are going to fall.

Master proof (**1**) A typesetter's PROOF, read and marked with corrections and queries. (**2**) A MARKED PROOF (**2**).

Masthead Details about the publisher printed on the front, editorial or contents page of a periodical.

Matrix The brass DIES used in HOT METAL composition.

Matt art A clay-COATED PAPER with a dull finish.

Matter Either MANUSCRIPT or COPY to

be printed, or type that is composed.
Measure see TYPE MEASURE.
Mechanical CAMERA-READY copy or artwork.
Mechanical tints Tints consisting of DOT or line patterns that can be laid down on ARTWORK before or during reproduction processing.
Media Information sources such as publishing, radio, television.
Medium face The normal form of a TYPEFACE, midway between BOLD and LIGHT FACE.
Mezzotint INTAGLIO printing process producing a range of tones.
Mf/mtf A mark used in COPY PREPARATION meaning More Follows or More To Follow.
Mid Describes a word space used in handset type, measuring one-quarter of an EM.
Millboards Strong gray or black BOARDS of good quality.
Mint condition Term used in secondhand book-dealing to describe a book with few or no marks of use.
Mock up The rough visualization of a publication or packaging design showing size, color, type, etc; a rudimentary DUMMY.
Modern face A TYPEFACE with vertical stress, strong stroke contrasts and unbracketed fine SERIFS; eg, Bodoni.
Moiré A printing fault whereby HALFTONE DOTS appear as a mechanical, woodgrain pattern.
Monochrome An image made up of varying tones but in only one color (generally black).
Monograph A publication, usually short, dealing with a single person or subject.
Monophoto The trade name of the PHOTOCOMPOSITION system produced by the manufacturers of MONOTYPE.
Monotype (**1**) The trade name for composing machines that cast single TYPEs. (**2**) The process of making a painting on glass or metal and then taking an impression on paper; only one impression can be taken.
Montage An assembly of portions of several drawings or photographs to form a single original.
Mutton/mutt A term for an EM QUAD.

N

Natural see CENTER FOLD.
Net Adjective applied to the prices of books which, according to the Net Book Agreement, cannot be reduced even for bulk purchasers. Compare NON-NET.
Net receipts In calculating the profits from a project, the monies received less the production and other costs — as opposed to the gross receipts, which are the total monies received. A PACKAGER may pay ROYALITES based on a percentage of either the net or the gross receipts.
Non-lining figures/numerals A set of numerals with DESCENDERS, unlike LINING NUMERALS; for example, 296 rather than 296.
Non-net Adjective applied to the prices of those books, usually educational, which may be reduced, in accordance with the Net Book Agreement, when selling in bulk to, for example, educational authorities.

O

Oblong/horizontal format (**1**) Applied to an image in which the width is greater than the depth. (**2**) Applied to a book which is wider than it is deep, and hence to the specification of its FORMAT, as in 'A5 landscape'.
Offprint A REPRINT of an article, or other part of a publication, produced as a separate item.
Offset lithography Method of lithography whereby the image is produced, not direct from the plate, but 'offset' first onto a rubber-covered cylinder (the 'blanket') which performs the printing operation.
Old face/old style Type form characterized by diagonal stress and sloped, bracketed SERIFS; eg, old face.
One and a half up Synonym for HALF UP.
One-piece film Film positive or negative that is in one piece as opposed to patched film which has captions, headings, etc, stripped onto a base film.
One-third reduction The amount of reduction (33 per cent) involved in printing an image prepared HALF UP.
Open circle A symbol used exactly as a BULLET, but looking like o rather than •
Option clause In an author's CONTRACT, a clause saying that the publisher shall have the first refusal of the author's next work of a particular type.
Origination *(UK)* See PREPARATION.
Orphan A single word standing at the top of a page when COPY has been set. Compare WIDOW.
Out of print No longer IN PRINT.
Out of register see REGISTER.
Overlay (**1**) A transparent sheet used in the preparation of multicolor ARTWORK. (**2**) A translucent sheet covering a piece of original artwork, on which instructions may be written.
Overmatter MATTER set which fails to fit within the appropriate space, and may therefore become DEAD MATTER (**1**).
Overprinting Printing over an already printed area.
Overs/over runs (**1**) Paper issued beyond the bare requirements, to allow for MAKE READY, SPOILS, etc. (**2**) SPOILS. (**3**) Any quantity produced over and above the ordered number.
Overstocks Quantities of BACKLIST titles in excess of the numbers that a publisher can reasonably expect to sell in the foreseeable future. Overstocks are normally reduced by partial REMAINDERING, as in the National Book Sale.
Ozalid A trade name referring to a method of copying PAGE PROOFS by the DYELINE process.

P

Packager A company offering a service or commodity as a complete unit or package, especially one which creates international CO-EDITIONS but does not itself publish.
Page One side of a LEAF (**3**), or the MATTER appearing on it.
Page make up (**1**) Synonym for MAKE UP. (**2**) In PHOTO-

COMPOSITION, a display showing copy as it will appear on a page.
Page-on-galley proofs PROOFS supplied on galley SLIPS, but typeset as pages.
Page proofs The proofing stage after GALLEY PROOFS but before MACHINE PROOFS, in which the MATTER has been segregated into pages (with or without illustrations).
Page spread see SPREAD.
Pages to view The number of pages visible on one side of a SHEET that has been printed on both sides.
Pagination (**1**) The numbering of the pages of a book. (**2**) The division of a copy into separate pages.
Pamphlet A short, unbound publication.
Pantone matching system Registered trade name for an international system for specifying colors to printers and for matching designers' materials such as inks, papers, marker pens.
Paperback/paper-bound/paper-covered Adjectives describing books whose COVERS are made of paper or thin card.
Pass for press To give the final OK to PROOFS.
Paste-up A LAYOUT of a number of pages (perhaps of a whole book) used to plan and direct the positioning of illustrations, captions and text.
PE/printer's error An error that is the responsibiity of the typesetter rather than of the author or editor.
Percentage reduction/enlargement The indication of SCALING, expressed in percentage terms, for reproduction of an image.
Perfect binding A binding method in which the leaves of a book are trimmed at the back and then glued rather than sewn. Distinct from thermal binding, in which a microwave technique is used to fuse the trimmed backs of the pages.
Period The full stop.
Photo engraving A PHOTOMECHANICAL method of producing etched line or HALFTONE plates.
Photocomposition The production of display lines and text by photographic means on film or paper. Photocomposing machines assemble lines of letters from various forms of photo matrix (storage devices holding FONTS), but the term is also used to include digital typesetting.
Photogravure Gravure is a technique of printing whereby variations in tone are produced by the amounts of ink held in indentations in the plate. Likewise, photogravure is the process of printing from a PHOTO-MECHANICALLY prepared surface, which holds the ink in recessed cells.
Photomechanical (**1**) Describes methods of making printing PLATES that involve photographic techniques. (**2**) The assembly of type or illustrations for transfer to a printing plate.
Photomechanical transfer (PMT) A mechanical method of quickly producing photoprints from flat originals for use in PASTE-UPS, PRESENTATION VISUALS, etc.
Photomontage The use of images from different photographs combined to produce a new, composite image.
Pica The correct term for 12 POINTS (1 pica EM), a unit of measurement used in setting.
Picture agency/picture library An organization which stores photographs and/or illustrations and leases the reproduction rights for them. Specialty agencies deal in sport, natural history, fashion, etc.
Picture credits CREDITS relating to illustrations.
Picture research The function sometimes, but not always, considered a part of EDITORIAL WORK, in which the aim is to find existing illustrations which may be used to complement the text.
Pie/pi Odds and ends of type which have been accidentally mixed.
Plagiarism The deliberate or accidental use of somebody else's copyright work (see UNIVERSAL COPYRIGHT CONVENTION).
Plant A printer's or typesetter's machinery.
Plate (**1**) An electro or stereo (one-piece duplicate) of set-up type and/or blocks. (**2**) A sheet of metal bearing a design, from which an IMPRESSION (**2**) is printed. (**3**) A full-page book illustration, printed separately from the text, often on a different paper. (**4**) A photographic plate; a whole plate measures 215×165mm (8½×6½in), a half plate 165×101mm (6½×4in).
Point A standard unit of type size. In the US/UK system it is 0·01383in (0·35mm approximately), or roughly 72 to the inch. The DIDOT POINT is rather larger.
Point size Specification for size of type in POINTS, eg, 11 point.
Portfolio The collection of earlier work shown by an artist to a potential client.
Portrait The converse of LANDSCAPE (**1**) and (**2**).
Positive (**1**) An image made photographically on paper or film, usually derived from a NEGATIVE. (**2**) A photographic color TRANSPARENCY or film with a positive image, used in platemaking.
Postlims see END MATTER.
Preface An author's or publisher's statement in the PRELIMS of a book. Compare FOREWORD.
Prelims/preliminary matter The pages preceding the BODY (**2**) of a book. They usually consist of HALF TITLE, TITLE PAGE, PREFACE and CONTENTS page, with their appropriate VERSOS.
Preparation The processes of COLOR SEPARATION, of preparation of a HALFTONE block, of TYPESETTING, or any other process which involves the first transformation of an original towards its final printed form.
Presentation visual Material prepared as a sample of the proposed appearance of a printed work. It may consist of drawings, typeset COPY, photographically produced prints, etc.
Press (**1**) A printing machine. (**2**) A printing company. (**3**) A publisher.
Press clippings agency An agency which, for a regular fee, searches through a wide diversity of printed media for references to a company and its products, or to a single product such as a book, and which supplies clippings of those references.

Press proof The last PROOF to be read before giving authorization for printing.
Press run see PRINT RUN.
Primary colors Pure colors from which all other colors can be mixed. In projected light, these are red, blue and green. Their complements, the secondary colors, are produced by mixing two out of the three; they are yellow, MAGENTA and CYAN.
Print origination see ORIGINATION.
Print run (**1**) The total number of copies produced in one printing. (**2**) Where several editions are being produced simultaneously, the number of copies for a particular edition (eg, the 'UK print run').
Printer The FILM (or plate) of a single color produced in COLOR SEPARATION.
Printer's latin Sections of typeset dog Latin, totally meaningless, used as BODY COPY (**3**).
Process camera A camera designed for process work in PHOTOMECHANICAL reproduction techniques.
Process colors Yellow, CYAN and MAGENTA, the secondary colors. See PRIMARY COLORS.
Production Generally (definitions vary) all the functions involved in the creation of a finished book or periodical other than COMMISSIONING, EDITORIAL WORK, design and picture selection and research.
Production schedule A document, generally updated several times, giving the DEADLINES for the various stages in the creation of a finished project.
Progressive proofs The PROOFS taken in color printing as a guide to shade and REGISTER (**2**). Each color is shown separately and imposed on the preceding color.
Proof An IMPRESSION (**2**) obtained from an inked plate, stone, screen, block or type in order to check the progress and accuracy of the work. It is also known as a 'pull', because in LETTERPRESS it is always used to involve pulling a roller over a sheet of paper placed on top of the material in the FORM.
Proof copy A copy of a PROOF, especially one imposed, folded, trimmed and bound in some cheap material (such as card) for advance promotional purposes.
Proof-correction marks Standard set of signs and symbols commonly understood by all those involved in turning COPY into final printed text.
Proof-reader/reader A person who reads PROOFS against the original MANUSCRIPT, both searching for PEs and corrections and revising COPY where necessary.
Proofing press A press, sometimes hand-operated, usually smaller than that used for the full PRINT RUN (**1**), on which typeset COPY or separated illustrations are COPY PROOFED.
Proportional spacing A method of spacing characters in COLD COMPOSITION, to accommodate the different widths of the letters and numerals.
Proud (**1**) Description of type matter that is designed to stand in isolation from the general text of a page. (**2**) Description of MATTER in a FORME that is inadvertently or deliberately higher than the other matter.
Published price The price of copies of a publication to the public.
Publisher The company (often called a 'publishing house') or individual responsible for the creation, distribution and marketing of published works.
Publisher's representative/rep Person responsible for visiting bookshops and wholesalers and persuading them to place orders for a publisher's books.
Publication date/publishing date The date specified by the PUBLISHER on which copies of a publication may be put on general sale.
Publishing house see PUBLISHER.
Pull see PROOF.
Pull out see FOLD OUT.
Pull-out section Pages of a periodical that can be detached all together and kept as a separate entity.
Put down/up Instruction to the typesetter to change characters from CAPITALS to LOWER CASE (down) or vice versa (up).
Put to bed (**1**) The state of printing PLATES (**1**) and (**2**) or FORMES when they are secured to the press ready to print. (**2**) As a verb, to take a project through to the stage immediately prior to final printing.

Q

Quarter-bound Description of a case-bound book using a stronger material for the back than the sides.

R

R Symbol denoting a registered design, a design officially registered by a patent office, such as a trademark, to give protection against PLAGIARISM.
RIP Instruction in SCALING (Rest In Proportion), where the other dimensions or images are to be reduced or enlarged in proportion to a given dimension.
R type A direct process of producing photographic color prints. R19 is the production of a print from ARTWORK; R14 from a TRANSPARENCY
Ragged left/right Typeset copy UNJUSTIFIED at left or right.
Raised capital A CAPITAL that projects above the line of type.
Ranged left/right A form of setting in which lines of unequal length are JUSTIFIED on one side and UNJUSTIFIED on the other. If the left-hand side is justified, the MATTER is 'ranged left', and vice versa.
Reader Consultant, reviewer of manuscript. See PROOF-READER.
Reading copy (**1**) A copy of a book supplied gratis to the potential placer of a large order, such as a schoolteacher. (**2**) An ADVANCE COPY, which may not have been brought up to the final published standard, supplied to, for example, a reviewer. (**3**) An INSPECTION COPY.
Ream Most commonly 500 SHEETS of paper, although sometimes 480 (short ream) or 516 (printer's ream).
Recto A right-hand page.
Register (**1**) The correct ALIGNMENT of pages with the MARGINS in order. (**2**) The correct positioning of

one color on another in color printing. In both (**1**) and (**2**), incorrect positioning is described as 'out of register'.
Register marks In color printing, marks used to ensure that the printing is not out of REGISTER (**2**).
Rehash To take previously published copy and use it in a different form — for example, with different illustrations and in a different format.
Reissue The republication, by the original publisher, of an OUT OF PRINT book.
Rejection fee Fee paid to a FREELANCE who has been asked to produce a ROUGH or DRAFT for material that is not used or preliminary work that is not to be taken further.
Relief printing Printing in which the image is obtained from a raised surface, such as LETTERPRESS.
Remainders Books sold at less than the PUBLISHED PRICE, either to reduce OVERSTOCKS (partial remaindering) or to completely sell out a printing of a book that is no longer selling at a sufficient rate. In some cases, books are produced specifically for cheap sale, with only one copy placed in a bookshop at the 'published price' (instant remaindering).
Rep see PUBLISHER'S REPRESENTATIVE.
Reportage (**1**) Style of photo-journalism conveying information through graphic images. (**2**) Style of writing that merely reports, but does not interpret.
Reprint Second or subsequent printing of a publication, article, etc.
Repro house/ reproduction house *(UK)* see SEPARATOR.
Repro proof/ reproduction proof A high-quality PROOF on art paper that can be used as ARTWORK.
Residual rights Those rights not specifically discussed in an author's CONTRACT.
Retainer fee Fee paid to a FREELANCE of any kind to retain his/her availability, rather than a fee paid for work done.
Retouching Any method used to correct, improve or change the character of a visual image.
Returns Copies of books or magazines which have been SUBSCRIBED by booksellers, newsagents etc, but returned unsold to the publisher
Reverse left to right Instruction to the printer to amend a FLOP, meaning to produce a mirror-image of the proofed one.
Reverse out/save out To reproduce text, lettering, etc, as a white image on a solid (usually black) or HALFTONE ground by PHOTOMECHANICAL techniques.
Reverse/wrong reading COPY that reads backwards, as on a LETTERPRESS printing surface. Compare RIGHT READING.
Reversion of copyright The return to the author of the rights which he or she has leased to the publisher, under conditions specified in the CONTRACT.
Review copy A gratis copy sent to a periodical or individual for the purposes of reading and review.
Review list A list, generally prepared by the publicity department, of those periodicals and individuals to whom it is proposed to send REVIEW COPIES.
Revise A revised version of a particular stage of PROOFS, usually produced owing to particularly heavy corrections on the original set. Thus a revised GALLEY might be produced before going to PAGE PROOFS.
Right reading COPY reading in the normal way, from left to right. Compare REVERSE/ WRONG READING.
Rights (**1**) Those parts of his/her copyright (see UNIVERSAL COPYRIGHT CONVENTION) which an author leases to a publisher, as specified in the CONTRACT. (**2**) Sub-leased permissions to publish a work in a different form, market or language (eg, movie rights, UK rights).
Rivers Streaks of white spacing produced when spaces in consecutive lines coincide, or almost coincide.
Roman Ordinary vertical type, as distinct from ITALIC.
Rough Sketch showing a proposed design.
Rough draft Initial stage of a MANUSCRIPT, subsequently to be rewritten.
Rounded and backed Describing a concave appearance at the FOREDGE of a book and a convex back with a projecting SHOULDER.
Royalty Monies paid to an author or contributor, based on the sales of a published work.
Rules Metal strips, of type height, in various widths and lengths, used to print lines; also, more generally, printed lines. (See, for example, FINE RULE.)
Run (**1**) The number of impressions taken from a FORM at one time. (**2**) Short for PRINT RUN.
Run in heading A heading on the same line as the opening of the subsequent text, as opposed to one placed above the text.
Run of paper (**1**) More commonly 'print to paper', instruction to print as many copies as possible using a given supply of paper, rather than a specified number of copies. (**2**) Position of advertising matter in a periodical which gives no display advantages.
Run on/follow on (**1**) Instruction to typesetter to make the text read directly on, without a paragraph break. (**2**) In a PRINT RUN, additional copies printed after those over which the FIXED COSTS have been amortized.
Run on edition An extra edition, over and above the originating publisher's own, sold to another publisher at a price calculated on the RUN ON (**2**) costs.
Runaround Text set to fit around an illustration that intrudes into the column width.
Runners Numbers placed in the text MARGIN in order to key in references to particuar lines.
Running costs The costs of actually printing, binding, etc, a particular edition, as opposed to the FIXED COSTS.
Running head The line of type which repeats, say, a chapter heading at the top of a page.
Running text A BODY of text running consecutively over several pages, even should illustrations, etc, intrude.

S

Saddle-/wire-stitching Method of stitching

brochures: they are opened over a saddle-shaped support and stitched or stapled through the back.
Same size/ss Instruction to REPRO HOUSE to reproduce a piece of visual material at the same size as supplied.
Sans serif A typeface without SERIFS or, usually, stroke contrast.
Scaling/scaling up Determining the degree of enlargement or reduction necessary to reproduce an original image within a given area of a design. The scaling may be represented as a percentage of the original image area (eg, HALF UP) or in figures proportionate to the dimensions of the original.
Scamp Rough sketch showing the basic idea for an advertisement or design.
Scanner Device using high-intensity light or a laser beam in association with a computer and film processor to produce high-quality COLOR SEPARATION films for printing.
Scatter proofs PROOFS for checking the quality of illustrations in PHOTO-MECHANICAL reproduction. To reduce proofing costs, as many images as possible are reproduced on each sheet, with no reference to correct positions in the LAYOUT.
Schedule A PRODUCTION SCHEDULE or similar document.
Scissors-and-paste job Reorganization of a section of manuscript by cutting it up and sticking the pieces back down again in a different order, with necessary minor editorial alterations to preserve sense. Also applied to revising design layouts in a similar way, especially during REHASHING.
Screen The pattern of DOTS produced by a HALFTONE SCREEN.
Screen angle The position of a HALFTONE SCREEN, as arranged in converting images to HALFTONE when two or more must be overprinted, to avoid MOIRÉ. In four-color printing the screen angles are: black 45°, magenta 75°, yellow 90°, cyan 105°.
Screen clash Disruptive pattern in an image produced when two or more HALFTONE SCREENS have been positioned at incorrect angles, or when a DOT-FOR-DOT reproduction has been unsatisfactorily executed.
Screen tint see TINT (**2**).
Section (**1**) A sheet folded to create four or more book pages, often called a signature. (**2**) A division of a publication, either smaller than a chapter or consisting of more than one chapter.
Section opener The introductory page or pages of a new SECTION (**2**), containing the HEADING, sometimes an explanatory paragraph outlining the contents of the section, and generally the first batch of text of the section, often with an introductory photograph or illustration. A chapter opener is the same, but for a chapter.
Section-sewn book One in which SECTIONS (**1**) are sewn together with thread after GATHERING.
See-through see LOOK-THROUGH.
Self cover A book whose cover is of the same paper STOCK (**2**) and printed at the same time as the leaves.
Self ends ENDPAPERS formed at the front of a book from a leaf of the first section and at the back from a leaf of the last section.
Separate ends Normal ENDPAPERS, as opposed to SELF ENDS.
Separation see COLOR SEPARATION.
Separation artwork ARTWORK produced with separate OVERLAYS for each color, so that COLOR SEPARATION is not necessary.
Separator A company whose prime concern is COLOR SEPARATION and/or the making of HALFTONE and LINE BLOCKS.
Serial rights RIGHTS granted to a periodical to reproduce part or all of a work, either spread out over several issues or in a single issue (one-shot or extract rights).
Serif The small terminal stroke at the end of the main stroke of a letter.
Set (**1**) The width (set width) of a type BODY (**1**). (**2**) Used as an instruction, as in 'set to 12 PICAS', or a description, as in 'handset'. (**3**) Short for TYPESET. (**4**) In a special sense, to describe the proportions of the EM of a size of type.
Set and hold Instruction to typeset MATTER for future use.
Set close Describes type set with the minimum of space between the words and no extra space between sentences.
Set off (**1**) Accidental transference of a printed image from one SHEET to the back of the next during printing. (**2**) In LITHOGRAPHY it refers to an impression taken from the block or plate containing the main outlines of a design, which is powdered with a non-greasy dye while the ink is damp, then placed on the stone or plate and passed through the press.
Set solid Instruction to set without LEADING between the lines.
Sheet feed Printing machine into which SHEETS are fed singly.
Sheet stock A mass of printed sheets held ready for binding.
Short page A page whose depth is either deliberately or accidentally shorter than usual. Compare LONG PAGE.
Shoulder The projection of the CASE down each side of a book's SPINE.
Show-through see LOOK-THROUGH.
Shrink wrapping Thin, transparent plastic film used in packaging; it is sealed tight around an object by heat. Often used to protect expensive books in the shops from the attentions of the customers' who are directed instead to an INSPECTION COPY.
Side heading A subheading set FLUSH LEFT or in the MARGIN.
Side notes Notes set in the MARGIN on either side of the text. Compare FOOTNOTES.
Side-stitching/side-stabbing A method of securing the SECTIONS (**1**) of a book using wires passed through close to the BACK.
Signature (**1**) The letter or reference mark at the tail of the first page of each SECTION (**1**) in a book, running in alphabetical or numerical order, which serves as a guide to the binder in GATHERING. (**2**) Traditional name for a SECTION (**1**).
Sign up To sign a CONTRACT between an author and publisher for

the writing of a COMMISSIONED project.
Single-color press Printing press able to print only one color at a time, and requiring separate runs in order to print in more than one color.
Sizing (1) See SCALING. **(2)** A gelatinous solution, also known as 'size', used to COAT PAPER to glaze or seal the surface and render the paper less porous. Size may be based on glue, casein (made from curdled milk), starch or similar substance.
Slip Broad strip of paper on which a GALLEY PROOF is printed.
Slip case Open-sided box to hold one or more books with their spines showing.
Slip page A GALLEY PROOF containing matter for one page.
Slug (1) A metal strip produced by a LINOTYPE machine, containing a full line of characters. **(2)** A thick metal strip of less than type height used for spacing in LETTERPRESS. **(3)** A metal strip bearing a temporary mark, as in 'see page ▮ ▮ '.
Small capitals/sc CAPITALS of smaller than standard size (often to the X-HEIGHT); the cross-references in this glossary are set in SMALL CAPITALS. They are indicated in MANUSCRIPT by a double underline.
Small face The smaller version of a typeface cast in two sizes on one BODY **(1)**. Compare LARGE FACE.
Soft cover (1) See PAPERBACK. **(2)** A COVER which is neither a CASE nor a SELF COVER.
Soft dot A halftone DOT with a soft EMULSION, and thus softer edges, making ETCHING correction easier.
Solid setting see SET SOLID.
Specification/spec Description of the components, characteristics and/or procedures of a particular job, product or activity; in particular, the numerical description (number of words, page format, etc) of a forthcoming project.
Specimen page A proof or specially made up page assembled as an example of a proposed style of design.
Spine The center of the CASE of a book, which runs down the BACK when it is CASED IN.
Spine lettering The lettering (usually title, author's name and publisher's COLOPHON **(1)**) BLOCKED on the SPINE or printed in the equivalent position on the JACKET.
Spin-off (1) A subsidiary, minor project generated as a result of the compilation of a major-one. **(2)** Describing the sale of non-MEDIA merchandizing RIGHTS **(2)**, such as that to show an image from a book on a T-shirt.
Spiral binding Binding method whereby a spiral wire holds the leaves together.
Spoils/spoilage Badly printed SHEETS discarded before delivery to the binder, or discarded by the binder because damaged during binding.
Spread/double spread/ double page spread **(1)** Two facing pages of a publication, often produced as a single unit at design stage, and printed thus in the case of a CENTER FOLD. **(2)** In LETTERPRESS, the word 'spread' can be used to describe the thickening of the strokes of letters, etc, owing to over inking, etc, and possibly causing FILLING IN.
Square-back book A book whose binding is collated and sewn, but not ROUNDED AND BACKED.
Standing type/plates/ matter/form Type MATTER composed, used and then held ready for REPRINTING, rather than PIED.
Stock (1) Metal part of a printing roller, covered with COMPOSITION. **(2)** Printer's term for paper, etc, to be used for printing.
Stock paper sizes Those sizes of SHEET which are readily available, rather than requiring a special making (manufacture).
Story-board see FLAT PLAN **(1)**.
Strapline (1) A subheading appearing above the main HEADLINE **(1)**. **(2)** An explanation of a cryptic book title on a front cover.
Straw-board A thick board manufactured from straw pulp and often used to make BOARDS.
Strike-through The effect of ink soaking right through a SHEET.
Stripping in In the preparation of CAMERA-READY text, the replacement of a line by an amended one; the analogous insertion of typeset material onto ARTWORK.
Style sheet (1) A document containing details of a HOUSE STYLE. **(2)** A document sent to the typesetter along with the manuscript detailing particular points of style, especially in cases where the COPY-EDITOR believes he or she may have been inconsistent.
Stylist (1) A person who makes minor amendments to a MANUSCRIPT so that it is rendered in consistent style (see HOUSE STYLE). **(2)** Someone who advises on the content and styling of commissioned photos.
Subhead A HEADING for an internal division of a chapter.
Subscribe On the part of a bookseller or wholesaler, to order copies of a book in advance of publication. The total number of copies ordered in this way is called the 'subscription'.
Subscript A letter or figure printed inferior to (ie, below) the line, as in H_2O.
Subsidiary rights RIGHTS other than that allowing first publication of a book.
Superior figure/letter see SUPERSCRIPT.
Superscript A figure or letter printed superior to (ie, above) the line, as in $12^2 = 24$ or when a numeral is used to indicate a FOOTNOTE.
Supplement Material added to a publication separately (such as an updating volume) or included in a REPRINT to supply added detail to the original text.
Surface paper see COATED PAPER.
Swash characters Old face italic characters with calligraphic flourishes.
Synopsis A condensed version of the thesis and contents of a book, giving a clear breakdown of the likely or actual progression of the text, and often enough listing putative selling points.

T

Tabulate To arrange COPY such as the text or figures in the form of a

columnar table, according to fixed measures.
Tail The bottom edge of a book, or the area close to the bottom of the FOOT MARGIN.
Tailband see HEAD-AND TAILBANDS.
Tail margin The FOOT MARGIN.
Tailpiece A design or illustration at the end of a chapter, SECTION (**2**) or book.
Take back PROOF CORRECTION requiring the typesetter to take back CHARACTERS (**1**), words or lines to the preceding line, column or page.
Take in Instruction to typesetter, on PROOF or MANUSCRIPT, to include extra COPY supplied at the place marked.
Take over PROOF CORRECTION requiring the typesetter to carry over CHARACTERS (**1**), words or lines to the next line, column or page.
Text The written or printed MATTER, including tables, forming the main BODY (**2**) of a publication.
Text type/matter Any TYPEFACE of a suitable size for printing TEXT, usually between about 8 point and 14 point (see POINT SIZE).
Thick Describes a word space used in handset type, measuring one-third of an EM.
Thin Describes a word space used in handset type, measuring one-fifth of an EM.
Thumb index An index guide, found primarily in alphabetically arranged books such as encyclopedias, whereby rounded sections are cut from the FOREEDGES of the book and the resulting 'gaps' labelled with the appropriate letters or legends.
Tight Describes an image that is usually small and detailed, with clear definition and very little space in its design.
Tight setting Text setting in which a line or lines have too little space between characters and/or words.
Tint (**1**) A shade of a color produced by the admixture of white. (**2**) The effect achieved by breaking up color into a percentage using DOTS which allow white paper to show through; in such a screen tint, a 10 percent tint would be 10 percent color and 90 percent white, and so on.
Tip in/tip on An illustration or other piece of matter printed on a single page and stuck separately into a book by paste along one edge.
Title page The right-hand page, usually following the HALF-TITLE, which bears the title, the author's and publisher's names, and other relevant data.
Title sheet/title section The first printed SECTION (**1**) of a publication.
Title verso The VERSO of the TITLE PAGE, usually carrying copyright data, the ISBN, etc.
Trade books Books produced for general retail sale through bookstores rather than through BOOK CLUBS or mass-market outlets.
Trade counter (**1**) Traditionally, the section in a publisher's warehouse where retailers could directly purchase books. (**2**) By analogy, the department of a publisher which processes retailers' orders.
Transparency A photographically developed image on transparent film. The term usually refers to a POSITIVE image in color, but is applicable also to any image on a transparent base.
Transpose To correct the wrong order of characters, words, lines or images on a MANUSCRIPT or PROOF.
Trichromatic inks Inks that use the three secondary colors (see PRIMARY COLORS) in different proportions to produce other colors.
Trim marks Marks incorporated on a printed sheet to indicate the correct trim.
True double Colloquial term for CENTER FOLD.
Turn up A piece of type inserted in a PROOF upside down to show that a specific character is temporarily unavailable.
Turnaround The time taken for a specific job to be done.
Turned-over cover A COVER (**1**) whose FLAPS are turned inside at the FOREDGE.
Twice up ARTWORK or COPY Prepared at twice the size at which it will be reproduced.
Type The raised image of a character cast on a rectangular piece of metal used in LETTERPRESS printing. See also TYPEFACE.
Type area The area of the page designed to contain text MATTER, illustrations, tables, etc, forming the BODY (**2**) of the work.
Typeface/type A particular design of type which, though it may be rendered in BOLD, ITALIC, etc, is distinguishable in its characteristics from other typefaces. Typefaces in common use include Bembo, Baskerville, Times, Plantin, Helvetica and Univers.
Type family All the variations and sizes of a basic TYPEFACE design, as well as its BOLD, CONDENSED, EXPANDED, ITALIC, LIGHT FACE, etc, manifestations.
Type mark up/mark up Instructions marked on COPY to be typeset indicating to the COMPOSITOR details of POINT SIZE, TYPEFACE, TYPE MEASURE, etc.
Type measure The width of a column or page setting expressed in PICA EMS.
Type page *(US)* Term for TYPE AREA.
Type rules see EM RULE, EN RULE, RULES.
Type scale/type gauge Rule marked with a scale of type measurements, POINTS, EMS, PICAS, etc.
Type specimen sheet Sample sheet showing the forms of letters, numerals, punctuation marks, signs, etc, available in one or more given TYPEFACES, often including an example of the type as set.
Typescript/ts A typewritten MANUSCRIPT.
Typesetting Methods of assembling TYPE for printing by hand, machine, or photographic techniqes, including digital typesetting.
Typo (**1**) Error in typewriting. (**2**) US Term for a LITERAL.
Typography The art, general design and appearance of printed MATTER using type, especially the design of TYPEFACES.

U

U & lc Abbreviation for 'upper and lower case', meaning that the piece of copy so referred to should be set in UPPER CASE and LOWER CASE as marked.

Underline/underscore A RULE printed beneath a word or portion of text.
Uniform edition see EDITION (**5**).
Unit cost The production cost per copy of a project, calculated by adding the FIXED COSTS and RUNNING COSTS and dividing by the PRINT RUN.
Universal Copyright Convention An international assembly that in 1952 agreed protection for the originator of a text, photograph, illustration, compilation, etc, to prevent subsequent use by another of material without permission or acknowledgement. The work must carry the copyright mark ©, the name of the individual or organization holding the copyright and the date of publication. This last is important because the period before the expiration of copyright varies from country to country; for example, in the US it is 28 years but is renewable, while in the UK it is 50 years after the publication of the work or the death of its author, whichever is the later. Authors may sublease some or all aspects of their copyright to publishers in the form of RIGHTS.
Unjustified Describes lines of type either (**1**) RANGED LEFT or right, with the other edge RAGGED, or (**2**) CENTRED, with both edges ragged. Compare JUSTIFICATION.
Upper case/uc The CAPITAL letters in a FONT of type.

V

Variable costs Alternative term for RUNNING COSTS, but implying those costs that will change in a production ESTIMATE if the PRINT RUN is changed.
Verso The left-hand page of a book or, more precisely, the other side of a LEAF (**3**) from a RECTO — see, for example, TITLE VERSO.
Vignette A small illustration or decoration without a border.
Visual A mock-up of the proposed appearance of a design or LAYOUT presented at any level of sophistication from a scanty ROUGH to a PRESENTATION VISUAL.
Volume A book, especially when it is one of a several-volume set.

W

Web-offset An offset press (see OFFSET LITHOGRAPHY) working from a reel or continuous roll of paper.,
Weight The degree of boldness of a TYPEFACE, such as LIGHT FACE, MEDIUM FACE or BOLD.
Widow A single word standing as the last line of a paragraph in typeset COPY, especially one which falls as the first line of a new page or column (more correctly called an ORPHAN).
Wire-stitching Stitching by use of wire staples, as, frequently, in SADDLE-STITCHING and SIDE-STITCHING.
Word break A division of a word at the end of a line of type, with part of the word taken over to the next line, in order to avoid excessive space between the words and letters of the line or, conversely, TIGHT SETTING.
Word spacing The adjustment of space between words in typeset COPY, using fixed or variable space widths according to the method of composition.
Work and tumble To print one side of a SHEET and turn it from front to back to print the second side, keeping the same ALIGNMENT of the side edges on the press.
Work and turn When MATTER for both sides of a SHEET is set in one FORME, after one side of the sheet is printed it is turned over end-for-end and backed up from the same forme.
Work and twist To print from the same FORME twice on the same side of a SHEET, turning the sheet through 90 degrees between impressions.
Work in progress In terms of a publisher's assets, those books which are currently in the process of editing, design or production, as opposed to those BACKLIST books still in stock or COMMISSIONED future projects.
Wrap A section of printed illustrations, usually four pages, wrapped around a folded SECTION (**1**) of text matter before GATHERING; rarely, when a book is of unorthodox page-length, a four-page text wrap may be put around a folded section of text; almost equally rarely, except in art books, a text-wrap may be put around a section of illustrations.
Wraparound A JACKET Illustration or design that extends over front, spine and back of a book.
Wrong reading Alternative term for REVERSE READING.

X

x-height The height of letters with neither ASCENDERS nor DESCENDERS, such as the LOWER CASE x.

Computer glossary

A

Alphanumeric sort The capacity to arrange items in alphabetical or numerical order. Necessary for INDEXING.

B

Back-up A duplicate copy or copies of the DATA on a DISK, made in case the disk is lost or damaged. Back-up copies are generally made both on disk and on paper — see HARD COPY BACK-UP.
Bit Short for BInary digiT. The smallest piece of information that can be stored in the computer's MEMORY. See CAPACITY.
Byte Eight BIT.

C

Capacity The amount of DATA that can be stored in a computer's MEMORY or on a DISK. It shows roughly how many characters the computer or disk can hold, and is measured in BYTES or KILOBYTES.
Compatible Two computers or PROGRAMs are compatible if they can exchange DATA without an INTERFACE — that is, if DISKs from one computer and program can be read by the other.
Count On a TYPESETTING TERMINAL, to decide where line endings fall.
Cursor A mark on a VDT screen — usually a flashing square — that indicates where the next character will appear if a key on the KEYBOARD is pressed.

D

Data Any information, code or instruction that the computer can store in its MEMORY.
Database A collection of DATA stored in the computer's MEMORY in such a way that it can be retrieved in a different order. For instance, a picture catalog stored as a database can be set up in such a way that lists of pictures by a particular photographer, or from a particular agency, of a particular subject or due back on a particular day, can be called up by the computer.
Daisywheel see PRINTER.
Dedicated A dedicated computer is one that is designed for a specific purpose — to be a WORD PROCESSOR, for instance. It cannot be used for any other purpose. Many MICROCOMPUTERs are non-dedicated — they can do nothing until a PROGRAM is inserted, but with the appropriate program they can become, for instance, a word processor, a DATABASE system or a SPREADSHEET system, and are therefore more flexible than dedicated computers.
Disk A thin, circular plate on which DATA can be stored magnetically and retrieved. Disks can be flexible – floppy – or rigid – hard (Winchester). Hard disks generally hold more information than floppy disks of the same size, and are less vulnerable to damage by rough handling, coffee stains, cigarette ash etc.
Disk drive The unit — it may be free-standing or physically part of the computer — that retrieves information from the DISK and transfers it to the computer's MEMORY. It looks like a slot into which the disk is inserted.
Dot matrix see PRINTER.

F

Facsimile machine A method of transmitting material, generally through a MODEM link, in facsimile form.
Floppy disk see DISK.

G

Gigo Garbage in, garbage out — the principle that the results you get out of a computer can only be as good as what you put in. That is, a computer is nothing more than a machine, and how useful it is to you depends on your skill in using it.

H

Hard disk see DISK.
Hard copy back-up A printed copy of the DATA on a DISK. It is useful to get into the habit of keeping hard copy back-ups of finished disks in case a computer fault prevents information being retrieved from a disk.
Hardware The physical objects that make up a computer — VDT, DISK DRIVE, PRINTER, KEYBOARD (see also SOFTWARE).

I

Indexing The editor or author marks on the manuscript that has been KEYED in to the computer the words that he or she wishes to include in the index. The computer not only puts them into alphabetical order (see ALPHANUMERICAL SORT) but, once pagination has been decided, adds the page numbers. Requires a PROGRAM that includes indexing.
Interface (**1**) A device that allows two computers that are not COMPATIBLE to exchange information. (**2**) The link between, say, a word processor and a printer.

K

Key To type copy into a computer's memory using the computer KEYBOARD.
Keyboard Like an ordinary typewriter keyboard, but with extra keys for WORD PROCESSOR commands such as 'delete' or 'insert'.
Kilobyte A thousand BYTES.

L

Load To transfer a PROGRAM or DATA from a DISK into the computer's MEMORY.
Letter-quality see PRINTER.

M

Mainframe computer A large and powerful computer with several TERMINALS that can perform several functions — DATABASE, SPREADSHEET, WORD PROCESSOR, for example — at the same time.
Memory The computer's capacity to store DATA. The memory is divided into ROM (Read Only Memory) and RAM (Random Access Memory). The ROM is installed physically inside the computer at the time of manufacture and contains *permanent* DATA and instructions. The RAM is the part of the memory that contains the DATA and PROGRAM currently in use. This information is *temporary;* it is transferred into the memory from DISKs via the DISK DRIVE. The RAM is lost if the computer is switched off. The

CAPACITY of the memory is measured in BYTES.
Microcomputer The smallest, cheapest computers currently available, and the kind on which word processing PROGRAMS generally used in publishing run. Can be DEDICATED or non-dedicated.
Minicomputer Between a MAINFRAME and a MICROCOMPUTER in size and price. Rapidly being overtaken by microcomputers of increasing power.
Modem Short for MOdulator/DEModulator. A way of sending computer DATA down an ordinary telephone line.
Milking machine Slang for text retrieval terminal. A way of transferring information between two computers or PROGRAMs that are not COMPATIBLE. The DATA from the DISK is transformed by the milking machine into signals that can be fed directly into the receiving computer's MEMORY.
Multidisk reader A computer that can interpret DATA from a number of non-compatible DISKs and transfer it onto disks that can be read by other (given) computers and PROGRAMS. So, for instance, disks from a computer using one word processing program can be converted so that they can be interpreted by a computer using a completely different WORD PROCESSOR.

N

Network A system that allows a number of different linked terminals to share facilities such as MEMORY, DATABASES, PRINTERS.

P

Printer Used to print the DATA in a computer MEMORY onto paper. Dot matrix printers form letters from dots. Daisywheel printers print individual characters arranged at the ends of the spokes of a wheel — the arrangement looks rather like the petals of a daisy, hence the name. Dot matrix printers are generally cheaper and faster than daisywheel printers, and are quite adequate for proof-reading copy from PRINTOUTs. Good dot matrix printers and daisywheel printers are of letter-quality — good enough for office correspondence.
Printout Paper copy of the DATA in the MEMORY of a computer.
Program A set of instructions that tells a computer how to perform a certain task — how to become a DATABASE, SPREADSHEET or WORD PROCESSOR, for example.

S

Save To transfer DATA from the computer's memory to a DISK.
Single-stroke key capture The system by which copy is keyed in to a DISK using a WORD PROCESSOR, and the disk is sent to the typesetter for typesetting without being rekeyed. That is, the original manuscript is keyed only once — which means there is no room for origination of literals at the typesetting stage. Currently the subject of much debate by the print unions.
Software The computer instructions — PROGRAMS — that make the HARDWARE work. For instance, software is what can turn a MICROCOMPUTER (hardware) into a DATABASE, SPREADSHEET or WORD PROCESSOR.
Soft keys Keys on the computer KEYBOARD that have no fixed value but can be designated to represent typesetting characters not on the keyboard, strings of ordinary characters, or computer commands.
Spreadsheet A PROGRAM that holds DATA on a 'sheet' in the computer's MEMORY. The data is laid out in rows and columns in such a way that altering one item alters all related items — which makes it very useful for working out, for instance, how various factors can influence projected budgets.

T

Terminal A VDT and KEYBOARD linked to a MAINFRAME computer or linked to other terminals through a NETWORK.
Typesetting terminal A TERMINAL on which copy can be typeset. The typesetting PROGRAM allows the operator to make decisions on line endings, hyphenation, etc, for any given typeface, size, leading and measure.

V

VDT Visual display terminal. The television monitor screen on which the DATA in the computer's MEMORY is displayed.

W

Winchester disk see DISK.
Word processor A DEDICATED computer or PROGRAM that allows a non-dedicated computer to perform word-processing functions — to KEY, delete, insert, move text.

Bibliography

Copy-editing, grammar and usage

A Civil Tongue, Edwin Newman, Bobbs-Merril, Indianapolis, 1976.

College Handbook of Composition, Langdon Elsbree, et al, 9th edition, D C Heath, Boston, 1977.

MLA Style Sheet, William Riley Parker, 2nd edition (revised by John H Fisher, et al), Modern Language Association, New York, 1970.

On Writing, Editing and Publishing, Essays Explicative and Hortatory, Jacques Barzan, University of Chicago Press, Chicago, 1971.

The Careful Writer, Theodore M Bernstein, Athenuem, New York, 1965.

The Elements of Style, William Strunk junior and E B White, 3rd edition, Macmillan, New York, 1979.

The New York Times Manual of Style and Usage, E Lewis Jordan, Quadrangle/The New York Times Book Company, New York, 1976.

University of Chicago Press Manual of Style, 13th edition, University of Chicago Press, Chicago, 1969.

US Government Printing Office Style Manual, revised edition, Washington, 1973.

Words Into Type, 3rd edition, Prentice-Hall, Englewood Cliffs, New Jersey, 1974.

The world of publishing

Copyright Information Kit, Library of Congress, Washington DC (Write for free information to: The Registrar of Copyrights, Library of Congress, Washington DC 20559.)

Folio, a magazine for the magazine industry.

Literary Market Place, R R Bowker Company, New York, 1984.

Publisher's Weekly, a magazine for the publishing industry.

The Hidden Job Market, Tom and Davidyne Mayleas, Times Books, New York, 1976.

The International Directory of Little Magazines and Small Presses, Dustbooks, Paradise, California, revised annually.

The Language of the Foreign Book Trade: Abbreviations, Terms, Phrases, edited by Jerrold Orne, 3rd edition, American Library Association, Chicago, 1976.

What Color is your Parachute?, Richard Nelson Bolles, Ten Speed Press, Berkeley, California, 1978.

You, Inc, Peter Weaver, Doubleday, New York, 1973 and Dolphin Books, Garden City, 1975.

Useful addresses

American Society of Journalists and Authors, Inc,
Suite 1907
1501 Broadway
New York, NY 10036

Editorial Freelancers Association
PO Box 2050
Madison Square Station
New York, NY 10159
(Provides useful job telephone service for employers who seek editorial help.)

Guild of Book Workers
521 Fifth Avenue
New York, NY 10175

PEN American Center
47 Fifth Avenue
New York, NY 10003

Society of Professional Journalists
Sigma Delta Chic
Suite 801W
840 North Lake Shore Drive
Chicago, IL 60611

Volunteer Lawyers for the Arts
36 West Forty-fourth Street
New York NY 10036

Index

Page numbers in *italic* refer to illustrations and captions.

Picture credits

12, 14, 17, 18, 20, 21, 22, 24, 40, 46, Mick Hill; 15, 38, Andrew Luckhurst; 65, Peter Zeevy; 65, Visutek Ltd; 72, 74, 75, John Heseltine, 101, Agfa Gevaert Ltd; 107, Leslie Hubble Ltd; 118, 119, Heidelberg UK Ltd; 118, Crosfield Electronics Ltd; 126, Carlton Publishing Ltd.